AF483587

LYLA DAVIS

Following Her Rainbow

Ivory Pages Publishing

Foreword

To All the Angel Momma's Out There...

I hope you will find comfort in this book. No mother ever wishes to bury her child, and the pain of that loss is unbearable. A piece of your heart leaves this Earth with your child, and you can never get that back. Still, there is hope.

I lost my sweet baby boy, Colin, over 22 years ago, and it took me years of heartache to realize that it is okay to ask for help. Even though your precious baby is not in your arms, he or she is in your heart, and they made you a mamma. No person and no distance can ever take that away from you... not even death. From one angel momma to another... I wish you all the love I can give, and the patience you need to help your heart heal. Remember... often times the worst storms bring the most beautiful rainbows...

TRIGGER WARNING: This book talks briefly about the loss of a child. While it focuses mostly on the healing and the hope of moving forward, it does describe the loss in the forward. This may be skipped and will not affect the book.

One

Prologue

"Just breathe, baby," Molly heard Waylon saying through her cries.

Molly glared at her husband. She wasn't a violent person, and she loved him, but right now, she just wanted to tell him to…

"Remember what we learned in class, slow deep breaths," he continued, interrupting her thought and obviously oblivious to her current state of mind.

It hurt so much more than she had ever imagined it would, and she wasn't sure she could do this anymore. She was beyond excited to meet her baby girl, but she hadn't prepared herself for this pain!

"I can't do this!" she yelled at him, pulling her hand away as he tried to comfort her.

Waylon looked at his beautiful wife with concern. He wasn't sure what to say to help her right now, and he felt completely useless. Plus, he couldn't figure out why she was looking at him like she wanted to hurt him or something!

"Yes, you can, Mol. You are the strongest women I've ever met! You've got this! Just a little longer!"

Dr. Stanley sat next to Molly on the bed, easing her legs apart so she could check her progress. A smile filled her petite face. "It's time, Molly. You did it! Now, how about we meet this baby girl?"

Just like that, everything changed. The room began to buzz with activity as two nurses came in to help prepare the room. They wheeled a bed, of sorts, out of a closet area, and it had blankets and other baby things on it. It looked like a little spaceship on a wooden base. Molly knew from her classes that it was a special bed that would keep her baby warm and cozy after she was born.

Suddenly, Molly realized there was no turning back. She was about to become a mother, and she had no idea what she was doing. As panic began to fill her mind, she looked at Waylon. He looked scared too, which, oddly, made her feel a little better.

Leaning in to kiss his wife on the forehead, Waylon said, "I love you, Mol."

"I love you too," she said as she started to feel the next contraction mounting inside her. Her stomach grew tight, and she felt pain in her bottom. This was it… could she really do this? She was beginning to think she'd gotten herself in *way* deeper than she was ready for!

"Okay, Molly, I want you to pull your legs back towards your chest, hold your breath, and bear down as hard as you can. Ready?"

Molly wasn't ready, but she nodded her head anyway. Listening to the doctor, she did as she was told, pushing as hard as she could.

"One, two, three, four, five, six, seven, eight…" the doctor counted rhythmically as Molly pushed.

Out of air, Molly stopped, gasping.

"Good job, Molly! Now take some deep breaths and let's get one more push on this contraction, okay?"

Molly breathed deeply and then pushed again, this time making it to 7. After that, she rested her head back and did her best to calm her breathing and her pulse down. She was scared to death, and excited too. How was it possible to feel both at once? Closing her eyes, she thought about all the fun she and Waylon had been having getting the baby room ready for Hannah. She had picked out the colors, and he had painted the room just the same way she had imagined. He had even painted a little mural in the corner where her rocking chair was sitting, awaiting her and Hannah to come home and snuggle in it. They had gone to the local baby store together and purchased an adorable outfit for Hannah to come home from the hospital in, and packed her hospital bag so they were ready to go at a moment's notice. She was so happy and excited… and nervous.

Feeling another contraction mounting, Molly prepared to push again, this time feeling Hannah move closer to the world with each push. Before long, her head was out, and Molly heard the doctor tell her to stop pushing. Molly was so exhausted; she couldn't hear a word anybody was saying anymore. She just wanted this to be over and to meet her little girl.

"Okay, Molly, one more push and we can meet this sweet baby girl," the doctor said.

Molly pushed as hard as she could, and Hannah Mae Walker was born. Waylon leaned down and kissed Molly again, telling her how amazing she had done. He looked so happy. Both he and Molly were crying tears of joy.

Molly looked down at the doctor, awaiting her little girl in her arms. She knew Waylon was going to cut the cord, and she didn't want to miss that moment. What she saw, though, was a look of concern on the doctor's face.

"Molly, I'm going to go ahead and hand Hannah over to the nurses so they can take a look at her, okay?"

"Okay… what's wrong with her? Is she okay?" Molly asked, concern filling her voice.

"Hannah seems to be struggling with her transition into the world right now, Molly. I'm not sure why yet, but we are going to do our best to help her, okay?"

Molly felt like the world was spinning around her and she didn't know how to make it stop. Why was Hannah so purple?

She looked at Waylon who was pale and looked like he was going to faint. "Waylon…she's not crying… *why isn't she crying*?" Molly asked him, begging him to help her understand what was happening.

Waylon looked at her, fear filling his face. "I don't know, Mol… I just don't know." He began to cry again, only this time not from joy. She could see how scared he was, and it made her even more worried. Waylon was always so strong and steady. Seeing him like this made her feel like the world was crumbling around her.

The next minutes felt like hours as more and more people rushed into her room. She couldn't see Hannah anymore because there were so many doctors and nurses around her. They all spoke quietly but with an urgency that told her things were not going well over there. She just wanted someone to tell her what was going on!

After Dr. Stanley finished with Molly's delivery and all that came after, she cleaned everything up and came up to Molly's bedside. "I'm going to go talk with the doctor that is working on Hannah and then I'll be right back to update you, okay?"

Molly couldn't speak. She just nodded, feeling completely numb. Why wasn't Hannah crying yet? The silence felt deafening to her. Just one little cry… that's all she needed to hear. Still, that one little cry never came.

After a few moments, Dr. Stanley returned, this time with another doctor alongside her. The other doctor was an older man with kind eyes. The look on their faces didn't make Molly feel any better than she had before. Tears filled Molly's eyes as she prepared herself for the words that were about to come. She knew in her heart that it wasn't going to be good news, but nothing could have prepared her for the reality that came out of the gentle doctor's mouth next.

"Molly… Waylon… This is Dr. Marten, our resident pediatric neonatologist," Dr. Stanley said. "He has been taking care of Hannah."

Again, no words could seem to find their way to Molly's mouth. She just nodded. Waylon sat on the bed next to Molly, apparently unable to speak either. He grabbed her hand, both of them needing to feel the support of the other.

"Hello, Molly," Dr. Marten said in a voice that sounded as smooth as silk.

Molly imagined that he was probably amazing at talking to children and calming them down with that soothing tone.

"There's no easy way to say this, so I'm just going to be straight to the point with you. Hannah was not breathing when she was born. We worked on her for a long time, but her lungs never took a breath of air. I'm very sorry to have to tell you both this, but Hannah was what we call 'stillborn'. It means that for a reason that we often never know, she was born directly into Heaven.

I truly wish there was something we could have done for her, but her little body just wasn't able to survive outside the womb. I'm so very sorry for your loss."

Molly looked at the doctors… she could hear them, but she felt like they were a million miles away. This couldn't be real! She needed to pinch herself or something, because there was no way this was happening!

"No!" she heard Waylon say as a sob escaped his throat. "Please… no!"

Molly felt Waylon grow limp next to her, sinking into the bed with her. He was sobbing. She felt nothing. This was wrong… it was all wrong… she was going to wake up anytime now and be in her bed, still pregnant, and this would just be a nightmare. She was sure of it! She closed her eyes, willing herself to fall asleep so she could wake back up and it would all be over. Only… it wasn't. No matter how hard she tried, it didn't stop!

Dr. Marten broke the silence as he softly asked, "Molly… would you like to hold Hannah?"

A nurse walked towards her with her baby girl, bundled up in a blanket with a little hat on her head.

What is happening right now? she thought to herself.

Molly held her arms out, feeling like a robot that was being controlled by someone else. The nurse placed the little bundle in her arms, and she looked down… *Hannah.*

In that moment, Molly's world came crashing down upon her. She felt her heart burst into a million pieces. Her little girl, lifeless in her arms, was the most beautiful baby she had ever seen. She was perfect… ten tiny fingers and ten tiny toes. She had her daddy's little nose and her mommy's long eyelashes.

Molly's eyes flooded with tears, and she let them fall. She held her baby girl close, willing her little eyes to open. How could this have happened? They were supposed to be a family! She wanted to teach her so many things and take her so many places! They had plans for her future! None of this made any sense.

For the first time, Molly looked into her husband's eyes, seeing a mirror image of her own pain and grief. He was hurting too, and he looked as lost as she felt. She leaned into him and sobbed. She felt as though she'd never be able to stop. A piece of her heart was gone, and she knew it could never be replaced. Her precious baby girl was gone, and her life would never be the same.

Looking back down at her baby girl, she finally let an agonizing sob escape her lungs. She didn't know how else to get the pain out of her.

Together, she and Waylon held Hannah for hours. They needed these moments to last a lifetime. Molly sang to her, rocking her in the bed. Waylon held her, desperately wishing he could somehow go back and change the outcome of this day. The nurses helped them cut a lock of Hannah's hair to keep as well as take her handprints and footprints for her baby book. The nurses were so kind to them, taking time and talking them through each part of the process. They even did molds of Hannah's hands and feet. They dressed Hannah in a special gown that a wonderful volunteer had made for babies such as her. It was beautiful and looked like it had been made from a lavender satin gown.

At some point that evening, it was time to say goodbye and let the nurse take their little girl. Molly guessed they probably needed the room for another mother, so they were moving her to a different area on the floor.

Molly leaned down and kissed her baby girl one last time. "I love you, my sweet Hannah Mae. Daddy and I will never forget you."

With that, she handed her precious angel to the nurse… all her dreams, her hopes, and her love were bundled up in that tiny lavender blanket. All that was left were empty arms and one question that lingered on… **why her?**

Two

Chapter 1

Molly Walker sat on an old wooden porch swing, rocking and listening to the adorable chirps of a little bird in the crab apple tree next to her house. She had thrown a soft blanket over her lap, one that her mother had made her a few years back. It was brightly colored and super soft, and it made her feel as though her mother was next to her as she snuggled it. She closed her eyes and felt the cool breeze on her face, smiling, happy that all seemed to be perfect at this very moment.

Her ears perked up as she listened closely… she could swear she could hear a quiet sound coming from the back yard. She squinted her eyes as she opened them to look towards the direction of the sound, trying to figure out where it was could possibly be coming from. Off in the distance, she thought she could see something floating in the lake that bordered her home, the waves swaying and pushing whatever it was back and forth gently.

Molly stood, putting her shoes back on her bare feet and heading down the wooden steps towards the water. She covered her eyes with her hands, willing herself to peer out into the water and make out the object that was bouncing around. The waves were getting choppier, and the once calm waters were now making the object tip from side to side.

As she got to the middle of her yard, she heard the noise again, only this time she knew the sound… it was a baby crying!

"Oh no!" she cried. Could there really be a baby out in the middle of the water? Who would do something like that?

Molly picked up her pace, going from a stroll to a sprint in seconds. She could hear the baby crying and was terrified she wouldn't make it to them in time.

Molly hurried down the hill towards the water, determined to save the crying child. She was running so fast, she didn't see the branch that was lying in front of her, and she tripped, falling hard to the ground.

"Oww!" she moaned, pausing to grab her throbbing ankle. As she looked down to make sure nothing was broken, she heard another shrill cry fill the mountainside. Her heart skipped. Alarm coursed through her veins. She had to save that baby!

Ignoring her injured ankle, she soldiered on, limping as she went. As if from nowhere, the mountainside was suddenly covered in fog, and she had to squint to try to see the water. She could barely see the ground ahead of her, so she trusted her ears as she followed the sound of the wailing baby. If she didn't get to the water soon enough, the baby was going to tip over and fall in the water. She was furious and terrified all at once.

Finally, she was at the bank of the water. She hopped from stone to stone, wincing at the pain in her ankle. When the water soaked her shoes, she shivered. It was so cold it stung the bottoms of her feet. She looked up at the basket that was floating ahead of her in the water. Panic pounded in her chest as she realized it was drifting farther away.

Diving into the icy water, she began to swim, struggling to keep her eyes open as she went. Not only was the water freezing, but it also stung her eyes. She paused to catch her breath, trying desperately to reach the baby. Suddenly, her heart stopped as she saw the basket start to sink into the water. The baby's cries turned into dreadful suffocating noises.

"No!" Molly screeched, swimming faster. The further she swam, the more it felt like something kept pulling her back. She struggled against the tides, crying in horror as the basket sank farther and farther into the water, until

it was completely out of sight. The sound of the silence around her became deafening.

Molly stopped swimming, sobbing as she floated in the now calm water. How could she have been so slow? Closing her eyes, feeling completely devastated, she allowed herself to be gently swallowed up by the water…

Molly woke up with a start, panting and gasping for air. She looked all around her, trying to figure out where she was and what was happening. Her panic slowly started to dissipate as she realized it was just another nightmare. Her heart ached from racing so fast, and she sighed as she tried to calm herself down again. These nightmares were coming more and more lately, and she needed to figure out how to make them stop. She was afraid her heart couldn't take too many more of them.

She shut her eyes for a moment and inhaled deeply, willing her body to relax. This was the third nightmare this month. She was starting to think things were never going to get better for her. Ever since her baby girl, Hannah, had been stillborn, she couldn't sleep. She felt sad all the time and she couldn't seem to figure out how to change that.

Tears began to well up in her eyes. As if on cue, her snowy-white cat Snowflake meowed and climbed into her bed, snuggling beside her. She smiled and gave her a pat on the head.

"Hey, Snow. I bet you are hungry, aren't you?"

Snowflake pushed her nose into Molly's hand and meowed, her feline way of saying yes.

"I'll go get you some grub, but first, I have to go to the bathroom," she sighed, giving Snowflake one more scruff under the chin.

She sat up, enjoying the feeling of the sun that was peeking in through the curtains on her bedroom window. It was one more reminder that spring was just around the corner. Tossing the blanket off her, Molly slowly slithered off the bed, rubbing her eyes. She looked over to the empty pillow next to hers and sighed. She was starting to get used to sleeping alone, and it scared her to think that her marriage was slipping away, one sleepless night after another. Waylon had been sleeping in the guest bedroom for almost 3 months now, and she was having a hard time seeing an end in sight to that pattern.

Molly quickly made her bed up and then lazily shoved her feet into her slippers, threw her comfy knit robe on, and made the six-step trek to the bathroom, feeling victorious as she closed the door. Everything she did felt like a battle lately… getting up in the morning, eating anything that took more than two steps to cook, wearing clothes that made her look something other than homeless.

She felt like the excitement and joy in her life had left the moment she said goodbye to her little girl. Now, she had no idea how to get it back. Honestly, she wasn't even sure she wanted to, or that she deserved to.

In the bathroom, she splashed some water on her face, looking in the mirror. A sad smile crept up her freckled cheeks, revealing a dimple on the right. She didn't even recognize herself anymore. Her once vibrant complexion was paler now, and her hazel eyes looked tired and old. It didn't help that there were dark circles underneath them. The only thing that had stayed shiny was her long and wavy auburn-brown hair.

Sighing, she grabbed her hairbrush and then set it back down. It felt like too much work to brush the mess of curls she had today, so she grabbed a ponytail holder that was on the counter and threw the whole mass up into a messy bun, her go-to look nowadays.

As she picked up her toothbrush, her dream flashed back. Was it always going to be this way? Was she ever going to get over the pain and heartache of losing a baby? Everywhere she went she felt like people were moving on without her… like she was stuck in the cement, unable to move, just watching the world pass by her, wishing she could move her feet and join them.

***

"It's going to be a good day," she said, pulling herself from the gloomy thoughts she was falling deeply into. She pasted a smile on her face, silently planning to make the best of the day that lay ahead, but Waylon's snores interrupted her thoughts, bringing her back to reality.

Waylon had returned home quite late last night, thoroughly wasted as usual. Molly couldn't seem to accept his new habits. She was frustrated and heartbroken by his behavior. She knew he was grieving just as much as she was, but she had really hoped he'd find a better way to cope over time. Still, after 10 months, nothing was changing. He was drinking away his sadness, and she couldn't seem to break through to him, no matter how hard she tried.

Molly headed back to her bedroom to get dressed for the day, grabbing her favorite leggings and a comfy sweatshirt. Some slip-on shoes completed the outfit… comfortable and relaxed, just like she preferred it to be. She went to the kitchen to make some coffee and toast. She didn't have much time this morning, so that was going to have to count as her breakfast. She put her toast on a paper plate so she could take it with her and filled her coffee tumbler.

Before heading out, she poured a cup of coffee for Waylon, adding hazelnut creamer and a little sugar to it, his favorite. No matter how frustrated she was with him, she still loved him, and she wanted their life back the way it was. Quietly, she opened the guest bedroom door and walked to the bed, hoping for a chance to talk to Waylon quickly before she left for the day. She could smell the alcohol on his clothes as she got closer to the bed.

Drinking had become Waylon's therapy ever since they lost Hannah. During Molly's pregnancy, they were ecstatic about becoming parents, investing heavily in Hannah's nursery and excitedly planning for their baby's arrival. They had felt like the luckiest people on Earth and were so hopeful about all that they would do together as a family of three.

However, their dreams and hopes had apparently not been in the cards for them. Instead, they had found themselves planning a funeral in the place of a baptism. Hannah's death had shattered the once loving couple, turning them into mere shadows of themselves. While Molly silently grieved every day and poured her energy into work, Waylon turned to drinking and staying out late at the club he worked at in the city, unable to confront the demons that were haunting him day and night.

Standing beside Waylon's bed, Molly called out softly, "Hey, Waylon. Can you wake up for a minute please?"

Waylon, feeling very groggy, slowly opened his eyes, taking a moment to register his surroundings before sitting up and holding his head with his left hand.

"Damn, my head is killing me," he croaked, letting out a sigh as he settled himself. Molly handed him the cup of coffee.

"Here, see if this helps."

"Thanks, Mol," he responded, taking a sip. Looking at her, he recognized her familiar disapproving expression, signaling a conversation was imminent.

"Heading out already?" he inquired, trying to change the course of the conversation.

"Yes, I just stopped in here quick to say goodbye."

"Alright, I'll see you later?" he asked, hoping silently that they could soon return to the days filled with laughter and beautiful conversations, not arguments or terse replies.

She looked at him with a sadness in her eyes, one that made him feel like he had just gotten socked in the gut. He could deal with her anger, or even her disappointment, but the look she had now killed him.

"How much longer are we going to keep doing this?" she asked, sitting on the edge of the bed so she could talk to him for a minute.

She didn't want to fight, but she couldn't just walk away and pretend like she was okay when she wasn't. "How long do you intend for us to go on like this, with you drinking and coming home late instead of talking to me about stuff so we can try to move forward?" she asked.

"Mol please, not again, not today," he snipped, upset with her for jumping into a conversation he wasn't ready for. He was tired of her constantly getting on his case about this. He abruptly set his cup of coffee on the nightstand and sat up so he could be next to her. When he reached out for her hand, she pulled away, turning away from him.

She took a breath and turned to face him again. Her tone was serious but genuine. "Way, you need Help, we both do, this is …."

"I told you I was fine, Mol!" Why did she have to be like this all the time? Couldn't she just leave him alone about it and let him figure it out on his own? "I don't need some therapist messing with my head… *I'm* handling me!"

Molly flinched as though he had slapped her. She was only trying to help, trying to get back to where they were. She didn't want to give up on him, on them, but she starting to worry that there was no other option.

"We are in this together, Waylon. We both lost Hannah, not just you. I know people deal with things differently, but your way of dealing with this isn't helping anybody... It's destroying what's left of us!" she cried, tears streaking down her face.

After taking a breath, she added, "I'm sick and tired of this, Way! I have asked you to get help with me *so* many times, and you always refuse. You just want to drink your sorrows away instead of talking to me. I'm hurting too, Waylon... Please just talk to me so we can try to fix this before it's too late."

"Mol, I've told you a hundred times... I won't go to anyone to talk about things I consider personal to myself, even if you keep begging me... it's not going to work! Why can't you just let this go so we can move on?"

"Waylon, you need help, which means there's no chance for moving on." She stood, aggravated and disheartened. This was *not* going the way she was hoping it would. After a moment, she looked back at the man she had planned to spend the rest of her life loving. She suddenly realized that that man no longer existed. They had lost Hannah together, but they had grieved far apart. Somewhere along that path, she had lost him too. Her heart felt as though it was breaking into pieces all over again.

"Way, you frown at us getting help, refuse to talk to me about Hannah, and want no part in even considering the possibility of having another child one day... I'd really love to know what moving on looks like to you?" She felt defeated, but she needed to know what he pictured as their future together. It was becoming harder and harder to envision to her.

He got up from the bed and crossed the room to her, grabbing her hands in his. "Molly honey, we can work on us, I promise... I want us to grow old loving each other, just you and me. We were fine before the baby, and we can still be fine without her now. I can't watch you go through such misery and pain again! *I* don't want to go through all this again, it's just *too much*," he said as his blue eyes turned red and tears dripped down his cheeks. He stared into Molly's eyes, pleading for her to understand.

Molly looked at Waylon, wishing she could find a way back to him. He was lost, and so was she, but they just couldn't seem to find their way back to each other. They were on two different planets when it came to their hopes and future wishes. She wanted to at least talk about having another baby one day, when they were ready, but Waylon had no intention of ever having a child again. How could they move past that? She wanted to talk, and he wanted to drink.

"I can't do this right now Waylon, I'm exhausted. I need some space to think," Molly said as she pulled away and walked toward the bedroom door. The room suddenly felt like it was caving in on her, and she needed to get out of it.

"Wait… you need space? From *me*? Are you *serious* right now? How is that possibly going to help things?" He was angry now, yelling at Molly. He winced at the pain in his head. How could she do this to him? He grabbed her hand, trying desperately to stop her from leaving.

"Molly, we need each other now more than ever!"

"No, I need you to listen and to talk with me, not at me! I need time to figure things out, and I need a break from the arguing. This isn't *us,* and it's not the way I want things to be between us. I'm scared, and I don't know what to do, and you're not helping matters. I need help and I'm going to get it, with or without you," Molly responded as she walked into the doorway.

As she left the room, she turned to say goodbye. "I'm going to stay at my parents' place tonight," she said.

"Molly! If you walk out that door, you're choosing a baby over the future of our marriage," he said pointing to the door.

She flinched again. "Waylon, having a baby was a *part* of our marriage, a dream we had *together* for a long time. I can't do this right now. I love you, but I can't watch you do this to yourself and to us." She sighed as she turned to leave.

Waylon started to go after her, but she stopped him with her outstretched hand.

"Goodbye, Waylon," she said as she left the guest room, shutting the door behind her.

Molly quickly grabbed her purse and keys and left their home, tears flowing freely down her cheeks. She closed her car door and laid her face in her hands on the steering wheel, allowing the emotions to pour from her like rain from a stormy sky. *How had it come to this?*

First, she lost her daughter, and now she was losing the man she had loved since the day she met him. This wasn't how things were supposed to be!

"What am I going to do?" she sobbed.

Three

Chapter 2

Molly pulled into her usual parking space in front of her shoppe. She took a quick look in the mirror, making sure the tears were all gone and that her eyes weren't completely bloodshot from crying. Deciding they were as good as they could get at the moment, she grabbed her stuff and got out of her car.

Molly smiled as she saw the beautiful new sign above the front door of her shoppe. It was bright and sunny, and perfect for her tastes. She didn't know they had been there to deliver it already, but she couldn't have loved it more. It said "The Sweet Sprinkle" in shades of magenta and pink, and it had a big cupcake next to it with sprinkles all over it. She instantly loved it and was happy that she had hired a local artist to create it for her. He had knocked her vision out of the park!

The Sweet Sprinkle was Molly's dream, and the only place that made her feel "normal" anymore. She and her best friend, Mia Lewis, had made the leap a little over a year ago to buy the cute little storefront on Badger Lane. It was the perfect location for the cupcake shop the two of them had dreamed about running since they were little girls, right in the busiest part of the city. Mia had been Molly's best friend since they were eight, and she knew her better than anybody.

Thankful for the distraction of work, Molly grabbed her key and opened the front door. The familiar "ding" of the bell as she entered made her feel like she was leaving one world and entering another. This world, thankfully, was busy and professional, unlike the emotionally draining world she'd just left. She was happy to put that behind her and bury herself in work for a while. She'd have to figure the rest out later.

Molly tossed her things in the office and put on her apron, ready to tackle the first order for the day. The sweet almond and vanilla smell of frosting filled the air and gave her a sense of comfort and happiness that she hadn't felt all morning. It was refreshing.

Yesterday, a woman had stopped in to place an order for a little girl's birthday party on Saturday- they wanted two dozen chocolate cupcakes with turquoise and bright pink frosting… And, of course, sprinkles! The little girl apparently loved dancing, so Molly had decided to put some cute little picks in the cupcakes that had ballet shoes on them. She loved to add a special touch to her creations. She considered herself an artist of sorts, and her cakes and cupcakes were her masterpieces.

She checked the order slips quickly to see what else needed to be done for the weekend so she could do all the baking in one shot. She found that she needed a pink champaign cake and a dozen red velvet cupcakes for other customers that were coming in today as well, so she grabbed all the ingredients for those too.

As she baked, Molly couldn't help but think about how excited the little girl would be when she saw her cupcakes for her party. That was Molly's favorite part… watching the happy reactions of her customers when they first saw their completed order. Soon, her mind traveled back to flashes of her morning argument with Waylon. She thought about her marriage, how it turned out to be such a mess somehow.

Molly knew that things were going to be hard after they lost Hannah, but she truly had thought they could find a way to get through the devastation together. She had signed on for the good and the bad when she shared her vows, but Waylon's drinking was getting out of hand, and he was refusing to talk to her or get help. She wasn't sure what else to do to try to find her way back to him anymore. Marriage took two people working, not just one!

Molly was deep in her thoughts when Mia walked in… so far in that she didn't even hear her come through the door.

"Mornin'!" she called out, nearly giving Molly a startled coronary.

Mia Lewis was always smiling. She had a happy-go-lucky personality that blended well with Molly's more serious attitude. They balanced one another out well, and that was what Molly loved so much about their friendship. She was of average height, standing just a bit shorter than Molly. Her beautiful black curly shoulder-length hair was pulled back in a clip today, though she usually wore it down. Mia's face was smooth and always looked well-kept.

As she approached the baking area, she smiled, showing the deep dimples in both of her freckled cheeks. Molly smiled back, finally getting her heartrate back under control after being startled. "Hey," she responded, still trying to pull herself from the thoughts she had been so engrossed in only moments prior.

Mia's smile faded as she looked at her friend, realizing instantly that something was wrong. She stopped in the office quick to drop her handbag, then grabbed her apron and threw it over her head. She walked behind the counter so she could help Molly out in the kitchen.

"Molly, what's going on?" Mia said carefully, moving around the table where Molly was working to give her a hug. She could see the dried tears on her cheeks.

Molly hugged her, allowing the trapped tears to fall again. Damn… she was so sick of crying!

After a bit, Molly's tears stopped, and she and Mia sat down at the table. She had just put the cake and cupcakes in the oven, so she had some time to talk before she had to take them out to cool. They wouldn't be opening the shoppe until nine o'clock and it was only seven thirty now, so they had some time to talk in private before customers started to come in.

"What happened Mol?" Mia asked.

"It's Waylon. He came home drunk again last night. We had a huge argument this morning when I tried to talk to him about getting help," Molly explained, the sadness and exhaustion in her voice not lost on Mia. She went on to explain the argument they'd had and how she had left after telling him she was taking a break.

"I'm *so* tired Mia… Tired of us arguing every single day! I really want to be there for him, but he has completely shut me out, and I can't find a way in anymore," Molly added.

Gently touching her hand to reassure her, Mia said softly, "I'm sorry you are going through all this. Maybe a break would help you *both*. I really think that you and Waylon will figure this out… you've been through a lot together, and he's your soul mate, Mol! I believe he's just too hurt and confused right now, but I think that in the end, you'll work things out."

Molly nodded but wasn't quite as sure as her friend was that this was all going to sort itself out.

"In the meantime, Mol, you need to take care of yourself," Mia said.

"I know… actually, I wanted to ask you something. Do you remember the name of that therapist you told me about a while back?"

"Yeah… her name is Claire, but I can't remember her last name…" Mia said, trying to think. "Wait… I just remembered I had a card in my wallet for her office at one point. Let me grab it and see if I still have it."

Mia walked over to the office and grabbed her purse, returning to the table with it in hand. She searched her wallet, bringing out a small business card. "Here it is! Her name is Claire Dansen and her office is actually just a few blocks down on the north side of the street. I think you should pay her a visit," Mia said handing the card to Molly. "Her number is at the top of the card there," she said, pointing to the contact information.

"I am going to call her as soon as I get a break this morning. I'm not sure I think it will help, but I need to try something," Molly said, looking at the card before placing it in the pocket of her apron.

Mia gave her a hug. "You know what, Mol, I think you should go ahead and take some time off today. Let me handle the store… I think you could use some time to cool off and figure some things out."

"I appreciate that. I may take you up on that offer. I just have to finish these orders this morning and then I could head out after that. Are you sure that's okay?"

"Absolutely! You aren't going to be able to get much done here if you don't figure some things out at home anyway," she said with enthusiasm in her voice.

Molly thought for a moment as the two women headed back to the kitchen just before the first timer went off. She pulled the cupcakes from the oven and placed them on the cooling racks.

"*Actually*... I'm pretty sure Waylon will be heading to work by noon, and I told him I'd spend the night at my mom's. I think I'll call Claire to make an appointment and then head home to grab some things to take to my parents' house. That will give me some time to get settled and talk to my mom about everything before suppertime."

"I think that sounds like a great idea," Mia told her as she cleaned up the counters to get ready for making the frosting.

Mia and Molly had been friends for what felt like forever, but she and her husband, Jeff, were also friends with Waylon, so Mia wanted nothing more than to help them find their way back to each other. If a short break is what it took to get that to happen, she was happy to encourage her friend to try it.

Both ladies heard the bells of the front door chime.

"Hello, ladies!" They heard a familiar voice echo in the room as their mutual friend, Lily Stanton, boisterously entered the shoppe.

Lily Stanton was as elegant and poised as they came... she was tall, energetic, and full of life.

"Morning, Lily," Mia said, smiling at her friend.

Molly couldn't help but smile when she looked at Lily. Today, she was wearing dress slacks, a lavender button-up blouse, and two-inch heels. She had no idea how Lily could stand all day in such unpractical shoes. Her short blond hair was a very bold shade of teal today... Lily changed her hair color every few months to keep everyone on their toes. Although she didn't quite understand the excitement of it, Molly loved her carefree attitude. Lily owned Bedheadz Salon and Spa, a very trendy salon about two blocks from The Sweet Sprinkle, so she often stopped in to say hi to her friends.

"You look like you saw a ghost or something," she told Mia, giving her a hug. Then, she turned to Molly and added, "and you look like hell... What's going on over here anyway?"

Lily Stanton had a way of telling things as they were, and a very small filter.

"Molly wants to take a break from Waylon," Mia responded.

"*Okay….*" Lily responded as though she *still* didn't see a reason why they both looked the way they did. "I'm sorry, but I don't seem to understand why that's got your face all frowned up like that," she said, addressing Mia.

Molly narrated every detail from the start of the morning to Lily.

"Molly, darling, I think you are making the right decision! You need this… Things have been so tough this past year, and maybe what you really need is some fresh air and some perspective. Enough of this back and forth with Waylon. You deserve better than that!"

"Okay now… Lily, last time I checked, she was still married to Waylon, so I think you'd better slow down the 'new person' talk," Mia said, interrupting Lily. "Yes, Molly is having a hard time, but they both are! And, you have to remember that they've also had several years of good times! Marriage is supposed to be in the bad times too, not just the good."

"Molly made the decision to do this, and all I'm doing is showing her my support, Mia. She has had enough heartache for a lifetime, and she deserves to be happy. If he doesn't want to be helped, he shouldn't keep her from moving on," Lily argued.

Mia shook her head in disagreement, but Lily wouldn't let her speak. She interrupted by turning the conversation to Molly. "Mols, I have an idea… Why not move in with me instead of staying all the way out at your parents' place? It's much closer, and I have plenty of room in my loft," Lily suggested.

Molly thought for a minute, deciding maybe Lily was right. She wasn't exactly thrilled at the thought of moving back in with her parents at her age. It seemed a little ridiculous. Besides, she'd probably have more privacy with Lily.

"Actually, I think I'm going to take you up on that offer, Lil'."

"Perfect!" Lily exclaimed. "Ok… this has been fun, but I need to get to the salon now. I have a ton of clients today, and I want to get home before dinner so we can hang out tonight!"

"Ok… see you later," Molly said as Lily bounced out with the same enthusiasm she had come in with earlier. She smiled as she watched her head out, waving and talking to everyone she encountered along her short walk. She wished she could be more outgoing like Lily. She had always been more serious and reserved. She guessed that was why they got along so well, with each of them bringing something different to their friendship.

* * *

Molly pulled up to her house, checking carefully to make sure Waylon's truck was gone from the driveway. Seeing his empty space, she let out a breath she had no idea she'd been holding. She wasn't coming here for another fight… she just wanted to pack up some of her things and get this over with. A sense of dread and sadness was lurking over her shoulder, and she considered turning around and driving back to work.

She took a deep breath, shut off the engine, and got out of her car. She and Waylon had bought the beautiful ranch-style home 4 years prior when they had moved to Mill's Crossing. They had met in college, both attending the same university in Wisconsin. Molly had been studying a dual major in business and culinary arts, and Waylon had been studying restaurant management. They had several classes together and had gotten paired up on a final project one semester. From the moment he introduced himself to her, she had been a goner.

Molly sighed at the thought of how happy and simple things were back then. Now, she found herself standing in front of the home they had planned to become a family and grow old together in, and her heart hurt. She walked up the brick pathway towards the front porch, climbing the stairs as she approached the front door. She felt as though she had to physically force her feet to move forward.

She pushed the code on the front door to unlock it and walked in slowly. She knew Waylon's car was gone, but she still worried that he may be there. "Waylon?" she called out, listening for a reply. Nothing. She was alone.

Molly walked down the hallway towards the bedroom. As she got closer to the room that was supposed to be Hannah's, she noticed that the door was open. *That's odd,* she thought. She peeked in, seeing that it was just the way she had left it the last time she gone in.

Hannah's room was as girly as girly gets. Waylon had painted the walls pink, and the trim was hickory. Waylon had even painted a mural on the far wall. It was stunning… it had a tree with long branches, and birds perched together on them. There was a sun in the corner, shining on the scene. The base of the tree had beautiful tulips and roses painted, creating a garden of petals that they had dreamed their little girl would adore.

In the corner, under the sun, they had placed an antique rocking chair that they had scored at a local flea market just outside of the city. It had added a sense of timelessness to the room, and Molly had loved it. She had dreamed of all the times she'd spend rocking her little girl in that chair, and the tears flowed as she thought of all the dreams that had been lost that fateful day. She and Waylon had spent so much to ensure Hannah would have the perfect room to come home to, and their little girl had never gotten the chance to see it.

She knew that one day she would have to clean Hannah's room out, but neither of them had been able to face that challenge yet. It just felt too final to her. She knew Hannah was gone, but she couldn't bring herself to move anything.

Molly shook her head as if to clear the sadness out. Everything about this house was getting to her, she realized. She needed a change. Closing the bedroom door gently, she wondered again at the reason it was open. Shrugging, she assumed Waylon must have been in there after their argument that morning. She wasn't sure how she felt about that or why he would go in there since he normally steered clear of the room, but that was neither here nor there.

She hurried into the master bedroom to pack. She found her suitcases and filled them with as many clothes and personal care items as she could. After rolling them to the doorway, she went to the kitchen to grab a water from the fridge. Sitting at the island, she decided to call her mom since she had forgotten to return her call earlier. She dialed the number as she sipped her water. Her mom answered after the first ring, which made Molly smile.

"Well, it's about time, Molly!"

Molly knew her mom was teasing, so she laughed, saying, "Hello to you too, Mom."

"You sound kind of funny, sweetheart. Is something wrong?"

Molly took a deep breath and then told her mother everything that had happened that morning, as well as her conversations with Mia and Lily at work. She also told her that she had finally called the therapy office and had scheduled an intake appointment for the following Tuesday.

"I'm really sorry, honey," Laura Flynn responded after trying to process all the information Molly had just shared with her. *"Where are you now?"*

"I'm at the house, Mom. I knew Waylon would be at work, so I decided to stop by and pack up some stuff. I just finished up. Honestly, everything in here reminds me of memories that hurt, Mom," Molly responded.

"Molly, sweetie, you are going to be just fine. I know it doesn't feel like it now, but this is only a small piece in your life's puzzle. These feelings will not last forever... you just have to give it some time," her mother responded.

"I really hope you are right, Mom," Molly said.

"Your Dad and I will plan to meet you at Lily's in about 45 minutes... does that work for you? That way we can help you get settled in."

"That would be really nice of you guys... are you sure? I don't want you to change your plans if you had any. I can do it on my own, too," Molly said.

"Absolutely... we wouldn't have it any other way!" Laura replied.

"I love you, Mom," Molly told her, feeling very grateful that she had such supportive and loving parents to help her get through this stuff.

"I love you too honey. We'll see you soon," Laura responded before disconnecting the call.

Molly put her phone in her pocket and got up from her stool. "I guess I'd better finish up and head out," she said to herself as she headed to the bathroom to grab a few extra things she had forgotten.

As she stepped out of the house that had been her home for the last few years, she felt a mixture of hope and sadness. She and Waylon had shared *so* many good laughs and memories here, and she wished with everything in her heart that they could share many more in the years to come. Instead, reality threatened to paint a very different portrait than the one her dreams had created for her. With an aching heart, she got in her car and drove away, tears flooding her eyes. This wasn't how her life was supposed to go.

* * *

Waylon sauntered into Club Seven, the night club he bartended at, around six o'clock. It was already shaping up to be a busy night and he wasn't in the mood for people tonight. He still couldn't believe that Molly had just walked out on him like that. What was she thinking? Did she seriously want another baby so badly that she'd throw away everything they'd worked so hard to build? He just couldn't figure out what the hell she was thinking…

"Hey, man! It's about time you got here… didn't you get the messages I left you?" Mark, his boss and lifelong friend, asked, clearly annoyed at the fact that Waylon had arrived almost a full hour late for work.

"Look, Mark, I'm not in the mood for your crap tonight," he growled back, sending Mark a *don't- mess-with-me* look. "And no, I didn't. What's the problem?"

"Wow… one of those nights I see… we had a bachelor party call to let us know they are coming in tonight, so in addition to it being a full house, we also have over thirty rowdy men coming in around eight!"

Mark was shorter than Waylon, but he was built like a wrestler on steroids. In addition to being the bar's manager, he was also the guy that got called when someone was getting out of hand and needed a reminder to chill out. He was very intimidating, especially now that he had shaved his head bald. There was something about the new look that made people think twice about mouthing off.

"Sorry… it's been a day," Waylon remarked, still in a bad mood. "I'll get to work so you can get back to terrorizing someone else."

"Great idea… I think Sean over there is about to have a coronary. I hope he gets the hang of things pretty soon or we're going to have to look for a replacement. You'd think after a month he'd know the drinks and the regulars a little better than he does now. Plus, he's as jumpy as a cat on a tin roof!" Mark laughed, trying to lighten the mood a bit. Looking at Waylon's grumpy face he realized it wasn't working. "What the heck is your deal today anyway?"

"Nothing. I just want to get to work if you don't mind…" Waylon barked back.

"Okay, okay. I'll leave you alone," Mark replied, his hands in the air as a sign of retreat.

"Finally," Waylon mumbled, heading back behind the bar.

Mark shook his head and walked off, deciding to give Waylon some space to deal with whatever it was that was obviously bothering him today.

Waylon spent the next ten minutes getting everything organized and prepped behind the bar, knowing from experience that it was going to be a crazy night. He liked things a certain way when it was busy, and he had learned that a little preparation ahead of time meant much less headache later.

As he worked by himself behind the bar, he thought about the argument he and Molly had had that morning. He knew he'd been drinking a lot lately, but it was part of the job he did every day. Plus… it helped make all the depressing thoughts he kept having about Hannah go away, and it seemed to be the only thing that did. He couldn't talk to Molly about them because she would never understand. He never wanted to go through that horrible pain again, and he didn't want her to either. He had decided at Hannah's funeral to never take that risk again, and he wasn't changing his mind. If she couldn't handle that and didn't think that him loving her was enough, then screw her. He was done fighting every day about it.

Waylon was brought back to the present by the sound of breaking glass. He looked down, seeing that he had knocked a martini glass off the counter and onto the floor when he wasn't paying attention. Cursing, he reached down and grabbed the big pieces, tossing them in the glass bin under the counter. Then, he grabbed the broom and dustpan and cleaned the rest of the mess up. He needed to get his head on straight or he was going to hurt someone tonight… If he had any other choice, he'd be outta here in a second. He wasn't in the mood for a bachelor's party, or any other social interaction for that matter! He wanted to grab a bottle of whiskey and drown his anger in it until he slept off this whole stupid mess.

Heading back to the counter, he made a drink for the first customer he saw that hadn't been helped. Lucky for him, the guy bought him a shot too… smiling for real for the first time tonight, Waylon knocked it back. *Well,* he thought, *maybe this night won't be so bad after all…*

Four

Chapter 3

Molly sat in the small lobby of Heartstrings Therapy Associates, the office that her therapist, Claire, worked in. She had arrived a little early, as usual, and was nervous as she waited. She'd been here 4 times since her intake a few months ago, and every time she felt her nerves bunch up when she walked through the door.

Across from her was a little girl with her mother. They were reading a book she'd picked up from the little rack in the corner. She was adorable with her little blond curls and what appeared to be dry chocolate milk on her cheek. She waved her chubby little hand at Molly, who smiled and waved back. She loved kids, always had. Something tugged at her heart, but she noticed it didn't make her sad today… it made her feel something she wasn't sure how to define.

"Molly, you can come on back," Claire said, pulling Molly from her thoughts. She waved goodbye to the little girl and followed Claire down the hall towards her office. Heartstrings was a beautiful and calm office. There was always soft music playing in the lobby, and they had white noise playing in the hallway. It made her want to sleep, if she was being honest. Molly smiled at the thought. She was guessing Claire wouldn't be too happy if she took a nap for her session!

Claire closed the door behind them, and Molly sat down on the faux leather sofa that sat just across from Claire's comfy-looking maroon chair. The sofa was soft, but Molly always felt like Claire's chair was probably even more comfortable. In front of her on a small end table was a box of Kleenex and a sign that read:

Just in case you need to blow, while you're here or when you go!

Molly always got a kick out of the that sign. It was meant to make people feel at ease with the thought of crying and needing to blow their nose, she knew, but she appreciated the fact that it made her smile when she was feeling sad.

Claire grabbed her notebook and pen and sat down in her chair. Her smile was infectious. Molly had really grown to like Claire. She seemed like a genuinely kind person, and she loved the fact that she could tell her anything without having to worry about being judged or embarrassed. She was slowly starting to see why so many people loved to go to therapy.

"Well, Molly, how was the last couple of weeks?" she asked, starting the conversation.

"Pretty good. I feel like my nightmares are starting to get less and less, which is good. I even think I'm getting better sleep because I'm not so worried about them," Molly admitted.

"That's great to hear. Why do you think they are coming less frequently?" she countered.

"I'm not sure. I guess maybe it has something to do with me not thinking about it all as much now."

"When you say, 'thinking about it,' what do you mean?"

"I mean Hannah. I don't pass by her room everyday multiple times now that I'm not living there, so I'm not constantly reminded of losing her," Molly explained, tears threatening to fall.

"Molly, it's okay to cry. You've been through something heartbreaking, and you need to let those feelings out. When we bottle emotions like that, we often get to a point where they must explode to come out, and that is often much more damaging to ourselves and those around us than sharing along the way is," Claire told her, handing her the tissue box.

Molly took a minute to compose herself, willing the tears to stop falling. She wasn't one of those "pretty" criers… she cried ugly! Her face turned puffy and red, and her eyes looked like she'd been on a day-long bender.

"Can you tell me why that made you so emotional?" Claire asked her.

"I just feel guilty, I guess," Molly admitted.

"Guilty about what?"

"I feel like I'm moving on, and it doesn't feel like it's right to do that without my baby girl. I don't feel like I'll ever be happy again, and if I am, I feel guilty for feeling that way!" Molly said, emotion spilling from her heart.

"What you are feeling is completely normal, Molly. When we lose someone close to us, especially someone who was, quite literally, a *part* of us, we often feel guilty moving forward without them. That doesn't make you a bad person, it makes you human." Claire took a second to write something down in her notebook before addressing Molly again.

"I would like you to try something for me this next week," she told her. "I'd like you to find a special place that you can go that can be just for you and Hannah. You can decide where that place is, but I'd like you to try to find someplace that means something to you. Can you do that?"

"Yeah… but what do I do there?" Molly asked, confused by the request.

"I'd like you to simply spend time with her there. You can talk to her if you feel like it. You can read a book. You can close your eyes and just listen to the world around you and breathe. You can do whatever feels right to you, but I want you to shut the rest of the world out and *feel* her presence with you in that place. Does that make sense?" she asked.

"I guess so, but I'm not sure I understand how this will help," Molly admitted.

"The goal of this exercise is to help you feel connected to Hannah. You told me you feel like you are moving on without her, but there is no written rule that says that you can't take her with you, Molly. It won't look the way you had hoped it would, but it can be a very special time for the two of you to be together. And… if you don't feel comfortable after trying, you can always stop."

"Okay… I can try. I like the idea of something that's just for her and myself,"

Molly said, smiling a little for the first time since her session had started.

For the remainder of her session, Molly and Claire talked about Waylon and Molly's separation and Molly's thoughts on the direction her marriage was heading. She felt much better after she walked out the door an hour later. She wasn't sure where she would go to spend special time with her thoughts and memories of Hannah, but she was going to give it a try. After all, it couldn't hurt, right?

* * *

Molly slithered out of bed after her alarm woke her from the same nightmare she'd been having for the last 6 months. They were getting less frequent since she'd been going to therapy, so that was good at least. She looked out the window, happy to see that spring was finally creeping in and pushing the winter cold out. She absolutely loved spring… the birds and the smell of freshly cut grass… it promised newness and fresh starts, something she desperately needed right now.

Looking around the room, she couldn't believe what a turn her life had taken over the last year. She'd been living with Lily for 3 months now, and she was finally starting to find a rhythm to her life. Even though they didn't always see eye-to-eye, she and Lily got along well enough to live together for a while. Still, Molly hoped that once she and Waylon decided where their relationship was heading, that maybe things would settle down and she could start figuring out what was going to come next for her. She looked at the grey walls, feeling like they reminded her of the mood she was currently in.

"Okay," she said to herself, "that's enough of *that*. Time to get up and get to it."

She put on her robe and slippers and crossed the hallway to the bathroom. When she was finished, she headed to the kitchen where the smells of hot coffee and toast were making her stomach grumble. She heard a familiar meow as she felt Snowflake rub up against her leg, wishing her a good morning and wanting to be fed. Molly smiled and reached down to pet her.

"Good morning, Snowflake. Nice to see you, too!" she said as the cat pushed her face into Molly's hand. "I'll get you some food in just a minute… first, I need some coffee."

"Hey, Molly!" Lily chirped when Molly rounded the corner that led to the kitchen.

Molly groaned a barely audible response. How could anyone be so chirpy in the morning, anyway?

"I already made coffee and some toast. Here." She slid a plate over to the spot across from her as she settled on one of the wooden stools at the small table that sat in the corner of the kitchen. She smiled at Molly as she joined her.

Lily was glad winter was finally giving way to the warmth of spring. Nature was coming alive again. She knew how difficult the last year had been for Molly, and this winter had been long and cold, which wasn't helping her to get out and find something to do. She knew Molly needed to get her mind off everything that had happened lately, and some fresh air would probably do her a lot of good.

Lily knew how much Molly loved nature. It made her heart sink all those times when Molly would sit at the window and look out longingly as white flakes covered the ground all around them. She was glad it was all over for this year; colors were returning – greens and blues and reds, and all the others that had disappeared for months. Although it was very beautiful, Wisconsin was always a little depressing in the wintertime.

"Do you have any fun plans this weekend?" she asked, hoping to change the sad look she was seeing on Molly's face.

"Nah. I've got a lot of paperwork to catch up on from the shoppe, so I'll probably hang out in the office there and get some of that done. It's easier if I try to keep up on it instead of falling behind," she answered. "How about you?"

"I am working Saturday, but I plan to do some shopping on Sunday. I need to get some new spring clothes. I'm getting sick of the boring winter colors… time for some fresh new ones!" She smiled as she added, "Hey… why don't you come with me? It would be fun!"

"I don't know… can I think on it? I really do need to get some stuff done, but maybe if I get a bunch finished up on Saturday I could," Molly said, smiling but still not very convincingly.

Both women sat in silence for a few minutes, eating toast and drinking their coffee. Molly stared out the window, watching some robins on the feeder outside on the small patio that was attached to the apartment. She had put it out there yesterday because she loved watching birds and missed them terribly after the long winter.

"I almost forgot to tell you… Yesterday at the salon, I was dying Sally's hair and she told me that Jill Larabee is pregnant! Can you imagine that?" Lily scoffed audibly as she had another bite of toast. "I always knew she was going to get pregnant without getting married," she continued with her mouth full.

Molly looked at her, playfully rolling her eyes. "Do you dress up this early and run off to the salon simply because of all the juicy stories you hear there?"

Lily laughed. "Of course not," she said, nudging Molly in the arm and acting offended. Juicy gossip may have been part of the joy Lily found in working at her salon, but it wasn't her inspiration for dressing up in nice clothes each day. The real reason was that Lily loved to dress up… it was as simple as that. It didn't make sense to remain in PJ's when it was dawn. She had this "need" to look as beautiful as was possible every second of every day. As the owner of Bedheadz Salon and Spa, she was obsessed with style.

As usual, she was dressed like an executive. This morning, she had thrown on black dress pants and a fancy white button-up shirt. The bright white was a stunning contrast to her teal hair. Her natural beauty always amazed Molly.

"You look beautiful as always, Lil," Molly told her, a genuinely friendly grin making its way out to visit for a few seconds.

"Thank you! Ok… so I guess you're right on part of that… I do like hearing all the juicy stories too." She giggled. Working at the salon gave her free access to premium gossip about people and she loved it.

"Sally's the one who has all the stories, and even though I like her stories, I'm not a huge fan of her personality. Ever since I first started working on her hair and nails, I've felt like there was something off about her. She seems so judgmental all the time."

She finished the last drop of her coffee and stood to set the dishes in the sink.

"Her boyfriend came by the salon yesterday… He caught her red-handed talking up this other guy. She is a huge flirt. She had her hands all over him while she was chatting him up. The boyfriend came in and wasn't too happy about it! Then, the best part was that she introduced the two of them to each other and they both looked at her like she was crazy! The whole thing was hilarious! I knew Sally was unpleasant, but I didn't picture her as a player."

Lily grimaced. "By the way, there's only one can of cat food left for Snowflake."

"Oh, shoot," Molly said. She suddenly realized that it was the only reply she had given to her so far. Whenever Lily started to ramble about salon gossip, she often zoned out, having conversations with herself more than with anyone else in the room. Molly truly didn't care who got a new boyfriend or who cooked what last night. She cared more about the constant weight in her chest, her failed marriage, and all the work she needed to get done.

"Fear not. I'll stop at the supermarket after work this evening," Lily said in a dramatic tone.

"Thanks," Molly said as she stood up from the table. She went to the refrigerator, took out the can of cat food, and filled Snowflake's bowl. "I appreciate you doing that."

"No problimo!" Lily replied, leaving the room for a bit to finish getting ready.

"Snowflake," Molly called. "Your feast is served!"

It didn't take long before Snowflake came to the kitchen and began to eat.

Her phone lit up as a text message came in. Glancing at it, she saw it was from her mom. She opened the message to read it.

Hey, honey. Any chance you'd have some time to come have lunch with Dad and I tomorrow? We miss you!

She loved her parents but wasn't sure she could whip up the energy to go over there, especially since she had so much work to get done this weekend.

"I'm gonna head out, Mol," Lily said as she grabbed her purse and keys.

Before she walked through the door she looked back, adding, "See you later?"

"Yeah, I'll be here at some point," Molly said, giving her an uncertain wave.

Once Lily was out of sight, she plopped back into her seat, letting the tears fall. She was so exhausted from trying to pretend to be okay all the time. She just wanted to rewind time and go back to the days before Hannah was born when she and Waylon were truly happy. She had felt like she was on top of the world back then… like everything in her life was lining up perfectly. She wasn't sure she'd ever feel like that again.

Molly was pulled from her thoughts by the alarm on her phone. She looked down, seeing the reminder that she had an appointment with her doctor later today. She had completely forgotten about the appointment. It was her annual physical… one she'd prefer to skip but knew that she couldn't. She knew her doctor was going to ask her how she had been doing since Hannah's birth, and she hated trying to answer that question anytime someone asked it. She felt like if she said "I'm good, how are you?" that people would think she was lying, and if she said "I'm sad and lonely, how are you?" that people would feel uncomfortable. There wasn't a good answer to "How are you doing?" apparently.

As she wiped the counter off quickly, she thought about everything Claire had said the other day at her appointment. Therapy was going okay, but she had really hoped that she'd feel better by now… it was taking too long, as far as she was concerned. Still, she had to admit that it was helping some, and it had definitely been helpful to talk through all the feelings that were coming with her impending divorce from Waylon.

She headed into the bedroom and got dressed for the day. She decided she should at least look somewhat presentable, so she threw on a good pair of jeans and a floral blouse she had gotten a couple of years ago from her parents for her birthday. She loved the feel of the silk on her skin, and for the first time in a while she felt refreshed. Some slip-on shoes completed the outfit. She grabbed her phone and threw it into her purse, picked her keys up from the stand next to the door and headed outside.

Molly instantly felt the warm spring breeze on her face. She closed her eyes and breathed the scent of newness in. For Molly, nothing had the power to make her feel a little better than fresh air did. She was sure glad spring was here. Maybe there was a chance that her life could sort itself out… after all, if spring could find its way back every year after the depression that winter brought, maybe *she* could find her way back to *herself* too. One could hope, right?

The day was beautiful, so Molly decided she'd walk to work instead of driving the short six blocks. She hoped that the walk would help to clear her mind and get her into a good mood before she got to work. It was early still, so there weren't very many people on the sidewalks yet. As she got a few blocks from her shoppe, she decided to take a detour through a beautiful little park that was next to a school. She hadn't walked this way before, so she thought she'd try a new path.

Molly was about halfway through the park when she heard a dog bark off to her left. Molly absolutely loved animals, so she was drawn to the sound. She turned to find a gorgeous yellow lab coming towards her at full speed. She held out her hand and yelled, "Whoa… slow down there, fella!" The dog apparently didn't hear her because he came right to her feet. Luckily, he stopped just before plowing into her legs, and she was thankful she hadn't ended up on her butt on the path.

Smiling, Molly reached down to pet the friendly animal. His tail was wagging fiercely, and he was happy as could be.

"Hey there, buddy. Where did you come from?" Molly ran her hand over the smooth fur on the happy dog, and he laid down by her feet exposing his belly for a rub. She laughed at his antics. Molly looked around for his owner, knowing he must have one as he was wearing a green collar with tags dangling from it. Before she could read the tag, she heard a man's voice yelling from the other side of the park.

"Buck!" he yelled with a loud whistle. She could hear the aggravation in his voice as he called the dog. "Buck… Come back here!"

Molly stood as the man got closer to them, smiling at the look on his face. He seemed perplexed. She tried to hide her amusement, but guessed she wasn't doing a very good job at it.

"Buck! What in the world are you doing?"

Molly laughed. "I think he likes me," she said, still petting his belly.

As if on cue, Buck barked at them, causing both to laugh.

"I'm sorry my dog is such a pain in the neck," the man said. "My name is Owen West, and this, as you now know, is Buck."

Molly shook his extended hand, offering her name to him in return. "My name is Molly. It's no big deal, really. He sure is a beautiful dog," she said to Owen.

"Yeah, he may be pretty, but he's also naughty! I'm *really sorry* if he was bothering you. He got loose from the leash and took off. Apparently, I'm not as fast as I once was, because he got away from me, even running at full speed." Owen laughed, still red in the face from his race across the park.

Again, Molly found herself laughing at the whole situation. She hadn't realized how long it had been since she'd let go and laughed like that... all she knew was that it felt good.

"He truly didn't cause me any trouble. I do need to get going to work, though. It was very nice meeting you," she said to Owen. "And you too, Buck!" she said petting Buck's soft fur one last time before walking away.

Buck gave her a friendly goodbye bark as she waved, walking towards the opposite side of the park. With that, she finished the 2 blocks to her shoppe, feeling much better than she had when she had left Lily's apartment. She wasn't sure if it was the fresh air that had helped or her amusing interaction with the man named Owen and his dog, Buck, but either way, she was thankful for the change in mood.

Lily threw on her apron and got to work... mornings were her favorite part of the day when it came to work... she could be herself and do what she loved... bake!

Five

Chapter 4

Fridays at The Sweet Sprinkle were often utter chaos. People always seemed to decide they needed a last-minute cake or cupcakes on Fridays. Molly had no idea why people didn't plan ahead a little farther than that, but she had learned over the last few years to be prepared. She always kept a spare dozen and a few half sheet cakes in the freezer for this very reason. Of course, it didn't hurt that she had become a master at decorating cupcakes quickly and proficiently.

Today was no different than any other Friday. One mom had stopped by and was completely panicked because her husband was supposed to order the cake for her son's birthday party on Saturday and had totally forgotten. Another customer stopped looking for a small cake for her best friend's 1-year sobriety pinning on Sunday afternoon.

Molly was always happy to make someone's day by telling them it was no problem, and that she could get that ready for them by closing time. The satisfied look on their faces when they picked up their order always made her feel good inside. Just as she was about to hang her apron on the hook and take a break, she heard the door chime, letting her know a customer had just walked in. Sighing, she put on a smile and headed out to the counter.

The man who had walked in looked like he was on edge, and it made her a little nervous. She wasn't sure if he wasn't feeling well, or if something was wrong. Molly had had very few upset customers over the last three years, and she didn't recognize this man as a customer she'd had, so she wasn't sure what was going on. Smiling nervously, she greeted him.

"Hello! My name is Molly. Welcome to The Sweet Sprinkle! How can I help you today?"

"Hi. Um… I could really use your help. You see… I, um, well, I'm planning to propose to my girlfriend tonight, and I had this whole plan of putting it on a cupcake and all that fancy stuff, but my dog, Max, just ate it!"

He looked so miserable that Molly felt a little bad about the laughter that snuck out of her mouth. "Oh, I'm so sorry… that's just… that's hilarious!"

"Yeah, well, it *is* a little funny, but it's also a disaster!" he said, sighing, but smiling a little from the corner of his mouth as well.

"Don't worry… I've got you covered! Did you have a certain type of cupcake in mind?" Molly asked.

"Yeah… she really likes red velvet, at least I hope she does. I swear she told me that once, anyway…" he said, still looking a little pale.

Molly's heart felt for the guy. Here, he was trying to do a grand gesture of love for his unsuspecting girlfriend, and his dog went and ate the prop! She couldn't help but grin at the thought of his dog sitting in the car, gulping down a yummy, frosted cupcake.

"I have some of those on hand, so we're good there! Was there any certain color of frosting or design you had in mind?"

"Honestly… I'd take anything at this point! Her favorite color is purple, and she absolutely hates pink… does that help?" he asked, obviously frustrated and seriously rethinking his whole idea at this point.

"Ok, don't you worry. Why don't you have a seat at one of the tables if you have about twenty minutes and I'll see if I can work some magic for you," Molly said, pointing to the little table in the corner. "There's a magazine rack there if you'd like something to read while you wait. There might even be a bridal one in there in case this goes well for you!" Molly laughed, poking his shoulder in fun.

"Ouch… that was a low blow, ma'am," he said, laughing. "In all seriousness, thank you very much for doing this for me. You are a lifesaver!"

"It's no problem at all, really. I love helping people out, and I love what I do. I'll be back in just a jiffy. Sit and relax a bit."

Molly disappeared into the back room. She grabbed a few cupcakes from the refrigerator and got to work decorating them. She used a lavender base and then added small purple roses all wrapped around a circle with green leaves at their base. When she finished, they looked beautiful, and they had a space in the center for the ring to sit like it had been made exactly for that purpose. She added a little bit of cupcake glitter to give it an extra special touch. She imagined the diamond ring sitting in the center and thought it would be perfect.

Molly put the cupcakes into a carrier and headed back out to the nervous man in the other room. When he saw her coming back, he got up quickly and hurried up to the counter, obviously anxious to see what she had come up with.

"Holy crap… those are awesome!" he said, eyeing the cupcakes. "You just did that now? You are incredible… thank you so much!"

Molly laughed. The guy looked utterly miserable when he had come in earlier, and now she was pretty sure he wanted to hug her he was so happy. She smiled, saying, "I was my pleasure."

"How much do I owe you?" he asked, grabbing his wallet from his pocket.

"It's on the house," Molly told him. "Congratulations on your upcoming engagement… well, if the dog doesn't eat these ones too!"

The man laughed. "No kidding!" he said. "Thank you again… I will *definitely* be back for more soon. These cupcakes smell *amazing!*"

"Well, I made one for each of you… and the third one is for Max. Maybe if you give him his own, he'll leave yours alone!"

Molly handed the man his cupcake box and followed him to the door, locking it behind him and turning the open sign around so it would read 'closed.' She took her apron off and threw it on the hook in her office. Sitting down in her chair, she leaned back and took a deep breath. "Whew," she sighed. "What a day."

Just as Molly grabbed her purse to head out, the phone rang. She reached across the desk and grabbed it. "Hello, The Sweet Sprinkle, this is Molly speaking. May I help you?"

"Hello, Molly. My name is Amy Martins, and I am the district office manager over at Belleview High School. I am calling regarding the annual teacher's appreciate dinner that we put on each year for our staff members. I am wondering if you would be interested in catering in the desserts for our event this year?"

"Hello, Amy. We *would* be interested! What is the date and time of the event?" Molly asked her.

"It's on Friday, March thirtieth at seven o'clock in the evening. We are expecting about two hundred people to attend."

Molly quickly jotted the information down in her order planner. She wanted to make sure she had the date open first, and when it was all clear, she gathered the rest of the information she needed from Miss Martins. When she was finished, she thanked the nice woman for calling and assured her that they would be there by five thirty on the evening of the thirtieth to set up for the party before guests arrived. She hung up the phone and placed the order on her desk. Then, she locked up and left, wanting to hurry out before anyone else stopped by or called.

After a day like today, she wanted a hot bath, a book, and a glass of wine. Oh, and lots of bubbles! Nothing was as relaxing as a hot bath filled with bubbles!

* * *

With all the warm spring weather lately, Molly had fallen into the habit of walking to work almost daily. She loved hearing the birds sing and smelling the freshness in the air. It helped her clear her head, and it allowed her to stop at her new favorite bench and sit awhile with her coffee each morning. She had decided a while back that this would be her special place with Hannah...

the one Claire had told her to find. She loved her morning talks with Hannah. Most of the time, she just sat in silence and took in the sights and smells and sounds all around her. Other times, she told Hannah about her day, or about the silly things she had heard at work. Either way, this had become her most cherished and anticipated time of each day. Claire had been right… this had been a great idea.

Today, she was watching a robin up in the towering maple tree near her special bench. It was chirping away as it fed its babies in the nest it had built for them. "Isn't that adorable, Hannah? You can even hear their happy little chirps," Molly said, talking softly to her little angel. "She's probably telling them it's going to be a beautiful day."

Molly sat for a bit in silence, listening to the robin's song. Something to her left caught her eye suddenly, and she looked to see a beautiful butterfly with wings that seemed to glisten in the sun fluttering towards her. She watched the delicate creature land gently on her knee. She couldn't believe it wasn't scared of her. For several seconds, Molly watched the butterfly sit as if it was watching the world around it.

Molly began to talk to the butterfly. "You sure are a beautiful little one, aren't you? Just a sweet little butterfly enjoying a perfect spring day."

Molly figured that she was already crazy enough to be sitting here talking to the air, why not talk to a butterfly too?

"Maybe they'll add "butterfly whisperer" to my list of issues if they ever commit me!" she said, laughing to herself.

Before she could wait for the universe to answer her, the butterfly flew off, and she heard a familiar bark, followed by an equally familiar man's voice. Looking to her left, she saw Buck come flying over the hill again, on a mission to escape his handler. Laughing, she watched the whole scene unfold before her. As Buck got closer, she set her coffee down next to her to keep it safe and then waited for the excited dog to get to her.

Smiling, she greeted him, "Well, hello, Buck! It's so nice to see you again!"

Buck excitedly gave her a loud bark, rubbing his face into her petting hands. His tail was wagging furiously, signaling his happiness to see her.

Within seconds, she saw Owen come up over the hill in chase. She laughed again… this was quite the entertainment for so early in the morning!

Molly grinned as Owen got closer. "Good morning!" she called, still petting Buck.

"Good morning, Molly. I see that my very naughty dog has once again found you and proceeded to interrupt your morning," Owen said, rolling his eyes.

"He definitely knows what he wants," she replied, laughing as Buck leaned up and licked her face.

"Buck… stop it!" Owen said, grabbing the dog to pull him away.

"It's okay… he just wanted a little morning loving," Molly said, nuzzling Buck's face with her hands.

"Well, there's nothing wrong with some morning loving, that's for sure," Owen said, instantly regretting his choice of words. His face turned thirty shades of red. "I mean, for a dog, of course…"

Laughing wholeheartedly, Molly nodded in agreeance, "Yes, I suppose dogs *and* humans like some morning loving…"

"Do you mind if I sit down for a bit?" Owen asked, clearly still winded from running after Buck. "I'm a little tuckered out from my unwanted morning sprint."

"Of course," Molly said, moving her coffee out of his way.

Molly watched Owen move Buck out of the way so he could sit next to her. He was a pretty tall man, around six feet she figured. He was wearing a sweatshirt and athletic pants, so she couldn't see his figure very well, but the way he filled it out told her that he was a pretty muscular guy. His nose looked a little crooked, like he had broken it and not gotten it fixed or something… she decided she'd have to ask him about that some time.

"So, what is a beautiful woman like yourself doing in a park all alone this early in the morning?" he asked, opening their conversation.

"I have been trying to walk to work as many days as I am able lately. I really love to walk… the air is so fresh and clean, and I love the smell of new grass and dirt," she said, absent-mindedly closing her eyes and looking towards the sky, taking in the scents all around her.

Owen watched her, thinking she may just be the most naturally beautiful woman he'd ever seen. Her face was mostly free of makeup, and her eyelashes were long and full, encasing her beautiful green eyes. Something in her eyes looked sad, though, and he noticed a hint of it in her voice as well as she spoke.

"I also come here to sit with my thoughts, and to…" she trailed off, uncomfortable sharing the intimate meaning this little bench had to her. She was never sure how to talk about Hannah to people… it seemed like everyone acted so oddly when she brought up her name, kind of like they were weirded out by her talking about Hannah still. It really bothered Molly, but she tried to be understanding, knowing that most people probably just didn't want to hurt her. The problem was, she felt better when she talked about her. It was her way of keeping her memory alive, and she couldn't figure out how to help others see that she needed that.

"And *to…*" Owen interjected, pulling her from her daydreaming thoughts.

"Oh, sorry. And to… to remember, I guess," she said, finding words that would hopefully satisfy him without making her share any more than she currently wanted to with a stranger.

"Ah… yes. I understand that completely. My wife passed away three years ago, and I come to this park to clear *my* head as well. Sometimes I think about taking a different path for our walks, but something lately has kept pulling me here… something other than Buck, of course." Owen laughed, a low and booming sound that Molly found very smooth and silky.

"I'm sorry that you lost your wife. That must have been terrible," Molly said, offering her empathetic sympathy to him, knowing full-well the devastation that a loss of that magnitude can cause in your heart.

"Thank you. I appreciate that," he said, sitting quietly for a moment in thought. "You said you work near here… do you mind if I ask where?"

"Oh… yes. I own a little cupcake and dessert shoppe a couple of blocks from here called The Sweet Sprinkle. My friend Mia and I started it a few years ago. It's always been a dream of mine, and I absolutely love it… for the *most* part." Molly winked as she said the last words. Every adult who owned a business knew that it wasn't all sunshine and rainbows. Sometimes, it was a major pain in the butt, too.

"I get that for sure. I'll have to stop in sometime… I happen to love cupcakes very much!" he laughed, nudging her arm with his.

"I bet you do… and I bet Buck does as well. We make doggy cupcakes occasionally too… some people go all out for their pets, that's for sure!"

"I'll have to keep that in mind… I usually give Buck a steak and potatoes for his birthday, but a cupcake sounds much better."

Molly and Owen both laughed as Buck perked his ears up at the mention of his name. He was obviously loving his time with Molly, and Owen couldn't really blame the guy. He was really enjoying it as well.

"What do you do for work?" Molly asked Owen, continuing the friendly conversation.

"I'm a science teacher at one of the high schools nearby," he answered.

"Uffdah… I could never do that! I love kids, but I don't think I'd have the patience to deal with them every day… especially in large quantities!"

"It's definitely an acquired taste…" Owen said, laughing at the look on her face when she talked about a group of teenagers. He got it… they were a lot even on a good day! He still loved it, though. He had loved it since the day he started teaching. Some days were definitely more stressful than others, but it was worth it to him, for sure.

Molly and Owen continued to talk lightly for a few minutes before Owen looked at his watch. Seeing the time, he sighed, wishing he could stay longer to get to know Molly better.

"I hate to say this, but I need to get going. I have to drop Buck off before I head to school for the day," he said, standing up and addressing Buck. "Say goodbye, Buck. We need to go."

Buck looked at Molly, then back at Owen again. He looked confused about whether he should stay with her or go with him. Molly laughed. "Goodbye, Buck! I hope to see you again soon!"

"It was really nice talking with you again, Molly. I hope we can do this again sometime," Owen said, smiling at her. He had a very nice smile… one that seemed to light up his face.

"It was nice to see you again, too," Molly said. "I am here every morning, if the weather is nice, so I'm sure I'll see you again soon."

"Perfect," he said. "Until then…"

Owen and Buck turned and walked off over the hill again. As they disappeared from her sight, Molly picked up her coffee and decided to get on with her day too.

"Well, Hannah, off I go to another day of fun at the shoppe," she said as she started down the path ahead of her.

Molly was really starting to enjoy her conversations with Owen. It was nice to have a friend to talk to that she didn't either live or work with. He was funny, too. *I definitely need a little "funny" in my life right now*, she thought. As she rounded the last corner towards her shoppe, she smiled and said, "It's going to be a good day."

* * *

After work, Owen decided to head into town to grab some plumbing materials he needed for his house. His kitchen sink had started leaking whenever it felt like it, so he wanted to change out some of the O-rings to see if that would fix the problem. He was *definitely* not a plumber, but he knew how expensive it would be if he had to call one, so he decided he'd try this first.

As he was driving towards the hardware store, his mind flashed back to his encounter with Molly again that morning in the park. He'd thought about it on and off all day and he couldn't seem to get his mind off it. She was so beautiful, and he got the feeling she didn't have any idea that she was. She had such cute dimples and stunning emerald-green eyes that made him want to explore their depths. He knew there was so much more to her story than he had already learned, and he couldn't help but want to hear it all. He felt like there was something she had wanted to say earlier but had held back from, and it was eating him up inside now. What was the real reason she went to the park every day? She had said something about remembering… had she lost her husband like he had lost his wife? If so, why hadn't she told him that after he told her about his? Something just didn't add up.

His thoughts were interrupted by a beep on his phone, an alarm signaling that he had received a text message. Looking down, he saw that it was from his dad.

I need you to stop by and help me with something this weekend.

That was the whole message… typical. Owen's dad, Chuck West, was a dairy farmer. He and Owen didn't get along very well because he hated that Owen was a teacher. He had wanted his son to take over the family farm, but Owen had never intended for farming to be his life. His dad had loved it, but he never had. He respected the hell out of him for working so hard for his family his whole life, but farming wasn't Owen's cup of tea. He just wished his father could figure that out and respect *his* decisions too.

What do you need, Dad? Owen responded.

I told you… I need you to stop by and help me. Is it too much to ask that you take an hour out of your busy life to help me out with something? Chuck countered.

Annoyed, Owen sent a message in return, saying, *I never said that, Dad. I just asked what you need help with.*

Ten seconds later, Owen's phone rang. He didn't need to look at the caller id to see that it was his dad.

"Hello," Owen answered.

"What did I do wrong with you anyway? When I ask for your help, just do it! I don't understand why you have to argue and pry about everything. I need you, so come. It's that simple…" his dad said, clearly angry at Owen for asking what he needed.

"I wasn't trying to argue… I just wondered what you need help with so I know how long it will take and can make sure I'm prepared for whatever it is. That's it, so calm down!" Owen responded, aggravated at his father's tone.

When it came to his dad, Owen didn't think he'd ever be treated like a man. He still acted like Owen was a child, and it grated at him. Owen hadn't seen his dad in almost a year, so this conversation was the first they'd had in a long time, and it had caught him off guard. A year prior, they had been at a family wedding when his father had started a fight in front of everyone with Owen, calling him a child and a disappointment. Owen had decided then and there to keep his distance.

Chuck West was a stubborn man, and the only person that could make Owen's usually calm demeanor change in the blink of an eye.

"If you want help, tell me what you need. I have a lot going on right now, but I'll help if I can."

Owen heard the click of the phone. His dad had hung up. Balling his fists in frustration, Owen took a deep breath, trying to get the whole conversation out of his mind. His mood had very quickly changed from happy to ornery, and now he just wanted to grab the stuff he needed and get out of there.

Finding the supplies from his list, he checked out and headed back to his car. He took a deep breath, trying to clear the air, along with his mind. He was sick of his father making him feel like a little boy. He was done with him for good this time.

Six

Chapter 5

"It sure was gorgeous today… I'm really glad this is shaping up to be such a warm spring," Molly said to Mia as they drove towards Belleview High. They hadn't had many customers for a Friday, so they had gotten a lot done and even had had some time to get caught up on phone calls and paperwork… something that rarely happened.

"Yeah, this has *definitely* been a mild spring. I did hear, though, that it's supposed to be back in the thirties one day next week," Mia replied, watching out the window as Molly drove their delivery van.

"Yuck! Why did you have to burst my bubble like that?" Molly whined.

"Hey… blame the weather guy, not me!" Mia said, teasing back. "Isn't it funny how just five short months ago, in the fall, we were thinking that fifty degrees seemed cold, and now, in March, it seems warm?"

"Yeah… I guess it's all relative. Either way, I'll take it."

"Me too," said Mia, laughing when she saw a guy walking on the sidewalk wearing shorts and a t-shirt. "Huh… I don't think it's quite that warm!"

Molly looked at the guy that Mia was pointing out and laughed. "No kidding! I'd be *way* too cold in shorts right now. Only in Wisconsin I guess…"

"Definitely," Mia said. "So, how long do you think we'll be staying at this dinner thing tonight? Do we just set up and leave, or are we staying for serving and clean-up?"

"When I talked to the lady earlier today, she asked if we could supervise the serving for a little while in case there were any issues or questions, so I told her that was fine. I don't really think it will be overly long, though. I'm hoping to be out of here by six thirty at the latest," Molly told her, crossing her fingers while she talked.

Mia smiled, secretly hoping she was right. "Well, I have a hot date with my couch, some wine, and my sexy husband later, so I hope it doesn't go too late!"

Molly laughed, nudging her best friend in the arm. "Well then, by all means, don't let me keep you from *that!*" she teased.

Molly and Mia got along so well that they often finished each other's sentences. They had been friends for so many years that she couldn't even remember a time where they weren't anymore. As little girls, they used to love each other one minute and hate each other the next... her mom once told her that the only way you could stay friends for so long and get so mad at each other sometimes was because you loved each other. She supposed that was true. Either way, she knew that Mia loved her husband, Jeff, very much, and she was truly happy that her best friend had found such a great guy to spend her lifetime with. She only wished she and Waylon had found that kind of happiness together too. She couldn't see Jeff turning into a drunk like Waylon had... no matter what type of tragedy he went through.

A minute later, Molly pulled the van into the parking lot of the Belleview High School. There were a few cars, but plenty of spaces up front by the doors for her to park. She and Mia got out and loaded the boxes of cupcakes and mini cheesecakes onto their cart and carefully pushed it into the huge brick building. The pillars on the front were almost two stories tall, and they reminded Molly of the ones at the courthouse. The red brick of the school was offset by a beautiful shade of blue on the steel siding that started at window-height and went to the roofline. There was a great big bear emblem next to the entrance, so Molly assumed that must be their mascot.

When they entered the building, they were greeted by a tall, skinny woman with a suit coat and black calf-length skirt on. She wore high heels and looked very professional. She greeted them with a kind smile and an extended hand.

"Hello, Molly. I'm Amy. It's nice to finally put a face to the voice on the phone!"

"Hello, Amy. It's nice to meet you as well," Molly said, gesturing to Mia as she added, "This is my friend and business partner Mia."

Amy shook Mia's hand and then turned to show them to a beautiful library area, right in the center of the school. It had been decorated with twinkle lights, tables with white cloths on them, fancy dinnerware, and a small gift at each place setting. She instantly loved Amy's style.

"This looks beautiful," Molly told Amy.

"Thank you, we do our best to show our staff how much we adore and appreciate them every chance we get. We believe that the happier our staff is, the happier our students will be. Working with kids day in and day out can be very stressful, and we want them to sit back and relax, even if it's just for a while."

Molly loved this school already, and she had just gotten there. "I think that's an amazing way to look at things, and an even better way to treat your employees than most do."

"I appreciate you saying that. How about I show you where you can set up?" Amy said, gesturing towards the side of the library.

Molly walked over to the tables and took inventory of their space. Getting to work, she and Mia unloaded and put together the display stands for the desserts, filling them with elegantly decorated cupcakes and mini cheesecakes. When they were finished, they stepped back and assessed their display.

"Not too shabby if I say so myself," Mia said, smiling.

"Agreed! Now… let's get all these boxes back out to the van and move it out of the way before too many people start to arrive. Then, we can find a spot in the back room that Amy told me was available to us to relax in while we wait for the time to serve," Molly said, starting to gather the empty containers.

After they cleaned up the mess and loaded everything in the van, Mia and Molly sat in the small lounge area in the back of the library that had been set up for the caterers to gather in. They talked for a while about this and that, and then Mia decided to call Jeff to let him know when she'd be home. Molly decided to head to the bathroom quickly before they had to serve dessert. She snuck out the door, avoiding the dinner that was going on in the main part of the library, and found the hallway that led towards the bathrooms.

As she walked through the hallway trying to find the restrooms, she saw a man in a navy-blue suit standing with his back to her, talking on the phone. As she got closer, she could hear that he was arguing with someone. She was going to try to hurry by, but something stopped her. That voice… it was… familiar. She stole a glance at his face as she passed him, realizing why she recognized the voice. It was Owen!

Molly was shocked to see Owen here… suddenly realizing that he had told her he was a teacher, so this must be the school he worked at. He was still arguing, and he hadn't noticed her yet, so she kept walking. For some reason, she was still not finding a darn bathroom!

"Where is this thing, anyway?!" she said to herself, getting frustrated as she reached a dead end and turned to head back to the intersection where she had seen Owen.

As she approached Owen, he hung up the phone and looked up, locking eyes with Molly. He looked just as surprised as she had felt a minute ago when she first saw him!

"Molly?" he said, confusion written on his face. "What are you doing here?"

"Hey, Owen! We are catering the desserts here tonight for your dinner," she said, smiling at him. "I didn't realize this was the school you worked at. It seems like a wonderful place!"

"Yeah, they really do care a lot about the kids and the staff here. That definitely makes it easier to deal with some of the not-so-fun parts of teaching. I'm really glad to see you, Molly."

"It's nice to see you, too. Even if you don't have Buck with you," she teased.

"Trust me, he'd have come if he could!" Owen replied, laughing.

"Not to pry, but is everything okay?" Molly asked, concern written all over her face.

"Okay?"

"I heard you arguing with someone on the phone when I passed by. I wasn't listening in or anything… I just can't find the darn bathroom!" she said, smirking at him.

Owen smiled, "You turned the wrong way… it's just over there," he said, pointing to his right. "And yes, I'm okay. That was my dad, actually. It's a long story, but the short of it is that he wants me to give up teaching and come back home to be a farmer like he is. He and I don't get along very well, unfortunately. He's stubborn and I'm not…"

Molly laughed, "Oh really? Not stubborn at all?"

"Well, okay, maybe a little, but nothing like him. He's legendary!" he said, visibly losing any last bit of anger he had been wearing on his face when she had first seen him.

"Not to be rude, but we are serving dessert in about ten minutes, and I still need to use the restroom quickly. As much as I'd love to stay and chat, I need to excuse myself for a moment." she told him, already starting to walk in the direction Owen had pointed.

"Absolutely… go ahead!" he said, backing up so she could get by him and head to the restrooms. He watched her walk away, thankful she had worn the stunning red dress she had on tonight. Her shoes were practical flats, and she had no jewelry on. On her face she wore very little makeup, but she was still an impressive sight.

Something in his gut tugged. *Uh oh,* he thought. *Owen… you'd better check yourself. She's filled with mystery, and you promised to stay away from women that were complicated.*

Molly entered the restroom and found it to be empty, so she went in the first stall she saw. She was almost finished when she heard two women enter, laughing and chattering the entire way. Before she could get up to leave the stall, one of the women said something that piqued her interest, so she waited, listening to their amusing conversation.

"Did you see Owen tonight? *Hubba-darn-bubba!*" the first one said.

"Oh yeah… that suit makes him look like James Bond all the way!" the second one responded.

Both women laughed while they touched up their makeup at the sink.

"That man is so fine; I'd like to eat *him* for dessert!"

"No way… he's all mine. I just need ten minutes alone with him in a dark room," the second women interjected. Molly could see the outline of her body in their mirror through the crack in the stall.

"If wishes were horses…" the first woman replied, laughing.

"More like 'if wishes were *Owen!*' If that were the case, I'd *definitely* be going for a ride!"

Both women laughed at their naughty conversation, most likely oblivious to the fact that Molly was sitting in the closed stall just down from where their entire X-rated conversation had just taken place. Molly caught herself covering her mouth as she silently laughed at the entire scene. Obviously, Owen was quite the eligible bachelor amongst the staff. I mean… she *had* noticed that he was attractive, but she had been looking more at his *dog,* to be quite honest! She hadn't really thought of him in a "man and woman meet and fall in love and live happily ever after" sort of way.

Still, for some reason she felt tiny butterflies down in her belly, and she wasn't sure what they were doing there. She came out from the stall, washed her hands, and dried them with a paper towel. She stopped to look into the mirror, making sure she looked okay. When she looked up, she saw something new in her face… a smile that was real and true. A smile that had been lost for almost a year.

She thought about what had brought that smile on, realizing it was Owen. Could she have feelings for this guy somewhere deep inside?

Nope… no way, she thought. He was a friendly guy, and he was attractive. She enjoyed talking to him and hanging out with him, and Buck, in the park. That was it, though. She wasn't going to make any more of this than it was. She couldn't, at least not right now.

As quickly as the smile had entered her face, it now faded. Her happiness was instantly replaced by guilt.

"Oh, my goodness! How could I be this cruel?" she said aloud to her reflection. Silently, she went on scolding herself. *How could I even entertain such thoughts knowing fully well that I'm still married to Waylon?*

Suddenly realizing she'd been in the bathroom for *much* longer than she had needed or intended to be in there, she tidied her face a bit and headed out the door.

For Heaven's sake, she thought, *Owen probably thinks I've fallen in or something*!

With that, she took a breath, opened the door, and headed back to the party. It was time to do what she had *actually* come here to do before she'd turned into an international spy in the bathroom of a high school!

Seven

Chapter 6

Molly sat at her bench in the park watching the birds and listening to the kids playing on the playground nearby. She was guessing there was some sort of mommy and me group that was meeting over there, because it looked like quite a crowd for a Tuesday afternoon. Two weeks had passed since the dinner at Owen's school, and Molly had only seen him here once since… not that she was looking for him or anything.

"I'm not sure why I seem to think he'll just show up every time I happen to be here," she said aloud as she spoke softly to Hannah.

Still, she found herself hoping she'd hear Buck come running over the hill, barking his usual "hello!" at her each time she sat on she and Hannah's bench, but they never came. She wasn't sure why she felt so disappointed, but she guessed it was because she was really starting to enjoy the friendship that seemed to be growing between them. She knew Owen was probably teaching at the moment, so she wasn't sure why she thought he'd be in the park.

"I just really enjoy talking to him, and of course petting Buck as well," she said. "Oh well, maybe I'll come back on Saturday to visit and see if they are around."

Molly stood, grabbing her purse from the bench, adding, "Enjoy this beautiful afternoon, Hannah. I'm heading over to the mall now to grab a few things I need before I go home for the evening. I'll stop by again soon."

Molly had gotten much more comfortable talking with Hannah on their bench over the last few weeks. It was really helping her feel connected to her baby girl, something she never thought she would be able to do. Unless a person had been through that kind of loss. It was impossible for them to understand, but she really cherished that time. For Molly, it was finally giving her a sense of closeness with her daughter that she hadn't felt since she was snuggled safely inside her tummy. She wouldn't trade that feeling for the world, no matter how many people may think she was off her rocker.

As Molly walked towards her car, she thought about everything that had happened over the last year. Her life had changed so much, and she realized now that although she and Waylon had once loved each other very deeply, Hannah's death had changed them both, and instead of growing closer and helping each other through the trauma, they had grown apart, each handling it in their own ways. It was time that she and Waylon had a heart-to-heart about everything so that they could decide about their future, and whether that was a future together or apart. She couldn't keep putting off the inevitable.

Molly grabbed her phone from her pocket and messaged Waylon.

Hey... been a minute. I hope you've been good. Would you be up for meeting tonight before you head to work? We can talk over dinner at Mainstream Eatery at 5:30pm if that works for you?

Molly received a text back from Waylon almost immediately.

"I don't have to be in until 7 tonight, so yeah, that works. See ya at then."

Molly tried to push back the sense of dread that was building in her core. She'd lost enough sleep over this… it was time to see if the separation had been enough for Waylon to re-think his drunken ways and to want to work on the love that they had planned to spend an eternity sharing. Tonight, she'd know one way or the other.

* * *

Molly was a bit late for the dinner as she had to finish up a cupcake order and run some quick errands before the stores closed for the evening. When she got to the restaurant, she saw Waylon's truck parked outside. She hurried out of the car, aggravated that she was late. She was a very punctual person who would rather not go to something than arrive late. Taking a deep breath, she opened the door and entered. She looked around the cute little diner and found Waylon sitting at a table over by the window. He was looking at a menu, so he didn't see her right away.

"Welcome to Mainstream… is it just you tonight or are you waiting for someone?" the man at the counter asked politely.

"Oh, hello. I am joining my… I see the person I'm meeting over there," she stumbled through, causing the man to look at her a little funny.

"Okay, you can go ahead and join him then. Would you like me to have your server bring you anything to drink?"

"Uh… yeah… I'll have a mango iced tea please," she replied, moving past him to join Waylon at the table.

When she got closer, Waylon looked up from the menu and smiled. He had always had a handsome smile… it was one of the first things Molly had fallen for way back when they first met. She returned the smile and sat at the open chair across from him. The air felt thick and heavy, and she was instantly uncomfortable. Yes, they were technically still married, but there was something different between them right now, something she couldn't quite put her finger on. He felt more like a stranger she was meeting on a first date than the man she had loved for many years.

"Hey, Mol," Waylon said, breaking the silence between them. "You look fantastic."

"Thank you, Way. You look good too," she replied, wishing she could get the odd feeling in the pit of her stomach to go away. "I'm sorry for keeping you waiting, I had a big order that took longer than I had planned and then I had to grab some stuff in town before the stores closed."

"It's no issue," Waylon said with a grin.

The waiter stopped by and took their orders, giving Molly a chance to think of what she wanted to talk about first. She wasn't used to feeling so uncomfortable with Waylon, so it was throwing her off. When the waiter left, she took a sip of her drink and then directed her attention to Waylon again.

"So… how have you been?" Molly inquired as she tried to jumpstart a conversation.

"I've been okay… busy at work as usual," he responded. "How about you?"

"I'm good. The shoppe is buzzing with customers ever since that lady from the Sentinel stopped by and did that article on us a couple of months ago. I honestly didn't even know people read the papers much anymore, but apparently, I was wrong."

"That's great… I always knew you were going to make it big with the shoppe," Waylon said, looking genuinely happy for her. If there was one thing Waylon had always done, it was support her in her dream of and vision for The Sweet Sprinkle. He had been the one that had encouraged her to take the leap and open the shoppe up with Mia. She would be forever grateful to him for that.

They exchanged random conversation back and forth and were finally starting to feel a little more like they used to when the waiter brought their dinner and sat their plates in front of them. Molly thanked him and he excused himself so they could enjoy their meals.

Molly picked at her food for a bit before setting her fork down to take a drink of her tea. Seeing that Waylon had done the same, she decided it was time to have the conversation she had asked him here to have. She wasn't sure how to approach the topic, so she decided to just throw it out on the table and let it go wherever it decided to go.

"Waylon, I asked you here tonight because I wanted to talk to you about everything that has happened and where we are going from here," she said, clearing her throat softly.

"Molly, do we seriously have to do this right now… *here*?" Waylon asked tensely.

"Yes, I think we do. I'm not sure how you are feeling about everything, but I know I am *really* tired of living the way we have been since Hannah."

"Please, Molly. I just want to enjoy this moment with you and this meal. We can talk later about all of this stuff," he said, getting more frustrated with her.

Molly took a few bites of her food and then, knowing she needed to find the courage somewhere down deep to finish the conversation she came here to have, put her fork back down, took a drink, and addressed him again.

"No… you know what? I came here tonight to talk about this with you in a calm manner, and we are going to do just that. I can't keep doing this… it's not fair to me and it's not fair to you."

"Fine," Waylon said, now clearly annoyed with Molly. He put his silverware down and stared at her, his eyes cold and angry. Molly had seen those eyes before, only they were usually bloodshot too. She took a deep breath and went on.

"Over the last few months, I have been going to therapy, and I really like it. It has given me a much clearer understanding of things, and a chance at hope again. I feel like I'm slowly finding my way back to myself. I really think it could help you, too, if you would just give it a try."

"I've told you a million times, Mol, I have no intention of going to therapy. I'm glad it's working for you, but it's not something I want to do. I'm fine… my mind isn't the problem between us," Waylon said, raising his voice slightly and earning some curious looks from the other restaurant guests.

Molly took a breath, waiting for everyone to stop looking. Then, she lowered her voice to a raised whisper, saying, "Waylon, *you* see therapy as an intrusive process, but *I* am living proof that it can be healing and helpful. And… what do you mean that's not the problem? What, exactly, do *you* see as our problem if not that?"

"Our problem is that you have become so obsessed with having another baby that you've thrown what we had right out the window, all over whether or not I'll go to therapy or agree to have another baby."

Molly flinched as though he had slapped her. Tears were filling her eyes and she willed them to stay away. Molly knew Waylon was angry about losing Hannah and about her leaving, but she had no idea that this was what he saw as their issue… her need to be a mother? She took a drink, suddenly feeling as though she'd swallowed a tack.

Seeing that he had hurt her, Waylon softened his voice, offering her a pleading look. "Look, as I told you before, I don't want another baby… not now, not ever. I want to move on with you and I together and happy again, no kids, no ties to this place or any other. I want to travel the world with you and see all the places you and I both used to dream about when we were first together," he said, reaching across the table to grab Molly's hands in his. "Don't you want us to be happy like that again, Mol?"

Molly pulled away from him, picking up her purse from the chair next to hers. She had to get out of here before she made a blubbery scene of tears all over the place in front of everyone around them.

"Molly, please don't go. I didn't mean to hurt you, I just need you to understand where I'm at with this," Waylon said, begging her to stay and talk.

Molly took a breath, trying desperately to calm down. She closed her eyes for a second, trying to find the words she needed to show him what was in her heart. Opening them slowly, she looked at him, the look on his face slowly breaking her heart into even more pieces than she thought she had left after Hannah.

"Way, I'm done. We're done. I love you and a part of me always will, but we have grown in very different directions ever since Hannah left us. We want different things, and we apparently always will. My heart can't take any more of this. We'll talk in a few days after I figure out what I want to do next, but for now I need some time to think," she said, tears burning her eyes again.

With a final whispered, "Goodbye, Way," Molly took her wedding ring off and set it in his hand, walking away. She felt as though part of her life had just ended, but she hoped with all her might that whatever was yet to come would heal the hole that had just been left in her heart.

* * *

Molly walked into Lily's apartment, tossed her keys on the counter, and went to the kitchen to grab a glass of wine. She wanted nothing more than a bubble bath, some soft music, and some peace and quiet so she could cry all the tears out that had threatened her all evening. As she got into the kitchen, she saw Lily coming in from the balcony.

"Hey, Mol…" Lily started but stopped as she saw the condition of Molly's face. She had red eyes with puffy bags under them as though she'd been crying, and her cheeks were a blotchy pink color. Lily instantly knew something was wrong. She crossed the room to her instantly and hugged her. Molly hugged her back, letting the tears fall.

"Hey, Lil. I'm sorry… just been a long night is all."

"What happened? Where did you go?" Lily asked, firing questions at her to try to figure out what was going on.

"Can we go sit down for a bit and talk maybe?" Molly asked, exhausted from her long day at work and her conversation with Waylon.

The two women walked over to the sofa and sat together, Snowflake jumping down from the back of it to purr and rub up against Molly. Molly pet her for a while, needing a minute to collect her thoughts before having to rehash it all again with Lily.

Lily gave her a second, but then broke the silence, reaching over to put her hand on Molly's. "Molly, what's going on?"

"I met with Waylon tonight," Molly said.

"Waylon? What for? "Lily asked, giving a confused look, as though she had expected something else to be wrong.

"After my therapy session today, I asked to meet up with him and he agreed. I knew from the beginning that things weren't going well. We talked some, but then as soon as I asked him about our relationship, he turned into the same Waylon he was before I left."

Lily wanted to help, but she wasn't sure how. She just sat and listened to Molly as she told her about the interaction she and Waylon had had at dinner.

"I even tried to convince him to come with me to see a therapist, but you know how stubborn Waylon can be right?"

"Yes, I most definitely do…" Lily said, rolling her eyes. "it's not like you were asking for a kidney or something! I can't figure out why he's so dead set against talking to someone. You two went through Hell together… what's he so scared of?"

"I have no idea. He blamed me for everything, of course, saying that me wanting to have a baby again one day is the reason we are separated. Can you *believe* that?" Molly asked.

"Unfortunately, yes. Mol, Waylon isn't in his own right mind right now. The problem is, I'm not sure how in the world he's ever going to get to that point if he doesn't admit something's wrong in the first place," Lily offered.

"That's true, for sure," Molly said, grabbing a Kleenex to blow her nose into. Sniffling, she went on. "I told him we are done, Lil. It broke my heart, but I had to say it."

Lily moved closer so she could take Molly in her arms. Molly sobbed for what felt like hours, and Lily just held her, running her hand over Molly's back to comfort her. She felt terrible for her best friend, wishing she could somehow take this all away for her, but knowing she couldn't. When Molly's sobs lessened, she handed her another tissue. Molly blew her nose and then laid her head on Lily's shoulder, allowing Snowflake to jump up into her lap again. Snowflake always seemed to know when she needed some snuggles.

"I'm sorry for all that," Molly sniffled. "It's just a lot, you know?"

"I completely understand, and I'm always happy to wear your snot for you!" Lily said, causing both women to laugh.

"Sorry about that, too!" Molly said, pretending to wipe the wetness from Lily's shoulder. "Thank you for letting me unload that on you… I really do appreciate it."

"No problimo, Molls! You know I'm always here for you," she said, sighing. "Besides, that man doesn't know how good he had it! He hurt you instead of healing with you… he's a fool!"

Molly laughed, this time from her belly. Lily always had a way of making things amusing, even when they were heavy and serious. Together, they sat on the sofa watching some Hallmark movie that was on TV, until Molly fell asleep on Lily's shoulder.

"You'll be okay, my sweet friend," Lily whispered softly before falling asleep as well.

Eight

Chapter 7

Bedheadz Salon & Spa was just three blocks away from Club Seven, the nightclub Waylon bartended at. He often passed by the salon at one point or another during the day, and he used to stop in and say hi whenever he saw Lily through the window. The customers loved him because he had a contagious personality. Ever since Hannah died, though, things had been different. He'd still walk by, but now he just kept on walking, looking at the ground or the people on the sidewalk ahead of him, but never stopping to say hi or even taking a second to wave. Today was no different.

Lily felt bad for Waylon… she like him, but she also felt protective of her best friend. She knew he was in a bad way, and that he needed to get some help so he could process everything that happened with Hannah, but he was apparently too darn stubborn to do so. She watched him saunter by, looking like he had been through Hell and back, hands in his pockets, an ornery look on his face. Shaking her head, she continued to put the curlers in Margaret Klamont's hair.

"There goes that *fine*-looking gentleman again… I wonder what happened to make him so sad. He used to be filled with life, and now he just looks frumpy all the time," Margaret said, clearly oblivious to the situation with him.

Margaret was an elderly woman who only came in when her daughter found time to bring her. Her daughter, Stella, would drop her off, run errands for an hour or so, and then come back to get her, never visiting or showing any sort of interest in anyone in the salon. It was odd, but Lily assumed she was just a bit of an introvert. At the salon, Lily saw every type of personality possible… it was one of the things she loved most about her job.

"You know, I heard he's been sleeping around…" Kate Phillips clucked, gossip-sharing her number one favorite activity. She was engaged to the pharmacist at the Walgreens down the street, and she visited every few weeks to have her nails trimmed, filled, and re-polished.

"No way… are you serious?" asked Tamara Flannery, a thin woman with curly black hair and beautiful ebony skin that appeared to be made of silk. Tamara stopped in every Tuesday to get her nails painted a new shade of polish. She was quite eccentric and preferred colors that matched whatever brightly colored shirt she happened to be wearing that day.

"Yep! Clara over at the pharmacy told my main squeeze that she saw him leave the club with some lady the other night after he got off work. She said the lady was hanging all over him all night, and that he was kissing her outside the club before they got in his truck together and left."

"I can't believe he'd do that to Molly!" Krista Ban chimed in from under the hair dryer. She was here to get her hair dyed a new shade of auburn. She was certain she could hide her graying hair from everyone if she got the roots done every 2-3 weeks.

Vanity is sure expensive, Lily thought as she smirked at the ladies and their gossip. They seemed to love hearing themselves talk!

The conversation between the women continued for much longer than Lily wanted to listen to it. They talked about him being seen with other women, his drinking, and so on. Lily could have stopped the gossip to set the facts straight, but she figured it would do no good. Gossip was gossip, and as much as she loved her share of the fun, she was also *well* aware that it was fueled by ignorance, and those that spread it around cared little for the truth. They thrived on the fun of shocking people and spreading stories that seemed more interesting than the truth, be it whatever it was.

Lily wasn't sure what to believe and what to let go right out the other ear. She wanted to find the truth so that she could warn Molly about it, whatever *it* was, but she didn't want to get into it with these ladies. She smiled and listened as she finished up their nails. After the timer went off on Krista's dryer, she took her to the sink to wash out the dyes and get her hair ready to be styled. Once Kate and Tamara left, it got quieter in the salon, and she was thankful for the time to think.

"A penny for your thoughts," Krista said, watching Lily in the mirror.

"Huh?" Lily replied, not realizing she had been in her own little world of daydreaming.

"You look like you have a lot on your mind today. Would you like to share, or is it personal?" Krista explained. Lily knew Krista was a sweetheart, and she smiled as she towel-dried her hair.

"I'm sorry about that. I was just thinking about everything the two 'gabbers' were talking about before."

"I'm sure it's hard to listen to that stuff… you probably hear things you wish you didn't all the time around here, don't you?" she replied with a tone of empathy. "It wasn't very nice of us to talk about Molly in front of you. I know you two are really close. I'm sorry about that."

"Oh, that's no problem, really," Lily said, assuring her it was okay.

"I try to stay out of other people's business as much as I can. I was just shocked to hear them say those things. I don't really know Waylon that well, but I know Molly, and it all just seems a bit off," Krista said, confusion making her eyebrows furrow.

"It's a complicated situation, but Molly is okay. I'm not really sure what to believe and not believe about what they were saying before, but I really don't think it would do Molly any good to hear it right now. She has enough on her plate."

"Yeah, how is she doing lately? I feel terrible because I haven't stopped by The Sweet Sprinkle to grab a treat in months!"

"She's doing good, actually… she is starting to come back to herself again, which makes me very happy. I miss the way things used to be… I miss the 'old Molly.'"

"I'm sure you do… she's been through so much. Give her time, I'm sure she'll come back to you… I guess the most important thing to realize is that she'll never *fully* be that person again, Lily. She's been changed forever by what she went through with Hannah, and if *any* of what those two goons said was true, then her life is about to change even more," Krista said, concern in her voice.

"I suppose you're right on that," Lily said, thinking as she put some light mousse in Krista's hair to give it body so she could style it. "Okay, what do you think, my dear?"

"I love it, as usual!" Krista said, smiling at her reflection in the mirror.

"Great! I think we are all set then!"

Krista stopped at the counter to pay for her services and left, waving to Lily as she walked out the door.

Sighing, Lily cleaned up the mess she had from the day and switched the sign on the door to closed. Krista had been her last client, and she was beat! She just wanted a glass of wine and a soft couch to put her feet up on. First, though, she needed to make a phone call. Grabbing her phone from her pocket, she hit the button to call Molly. Molly picked up quickly.

"Hey, Lil!" Molly said, seemingly in a pretty good mood for the end of a busy workday.

"Hey, Molly… quick question… is there any chance you'd want to go for a walk in a little while, after you close up for the day?" Lily asked.

Molly could hear the tension in Lily's voice, and it made her worry. "Well, I have to run over to my parents tonight for dinner, but you could definitely come with! We could take a walk *there* if you want!"

"Um… yeah, that actually sounds great… I could use some of your momma's cookin'!" Lily said, smiling at the thought.

"Okay, great! I'll let my mom know you'll be coming with me. I'm sure she'll be really stoked to see you again!" Molly said, happy that Lily was joining her for dinner at her parents. "I'll be done here in a half hour or so, and then I'll head out. Meet you there?"

"Yeah, that works. I'll see you in a bit," Lily said, ending the call.

This will be good, she thought. There was nothing in this *whole world* that would help Lily to calm her thoughts and think clearly more than Molly's mom's delicious food. She wasn't sure what it was going to be, but her mouth was already watering just thinking of the possibilities...

* * *

Molly finished her last order for the day and cleaned up before she closed the shoppe. An alarm on her phone rang reminding her that she needed to get going to her parent's house to meet up with Lily. She had set the timer immediately after her call so she wouldn't forget. Lily sounded anxious, like she needed to tell her something important. She took her keys from her purse and unlocked her car.

As she drove to her parents, she kept wondering what Lily could be so anxious about. It wasn't like her to be anything less than peppy, so the way her voice had sounded on the phone was a little unnerving. As she traveled through town, she let her mind wander to the most likely possibility... she was probably going to ask Molly to find a new place. She knew Lily liked her privacy, and that she loved living the single, partying lifestyle that she'd grown accustomed to. Molly was probably cramping her style by living there and taking up space in her home.

Crap, Molly thought, I really like staying with Lily. What am I going to do now?

Molly's thoughts were broken up by a car behind her honking loudly at her. She shook her head, clearing her mind and concentrating on the road ahead. She hadn't realized she was dazing a bit and had put her car on autopilot... without that option actually being on her car! She better get her stuff together here, before she got into an accident or something...

Two blocks later, Molly turned onto the road her parents lived on. It was a newly paved road with adorable moderately-sized homes on it and trees lining the street. In the spring and summer months when everything was green and alive, it felt as though you were traveling through a nature-made tunnel of oak, maple, and ash trees. Each yard was beautifully landscaped, and it reminded Molly of a road you'd see on TV or something.

Molly had grown up on this road, loving every minute of her childhood. She'd had many neighbor children to play with and could walk the short 2 blocks to school each day with them. She smiled as the memories came flooding back now. Just ahead, she saw her parent's house, and she pulled into the familiar driveway, putting her car in park and turning off the ignition.

Molly's parents lived in a two-story house that had dark gray wood siding with brick along the bottom. The windows had shutters on them that were a deep blue color, something her father had put up last year after her mother had not-so-subtly "hinted" she wanted for about six months. Molly smiled as she saw the freshly planted flowers in each box below the windows. Her mother, and pretty much everybody else on this street as well, was a wonderful gardener… something she had *definitely not* passed on to her daughter. Molly was as black of a thumb as she could get.

She smiled at her mother and Lily, who were standing on the porch waving at her. Leave it to Lily to beat her! Lily was even more punctual than Molly was, and that was saying a lot!

Molly got out of her car and joined the other two women on the porch.

"Hey Mom!" Molly greeted her mother and gave her a hug.

"Hey honey," her mother responded and hugged her back.

"Hey Lil," she added as she nudged her friend in the arm with her elbow.

"I was pleasantly surprised to see Lily drive in," her mother said, giving her a look that reminded Molly that she'd forgotten to message her earlier to tell her Lily would be with tonight.

"Shoot… I completely forgot to message you… sorry," she said with an apologetic glance.

"No big deal… there is plenty to go around, and your father needs to learn to share anyway!" Laura Flynn was a self-proclaimed jokester who loved to pick on the ones she loved. She had a heart of gold but loved to razz people too.

"Lily, what's up with *you* lately? Have you found any good-looking men to trick into marrying you yet?"

"Mom!" Molly said, rolling her eyes.

"It's okay, Mol. Your mother knows what a catch I am, so it's probably quite confusing how I'm standing here right now without my harem of followers chasing after me!" Lily said, causing an eruption of laughter amongst the three women.

"Oh yes… sorry, you're probably right. We should probably get inside soon before one of them drives by and spots you!" Molly teased back.

"So true… so true…" Lily said, continuing to laugh.

Laura rolled her eyes as she turned towards the house. "You two coming in? I'm guessing it will be about 20 minutes or so before the chili is ready to eat."

"Actually, we are going to go for a quick walk if that's okay," Molly answered tentatively. "Lily came over because she wanted to talk to me about something, so I was thinking we'd walk and talk a bit before we come in to visit and have dinner."

"Oh… *sure*! You finally come over and it's to talk to Molly, the person you live with currently, instead of to visit me?" she asked Lily dramatically.

Lily instantly got a worried look on her face. "No, of course not! I just needed to tell her something and then I was really looking forward to catching up with you and eating your amazing supper!"

Molly laughed as her mother put her hand on Lily's arm, smiling. "I'm just kidding, Lily. I'm always happy to have you here!"

Lily sighed as she smiled back at her. "Whew!" she said, acting as though a weight had been lifted from her shoulders. "The last thing I need is the person who is making my supper to be upset with me! That doesn't seem like a very smart idea!"

Laura Flynn laughed as she opened the door and walked into the house, leaving the two friends on the porch together.

"Well, should we go for that walk then?" Molly asked her, wrapping her arm around her friend's shoulders.

"Yeah… that is probably a good idea," Lily answered, still shaking her head from her interaction with Molly's mom.

The two women walked to the end of the sidewalk and turned right, journeying along the familiar path that Molly had taken hundreds of times as both a child and an adult. The sun was to their backs as it lowered closer and closer to the horizon. Its warmth was a welcomed friend to the cool Wisconsin spring evening. Molly could smell the newness all around her as they walked down the sidewalk. It felt as though they were walking through a botanical garden display, and it was even more beautiful than the last time she had been here and taken a walk with her mom.

"Look, Mol, I'm going to cut straight to the point here… I heard some things today at the salon that I think you may want to hear too. I've been trying to figure out if and how to tell you, but I think I'll just repeat what they said. I haven't checked to see if it's true or not, so know that right off the bat… there's a chance that all of it is just gossip and nothing more, okay?" Lily stumbled through the words as though she was trying to convince each one to spill from her mouth.

Molly still had her arm hooked through Lily's, enjoying the closeness to her best friend. She looked at her now, concern filling her face.

"What did you hear, Lily?" she asked, her brow furrowing in apprehension.

Lily went on to narrate all she had heard at the salon earlier. She told Molly about Waylon's alleged escapades. Molly could see how nervous Lily was as she told her about Waylon. She knew it wasn't easy for her to tell her those things. The odd thing was that she didn't quite know how all of this made her feel. She knew she should be mad, or sad, or hurt… but she didn't feel any of those things right now. She felt…

"Mol, did you hear me?" Lily interrupted.

"Yes, sorry. I was just trying to process what you were saying…" Molly answered.

"Do you think it's possible that he really did those things? I mean, I know you said he's been drinking a lot, but cheating? That just doesn't seem like something he would do, does it?"

"No, it doesn't, but we *are* separated, Lil. To be quite honest, I'm not sure what the rules are during a separation. Besides… there's a very good chance those nosey ladies are just spreading rumors. I think you should just ignore them," Molly replied, still trying to figure out what all of this meant to her and for her. She felt sort of numb inside right now, and she needed some time to sort through all of it. The side of a street was not the place for that!

"You may be right, Mol, but I'm not so sure. That lady said she saw it with her own eyes… do you think you should talk to him? If it's true, I think he's spiraling out of control!" Lily said, obviously confused at the fact that she seemed to be more upset about this than Molly was.

"Lily, I appreciate you looking out for me, and I'm glad that you told me what you heard. The thing is, I know Waylon, and I can't ever imagine that he would cheat on me like that. He's totally lost right now, and he's *definitely* drinking way too much," Molly said, trying to explain her feelings on this to Lily even though she hadn't even worked them out to herself quite yet. "Even so, I would imagine they saw something and jumped to a conclusion that wasn't entirely correct, you know?" Seeing that Lily still didn't look settled on the matter, Molly added, "and again, he and I are separated and it's highly likely that it is a permanent decision, so I'm not sure that I would have any right to be upset either way."

Lily didn't want to push the matter any further, so she changed the subject. They walked along the path chatting about all the beautiful flowers and signs of spring all around them. Lily loved flowers, and she loved spending time with her friend even more.

As they rounded the last corner to start back towards her parent's home, Molly heard a familiar bark. She squinted her eyes towards the direction she'd heard the sound and saw Buck running straight through a yard and making a beeline towards her. He was coming at full speed, and she braced herself for the impact, laughing as he knocked her onto her butt on the grass. Buck licked her face and nuzzled at her hands as she petted him, laughing hysterically.

"Molly, oh my…" Lily screeched, trying to figure out what was going on. "Are you okay?"

Laughing, Molly answered, "Yeah, I'm great. This big goofball here is Buck!"

Lily looked at Molly as though she was speaking French or something. "Who the heck is Buck?"

Molly calmed Buck down for a second so she could address Lily. "Lily, meet Buck!" she said. "Buck… meet Lily!"

Buck barked a greeting but kept his attention on Molly.

"Okay… and that still doesn't answer my question, Mol!"

"Oh… so, Buck is…"

Molly was interrupted by a shouting man running between the two houses, the same pathway Buck had just come from. She smiled as he approached.

"Buck! You are about one bad move from my last nerve!" he yelled as he approached. Seeing Molly on the ground, he panicked. "Oh my God! Molly… are you okay? Did he knock you over? I'm so sorry!"

Owen ran straight to Molly, reaching down to help her up. His hand was strong and firm, and she felt like he could lift the world with it if he wanted to. She got up to her feet and smiled at him.

"Hey, Owen. It's really no big deal," she said, reaching down to pet Buck again. "He was just saying hello, weren't you, boy?"

"I don't know what it is about you, but he seems to be able to sniff you from several blocks away!" Owen said, perplexed.

"Well, I'm not sure that's a good thing! I probably should consider a different deodorant or something if that's the case!" she said, laughing again.

"Oh… I didn't mean that you stink!" Owen said, trying to pull the foot out of his mouth as his face turned a candy apple red.

"I was joking, Owen. It's fine, really." Molly said, enjoying his squirming for a bit.

Suddenly, she heard Lily clear her throat, realizing she had completely forgotten her best friend was standing there. Looking at her, she grinned.

"Lily, this is Owen."

Lily looked from Molly to Owen, clearly quite confused. "Hello, Owen, it's nice to meet you… whoever you are."

"Hello, Lily. It's nice to meet you, too. Molly and I have met in the park near her work a few times over the last couple of months. Buck, here, seems to be quite attracted to her, so he likes to play escape artist and run off every time she's there."

"Ah… I see. Well, I'm Molly's best friend and currently her roommate. We were just on a walk when Buck decided to make his presence known," she said, leaning down to pet Buck.

Lily was more of a cat person, but she tolerated dogs just fine. She just didn't want to live with one was all.

"What are you doing over this direction?" Molly asked Owen.

"Oh… I suppose that's a fair question. I live a couple of blocks down from here," he said, pointing towards the street behind her parent's place.

"Oh wow, that's crazy! My parents live just down this street," Molly replied.

"That's quite the coincidence," he said, smiling as he spoke.

Lily stood by Molly's side, staring at them, watching their interaction with one another. Owen seemed like he couldn't stop smiling while they talked, while Molly seemed a bit uncomfortable, like she wasn't sure what to do with herself or what to say. It was interesting… she felt like there was some sort of chemistry between them, but it was kind of hard to detect what type. Lily loved a good mystery, and these two were *definitely* challenging her!

Before Lily could wrap her head around what was happening, she saw a small boy walking towards them holding the hand of a middle-aged woman. He broke her grasp as soon as they rounded the corner and came running towards the three of them.

"Daddy! Buck! There you are!" he yelled, running happily into Owen's arms.

Owen picked the boy up as he got to him, grinning from ear to ear as he held the boy. Turning to Molly, he said, "Molly, I'd like you to meet my son, Oliver."

Molly felt her jaw hit the ground. She had no idea Owen had a son! She looked at the adorable little boy, smiling as she said, "Hello, Oliver. My name is Molly. It's very nice to meet you!"

Oliver was built like a mini wrestler, with chubby little freckled cheeks and sandy blonde hair that was spiked up on the top. He had his daddy's green eyes that seemed to sparkle in the light. He was squirming all over, so Owen sat him on the ground to play with Buck. She looked at Owen, wondering what other secrets the man had. Every time she saw him, she learned something new and interesting about him.

"Oliver is 5. My mother was just dropping him off after a trip to the ice cream shoppe when Buck took off," Owen said, trying to explain.

Suddenly, Molly remembered the lady that Oliver had been walking with. She looked around Owen's shoulder and saw her getting closer. As she approached, she smiled and extended her hand.

"Hello, I'm Cheryl Tannen, Owen's mother and this little cutie pie's grandmother. It's nice to meet you… I didn't catch your name?"

"Oh, my name is Molly," she said, excepting the handshake. "Owen and I have run into each other a few times at the park near where I work," Molly explained. Turning to Lily, she added, "This is my friend, Lily."

Lily shook Cheryl's outstretched hand, smiling.

The four adults talked for a bit while Oliver rolled around on the ground with Buck. Seeing the sun setting, Molly decided they'd better head back to her parent's house to eat.

"I hate to bolt, but Lily and I are due at my parent's place for supper, and we've already taken a bit longer than planned. It was very nice to meet you, Oliver!" she said as the little boy grabbed his dad's hand and got ready to walk back towards their home. "You too, Mrs. Tannen."

"Oh, you can just call me Cheryl, honey. Any friend of Owen's is a friend of mine!" Cheryl said, smiling as she grabbed Oliver's other hand.

"It was nice to see you again, Owen," she said, smiling as she and Lily turned to head back to her childhood home.

"See you, everyone!" Lily said.

They got about ten steps before Lily poked at Molly's arm teasingly. "You sly little devil… why did you never tell me about that handsome piece of man meat?"

"Lily! You are so… I'm not even sure what the word is for you! He's a really nice guy that I've seen a few times at the park. We've become friends, sort of. That's all!" Molly said, laughing.

"Sure… we'll call it that for now, but that man has a smolder in his eyes every time he looks at you," Lily said, a mischievous look in her eyes. "If I were you, I'd be exploring that further!"

Molly rolled her eyes, laughing at Lily's choice of words. Owen was becoming a good friend she enjoyed laughing with… and at! Just friends, that was it. He was nothing more than a friend… so why was it she couldn't seem to tear her eyes away from him as he walked away?

Nine

Chapter 8

Waylon sat alone at the bar, his calloused hands wrapped tightly around a cold glass of whiskey. The dim lights of the nightclub flickered casting shadows that mirrored the darkness he felt in his heart. The rhythmic thump of the bass from the dance floor seemed distant, drowned out by the cacophony of his thoughts.

Thoughts of his baby girl's tiny, lifeless body in his arms echoed in his mind, a haunting reminder of once wonderful dreams that now felt like a distant nightmare. He couldn't escape the grief that gripped him, a vice squeezing tighter with each passing day. The pain was unbearable, and the only solace he found was at the bottom of a bottle.

Work had become his sanctuary, a place where the alcohol temporarily numbed the ache in his heart. Waylon had lost count of the nights he had spent drowning his sorrows, desperately trying to forget the emptiness that consumed him, especially since Molly had left.

The familiar scent of spilled beer, the hum of conversations, and the clinking of glasses were his only companions in the silent battle against his lonely despair.

"At least *you'll* never leave me," he said to his glass of whiskey before knocking it back.

As the liquid courage flowed through his veins, Waylon's mind wandered to the crumbling remains of his marriage. Molly, once the love of his life, had become a distant figure in the rearview mirror of their shattered relationship.

"Hey, man. You look like you got chewed and spit back out by a bear or something... wanna get it off your chest?" a burly man who'd been sitting at the bar for a while asked.

"What?" Waylon barked, pulled from his thoughts.

"I just asked if you wanted to talk about whatever's on your mind, that's all. I have no life, no wife, and nowhere to be if you do. Plus... I'm probably not going to remember any of this tomorrow anyway!"

Waylon looked at the man, annoyed at his intrusion. "Oh hell... why not?" he said, unloading on the man.

"My soon-to-be ex-wife had divorce papers served to me today," he said, anger written all over his face.

The divorce papers he'd been served, just hours before, sat on the kitchen table at home, a tangible manifestation of the rift that had torn apart their once-happy life together.

"Shit... that sucks, man."

Anger burned within him as he replayed the arguments, the bitter exchanges that had fueled the demise of their marriage.

"Yeah... and it's all because she wants another kid and I don't! Can you believe she'd leave me over that? It's like nothing before this even matters to her!"

The mere thought of bringing new life into a world that had stolen his daughter from him was unbearable to Waylon. He couldn't fathom the idea of replacing the irreplaceable, and he couldn't understand why Molly would want to risk going through such incredible pain again.

"Why can't she see my side of this?" Waylon muttered to the man, his voice barely audible over the ambient noise of the nightclub. His hands trembled as he gripped the glass tighter, the amber liquid sloshing within.

"No clue, man. I've never been married... seems like too much of a headache to me. I'd rather be alone than have to deal with some woman telling me what to do all the time," the man said, joining Waylon in drinking away his sorrows.

"You might have the right idea, that's for sure," Waylon replied, clinking glasses with the man before shooting another drink back.

The realization that his wife was willing to let go, to move on and rebuild without him, fueled the flames of resentment. Their once-shared dreams and aspirations had crumbled into irreconcilable differences. The pain of loss had driven a wedge between them, leaving scars that could never fully heal.

Waylon's eyes stared blankly into the depths of his drink, the reflection of a broken man staring back at him. The weight of grief and anger bore down on his shoulders, threatening to crush him beneath the burden of his own emotions.

Before long, the man left, saying something about getting up early for work the next day, and Waylon was left to wallow in self-pity alone. As the night wore on, the patrons of the nightclub continued their revelry, oblivious to the silent storm raging within him.

At one o'clock in the morning, as his shift neared an end, Waylon poured himself another drink, the bitterness of the alcohol mirroring the bitterness of his heart. In the haze of intoxication, he found temporary refuge from the harsh realities that awaited him beyond the neon-lit haven.

This chapter of Waylon's life had taken a dark turn, a narrative of loss, despair and shattered dreams. Amid the pulsating beats and the swirling chaos in the nightclub, he clung to the only coping mechanism he knew – the numbing embrace of alcohol, a fleeting escape from a reality that refused to be silenced.

* * *

Rainy, gloomy mornings were commonplace in Wisconsin in April. As the dawn rose on a quiet spring morning, Mia got out of bed and headed to the kitchen, bound for a cup of coffee. She was a strong believer that nothing, absolutely nothing, should precede her morning coffee. Her husband, Jeff, followed closely after her, fully aware of her morning 'no talking until coffee' rule. He grabbed two cups from the cupboard as she hit the button on the coffeemaker and waited for it to perk.

Mia poured coffee into the two mugs, smiling at her handsome husband as he poured some creamer into both. He knew her so well, and she was thankful that he was always so kind and helpful to her. She had hit the 'husband jackpot,' that was for sure. Jeff had jet-black hair and a square jawline. He had stubble on his face as he hadn't shaved for the day yet. He liked to keep it clean-shaven because he said it itched him if it grew out, but she loved the look he had right now… it made her want to run her hands over his face and enjoy the rugged masculinity of it. She looked up to see him looking back at her, his brown eyes curious about her thoughts.

After a few sips, she followed him into the living room, and they sat together on the sofa. Normally, she turned the news on so they could watch the weather report and see all the stock market information, but today, they sat in silence for a bit, just enjoying the sound of the birds that were chirping outside her bay window.

Her gaze moved to her husband. He looked so handsome and comfortable as he sat snuggled up to her on the sofa. Their life was perfect in every way… for her, at least. Jeff had been talking about having children a lot lately, though, and she worried that he wasn't as happy as she was with everything. It wasn't like she didn't want kids… she was just really scared after what had happened to Molly. She didn't want to go through that! She knew he wasn't pushing it because of that same reason, but she also knew that them not talking about it was starting to fester up, and she didn't want to end up the same way Molly and Waylon were now.

"A penny for your thoughts?" Jeff asked, smiling at her as she came out of the fog she'd been in.

"What?" she replied, still confused.

"What is that beautiful mind thinking so hard about so early in the morning?" he asked, hugging her closer to him.

Mia sat both of their coffee cups on the end table and snuggled into her husband's arms. She felt safe and protected there, and so very loved. She was terrified that this, or something else, would ruin that.

"I was just thinking about how much I love you, that's all," she said, loving the soothing feeling his heart beating in his chest gave her.

"Well, I love you too, sweetheart, but there was more than that going on in there. As a matter of fact, there was something a bit 'spicy' going on in there in the kitchen, too, so I'd love to hear about whatever thought *that* was as well!" Jeff said, laughing softly.

"Goof," she said, nudging his ribs. "I guess I was just thinking about everything with Molly and Waylon. It's such a mess, you know?"

"Yeah, definitely not how I saw that all going, that's for sure."

"I've been trying to stay out of it, to let Molly have time to figure it all out herself, but she's been listening to Lily, who happens to hate Waylon by the way, and I don't think that's the best idea. I think she needs to go back home and work on her marriage! How can they ever have a chance to fix things if she doesn't even try to work on it?" Mia asked, frustration clear in her voice as she spoke.

Jeff sighed, knowing this was bothering his wife, but not sure how to tell her that she needed to continue to allow Molly to handle this the way that she felt was right. He didn't want to upset Mia… that never ended well for him!

"Honestly, I think she is doing what she needs to do right now," he said carefully.

"What?" she asked, sitting up to look at him. "How can you say that? Don't you want them to work this out?"

Jeff swallowed hard, knowing he was preparing for a battle that wasn't theirs to have. "Baby, I think that only Waylon and Molly can know what is right for Waylon and Molly. *Of course* I miss the way things were when we could all hang out and do stuff together, but things have changed. Waylon is lost and not handling things in a healthy way, and Molly needs to protect herself. If he isn't willing to do the work to make things better, what else can she do?"

"She can try harder! Waylon is just messed up right now, that's all. She needs to hang in there and try to fix this!" Mia said, clearly getting more agitated and frustrated with her husband.

"Sweetheart, calm down. I am just saying that it's not fair for Molly to have to fight for something that Waylon has no fight left in him for. Do you really want her to stay in a loveless, unhappy marriage simply because it's 'the right thing to do'?"

"No… but… she can at least give it a little more time." Mia said, still frustrated.

"I think it's fair if Molly needs and wants some space to heal from everything she's been through. Her home has become a toxic environment for her, and if she decides to end her marriage and move on, that's her decision, not ours," Jeff said, holding his wife's hands in his, trying to help her see the other side of this argument.

Mia pulled her hands away from his, angry now. "Toxic environment? You are making it sounds like Molly is the only one who went through this mess! Waylon is going through the same crap, Jeff! Yes, he's drinking instead of dealing with it, but he only does that to dull the pain! They need each other, now more than ever!" Mia had tears in her eyes now. She was so frustrated with this whole conversation that she stood up and started to pace the room.

Jeff stood, walking to her and pulling her into his arms. "All I know for sure is that *I* need *you*," he said, softening his voice to try to calm her down. Mia tried to push him away, but he only tightened his grip to hold on. She finally gave up and laid her head on his chest, crying. He hated to see her so upset, especially since this wasn't their burden to carry.

After a little bit, Mia's cries lessened, and she calmed. They returned to the couch to sip on their coffee again, her eyes puffy and red.

"I'm going to try to talk some sense into Molly," Mia said, staring into her coffee as she spoke. "I at least have to try, Jeff."

With that, she grabbed her cell phone from the charger on the end table and searched her contacts for Molly's name. Sitting back, she waited for her to answer.

"Hello?" Molly answered, sounding like she was brushing her teeth or something.

"Morning, Molly," Mia said.

"Is everything okay, Mia?"

"Yeah… sorry for the early call. I just had an idea that I wanted to run by you," Mia replied. Jeff motioned for her to say hi for him, so she added, "Jeff says hi, by the way."

"Oh… tell him I said hi, too!" Molly said. "So… what's this idea you have?"

"Well, I know we've all been really stressed out lately with work and life and everything; I'm thinking we should have a girl's night out tonight. You know, we could unwind, go to some fancy restaurant, and treat ourselves. What do you think?"

Molly thought for a second. "That sounds really nice, actually. I could definitely use some fun in my life right now!" Molly said. "I'm in. I'll ask Lily if she can come… I don't think she had any plans tonight."

"Lily? I was just talking about you and me, but I guess she can come if you want her to." Mia said with a pout.

"I don't have to ask her if you don't want me to… I was just thinking you had meant all of us, that's all," Molly said, confused at Mia's tone.

"No, that's fine. Do you want to meet at seven?" Mia asked.

"Sure… why don't you pick a place and text me later and we'll plan on meeting you there… does that work?" Molly asked, happy to have some time with her two best friends that *didn't* involve work.

"Yep, that's fine. I'll see you tonight," Mia said, disconnecting the call.

Mia put her phone on the table and looked at Jeff. He was watching her curiously.

"Why does she think she needs to bring Lily with her everywhere she goes lately?" she muttered angrily.

Jeff sighed. His wife was obviously on a mission, and he was guessing it wasn't going to end well for anyone involved. "This is not going to end well, you know…"

"What isn't?" Mia asked him in a tone that warned him to tread lightly with his answer.

"Whatever you have planned, that's what. I think you need to just leave Molly alone with this… it's *her* decision, Mia."

Jeff got up and walked to the kitchen to put his coffee mug in the dishwasher.

When he came back into the room, he added, "You just need to be there for her and support her in whatever decision she makes about this."

"I'm absolutely not going to support my friend if she is making decisions that will lead her to a being a divorcee at 25!" Mia snapped, setting her coffee cup on the stand and storming from the room.

Jeff sighed. "Well, that went well," he muttered under his breath.

* * *

The air buzzed with excitement as Lily, Mia, and Molly stepped into the vibrant restaurant, their laughter already filling the space. It was a much-needed night out, a chance for the trio to unwind and escape the demands of their everyday lives. The ambiance of the restaurant was warm, the soft white of hanging lights casting a cozy glow over each of the small round tables scattered throughout the room.

Seated at a corner table, the friends were ready for an evening of wine, good food, and most importantly, each other's company. Lily and Molly were excited about a night of friendship and laughter, not knowing that Mia had other plans for the evening as well.

Lily, with her infectious smile, suggested a round of wine to kick off the night. Their outspoken waiter brought their glasses, filled them with a taste of the house specialty wine, and placed one in front of each of the women.

"Cheers!!" Mia, Molly and Lily said in unison as they clinked their glasses together.

"Hmm… *nothing* beats a smooth red wine," Lily said and took another sip of her drink. The wine was earthy and smooth, and it really hit the spot after a long day on her feet.

"Good wine *and* good food!" Molly said with a giggle, taking a sip as well.

The women ordered their food and then spent the next half an hour talking, sharing stories from work that day, and simply enjoying the closeness of their friendship. Before they knew it, their food arrived, and they continued their banter back and forth as they each enjoyed their ordered dish. Their laughter provided a refreshing break from the chaos of their day-to-day routines.

Molly had ordered the filet mignon with a side salad and a baked potato. She had always been a meat and potatoes kind of girl, and tonight was no different. When she was feeling stressed or sad, she always went for her comfort foods, and this was, hands down, one of the best versions she had tasted yet.

Lily, on the other hand, had went for the beer cheese soup, a Wisconsin staple, with bruschetta and a side of fresh fruit. She had loved the regional favorite ever since she was a teenager and her aunt had made some for a family gathering. She fell in love with the soup instantly, and now ordered it as often as she could.

Mia, always on some sort of fad diet, had opted for the Caesar salad with roasted chicken. Molly couldn't remember ever seeing her eat anything with more substance than that. When they were teenagers, she used to worry that Mia may have a problem with eating, like maybe an eating disorder or something, but she had come to know that it was just a way of life for her good friend. She'd been at Mia's house once and heard her mother talking about the obesity crisis, and she'd instantly understood where her friend's obsession with healthy eating had come from. It seemed a little ironic that she now co-owned a cupcake shop!

After savoring a delightful meal, Lily proposed the idea of karaoke, an activity that never failed to bring joy and laughter. The trio waited for an opening in the entertainment and then made their way to the small stage, each holding a microphone with nervous anticipation. They had only done karaoke one other time, and it had been at Mia & Jeff's wedding several years back. The first notes of a familiar song played, and soon, the restaurant was treated to the harmonious sounds of Lily, Mia, and Molly's laughter-filled rendition.

Their inhibitions melted away as the song went on, and the karaoke session became a cathartic release for the friends. Lily danced freely, Mia belted out her part with passion, and Molly allowed herself to be swept away by the music, if only for a fleeting moment.

For Molly, it was a night of friendship, bonding, and forgetting the troubles that awaited her beyond the music-filled haven. She hadn't realized just how much she'd needed this until right now. As the music ended, they took their bow, earning an erupting applause from the audience. Then, the three took their seats again, laughing the entire way back.

"Oh, my goodness… I needed that *so* much!" Molly said as the laughter subsided.

"Me too, thank you for inviting me to tag along, Mia!" Lily said, taking another swig from her wine glass.

"No problem… I'm glad you are both having fun," Mia said, clearing her throat after taking a drink. She took a breath, clearly with something on her mind.

"Mia, I know you better than anyone, so I know when something's up. What's that mind thinking about?" Molly asked, concern taking the place of the joy that had just been on her face.

Mia, ever the straightforward friend, decided this was as good a time as any to bring up the topic that had been lingering in her mind all day, the reason she'd invited Molly here in the first place. "Molly, we need to talk about Waylon."

Molly looked back at her forlornly, a shadow crossing her face. "Mia, we are all having a great time here… let's not ruin it by talking about Waylon, okay?" she asked, touching Mia's hand and smiling at her friend.

Molly was really enjoying herself tonight, and she preferred to keep the topic of Waylon locked far away. Still, Mia seemed to have a mission, and she wasn't going to stop until she had her say, apparently.

"Molly… I just don't understand why you're so determined to go stay away from Waylon," Mia said, her brow furrowed. "It's only been three months since you two separated. Can't you give him more time? People change, you know… Maybe he's trying to heal in his own way… what if he just needs more time to come around?"

Molly's eyes hardened, a defensive glint replacing the warmth they once held. "Mia, you don't get it. I've given him enough time. I can't watch him drown his grief in alcohol any longer. I can't live in a constant cycle of pain and disappointment."

"But…" Mia started, stopping abruptly as Molly interrupted her.

"I filed for divorce this week, Mia. It's *over.*"

Mia's expression turned incredulous, her disbelief evident. "You did *what?* Molly, that's impulsive. You're making a *huge* mistake."

Lily, sensing the tension escalating, interjected, "Mia, let's not argue about this. Molly knows what's best for her."

Unfortunately, Mia was not easily dissuaded. "No, Lily, I won't stay silent when Molly is about to *ruin her life.* Waylon loves her, and grief makes people do things they regret. She can't just give up on him like this."

Molly's patience was wearing dangerously thin, and she shot back in a tone that was hushed, yet loud enough to cause people to start to look at them. "I am absolutely *not* giving up on him. I've given him more chances than anyone will ever know, because it's nobody's business but mine! The only thing I'm giving up on is a toxic situation. I deserve a chance at happiness, too! I can't keep sacrificing my well-being for the sake of a marriage that's been drowning for far too long… I refuse to go down with it!"

The disagreement escalated into a heated argument, the emotions pouring out like uncorked bottles of wine. Molly, feeling cornered and frustrated, finally declared, "I'm done, Mia. I won't listen to this anymore. Lily, let's go."

Lily, her eyes filled with unshed tears, glanced at Molly and then at Mia. With a decisive nod, she stood up, linking her arm with Molly's. "Okay. Maybe we can all talk about this another time, when everyone's calmed down."

As the two friends made their way toward the exit, leaving Mia behind, the tension in the air lingered. Molly felt a mix of sadness and relief. She loved Mia, but she couldn't allow her decisions to be dictated by someone who couldn't possibly understand the depth of her pain. A night that had started with laughter and camaraderie had abruptly ended with an unresolved rift, leaving the trio in a state of emotional disarray.

Ten

Chapter 9

Molly and Mia worked side-by-side for the next two weeks but shared no more than short sentences and comments to one another. Molly's heart hurt after what Mia had said to her, and she refused to be the one who brought it up to talk about. This one was Mia's fault, and Mia was going to be the one to apologize, not her!

After taking an order from a woman who needed cupcakes for her parents for their fiftieth anniversary, Mia came back into the kitchen, grabbing her icing knife again. Two seconds later, she sat it down, taking a deep breath and turning towards Molly.

"Molly, can we talk? Please?" she asked, urging Molly to put her task aside for a moment.

Molly slid her mixing bowl over, turning to face Mia, sighing, "Yeah… what's up?"

"Look… I'm sorry about that night at the restaurant. I realize I may have gone too far. I shouldn't have kept scolding you or questioning your motives like that," Mia said. " You're old enough to make your own decisions, and if you think divorcing Waylon is what's best, then I support you."

Molly thought for a moment, trying to decide if Mia was being sincere, or if she was just trying to get her to stop being mad. Smiling, she decided to give her the benefit of the doubt and believe that her intentions were honest and sincere.

"Thank you, Mia," Molly said and hugged her tightly. Molly was happy that Mia was supporting her with this. She needed all the support she could get. "I appreciate you saying that, and I do think that this is what is best. It took a lot of tears, plenty of doubt, and even more sleepless nights to come to this decision, so I can assure you it wasn't without its due diligence," she added.

The bell ringing on the front door jolted Molly out of her reverie. Someone was at the counter. "I'll grab that one," Molly said, using a cloth to clean the flower from her hands quickly before heading out front.

"Good afternoon and welcome to The Sweet Sprinkle," Molly said as she rounded the corner.

"Molly! Is that really you?" the lady said excitedly. "How are you doing? "

"Madison Montgomery… Oh my goodness! It's been a minute since I last saw you!" Molly replied, smiling as she realized who the customer was. "How have you been?" she asked.

Molly and Madison had gone to high school together, and Molly hadn't seen her since graduation. They had once been very good friends, but had lost touch in college, the way many do.

"I'm doing amazing, thank you for asking!" Madison said as she lifted a baby carrier onto the counter for Molly to see.

Smiling, Molly looked inside the navy and pink seat, seeing a beautiful baby girl asleep safely inside. Molly hadn't even noticed she was carrying the baby seat until now.

"Oh, Madison… she's beautiful," Molly said with tears welling up in her eyes. The woman saw the tears and instantly felt terrible.

"Oh my God. I'm so sorry, Molly. I didn't even think about how it might make you feel to see her," Madison stammered.

"Nonsense… no reason to feel sorry, Madison," Molly encouraged her with a smile. "I'm just really happy for you."

Molly felt a pain in her chest, but it wasn't the same kind of pain she'd felt for so many months… this was different. She longed for her little girl, just like she always had, but she couldn't quite put her finger on what *this* pain was. She felt like she wanted to hold this baby girl… but why would she want to do that? She'd never felt that before… usually, she veered away because she didn't want to see people so happy when she felt so darn sad, but not this time. She felt unsettled by these new feelings.

Shaking her head, Molly re-focused her attention on Madison. "What can I get for you two ladies today?" she asked, smiling at Madison.

"Oh right… sorry. Um, I need two dozen cupcakes for my daughter's baptism on Sunday, May sixteenth. Is that possible?"

"Absolutely! What flavor would you like?" Molly asked, starting a new order slip for Madison.

Looking at the list of cupcake flavors on the wall, Madison contemplated the choices, deciding on one dozen lemondrop with almond buttercream frosting, and one dozen pink champaign with raspberry filling and vanilla buttercream frosting.

"That sounds perfect," Molly said, adding, "Now, what color of frosting would you like?

"Oh boy… well, her dress is white, and we have pink napkins to go with it, so maybe do white and incorporate some soft pink in it somewhere too? Is that doable?" she asked.

"Absolutely! I'll have them ready for you to pick up on that Friday. You can refrigerate them until Sunday morning, then I recommend you bring them out to sit at room temperature until the party," Molly said, giving her all the instructions she'd need for pick-up and set-up.

"Thank you so much, Molly! I really appreciate this… it was so nice to see you again!" Madison said, smiling as she picked her daughter's seat up from the counter and left, waving back at Molly.

Once Madison was out the door, Molly went into her office and sank into her chair, crying the tears that had threatened to fall earlier. Seeing that beautiful baby girl had reminded her of Hannah, reminded her of all the things she had planned to be doing with her now.

After a few minutes, Molly stood up and went to the bathroom to clean her face. She decided to let Mia close the shoppe tonight so she could leave early and take a little ride over to see her mom. She needed someone to talk to about what she'd felt when she saw Madison's baby, and she knew her mother would understand more than anyone. She still had a few days before her next visit with Claire, and she felt like she needed to talk this through sooner than that. She hated letting things fester, knew she'd eventually lose it and blow up on someone who didn't have anything to do with the issue if she didn't deal with it now.

She went back into the kitchen to find Mia cleaning up, obviously finished with her decorating for the day.

"Hey, Mia. I'm not feeling so great. Since we're basically finished up here, I'm going to head out now and go see my mom. Are you okay with closing everything up? I'll help clean up this mess before I go."

"No problem," Mia said. "Is everything okay, Mol?"

"Yeah… just need to talk to her is all. I'm fine," Molly fibbed, not wanting to get into it with Mia, knowing she wouldn't understand.

"Okay. You don't have to help with this, though, I'm literally almost done," Mia said, smiling. "Go ahead and head out. Make sure to tell your mom hi for me, okay?"

"Sounds good. Thank you. I'll see you tomorrow morning," Molly said, putting her apron on the hook and grabbing her purse. It was time to face some more demons… at least with her mom by her side she knew she could work through this, just like she had with so many other obstacles in her life. Her mom was her hero, and she always knew what to say to make Molly feel better.

"I sure could use some of that amazing advice now," she thought out loud as she got in her car to leave. Hopefully, her mom was ready for a challenge today.

* * *

James Flynn was washing his hands in the kitchen sink when he saw Molly pull into the driveway. He had been outside tilling the fertilizer into the vegetable garden so it would have a month or so to work its magic before planting season started. Now that that was finished, he needed to get ready to head to the greenhouse just south of town to grab his seeds and potting soil. He always started his plants indoors, firmly believing that it was never a good idea to plant anything in Wisconsin soil before the end of May or beginning of June.

Molly's dad was a sturdy man, standing around six feet tall with a muscular build. As a community sanitation worker, he spent his days on the side of a garbage truck, hoisting heavy garbage cans for hours. He loved his job, but it definitely took a toll on his back.

Drying his hands with the towel, he hollered loud enough for his wife to hear him from the living room where she was folding laundry, "Honey… your baby bird has returned to the nest!"

Rolling her eyes, Laura got up from her spot on the sofa and went to look out the window. Seeing Molly getting out of her car, she got a concerned look on her face, responding," Very funny, dear." Molly very rarely just popped by to visit… there was usually a reason unless they asked her to come. Laura wondered what was troubling her daughter today. "I wonder what she stopped by for…" she said curiously.

Walking to the door, she opened it and greeted Molly. "Hello, sweetheart. Is everything okay? I didn't know you were stopping by for a visit today."

"Hey, mom. It's fine, I guess. I just really needed to talk to you about something that happened today," Molly replied, giving her mom a hug before following her inside.

"Hey, pumpkin!" her dad said, coming out from the kitchen to say hi on his way by. He stopped to give her a hug, and Molly let herself melt into his chest. There was no hug in the world that made her feel safe and warm the way her dad's hugs did. She could smell his aftershave, its familiar aroma making her feel grounded and home.

"Hey, dad," she said. "Where are you off to?"

"I need to run to the greenhouse and grab my seeds and soil and such. I'm already almost a week behind starting my plants for this year," he said, sighing as though it was a very big deal that his plants were getting in a few days later than usual.

Molly smiled. Her dad was a very unpunctual man. He was literally late for everything, but he liked to act like it was an unusual thing that he was behind. It was one of the things she loved most about him.

Grabbing his keys, her dad opened the front door to leave. As he walked out, he called behind him, "I'll see you two beautiful ladies in a bit!"

They said their goodbyes, and then Molly followed her mom to the sofa, finding a comfy pillow to hug.

"You must have closed up the shop early… Is something wrong, sweetheart?" Molly's mother asked when Molly had settled down on the couch.

"Yeah… something happened today that has me kind of confused. I was hoping you could help me sort it out, like you always seem to be able to do," Molly said.

"Oh boy… that's an overstatement I think, but I'm sure happy to try. What happened today?" her mom asked, smiling at her daughter.

"Madison Montgomery stopped by today to order some cupcakes," Molly began, swallowing hard before continuing to explain. "She has a new baby girl, and she is being baptized in a couple of weeks."

Molly's mom nodded, urging her to continue, knowing where this was probably going.

"Seeing that sweet little girl made so many memories of shattered dreams come flooding back to me, just like it always does when I see a little baby girl," Molly continued, a tear falling down her cheek. Madison looked so happy, Mom, and I wanted to be happy for her, but it is just so hard! *I* could have been happy like *her* if Hannah hadn't…" she trailed off, unable to get the words out of her mouth.

Molly tried to steady her voice and calm down, but the tears were falling down her face now, and she wasn't sure how to stop them. Her mom reached over and pulled her into a hug, letting her get the sobs out of her chest. When she finally found herself calmer, she sat up, looking at her mom again.

"Oh, honey. I'm so sorry you have had to go through all of this," her mother said, wiping at her own tear-stained cheeks. "No one deserves to go through what you're going through, and you are stronger and braver than you realize."

Molly squeezed her mom's hand, thankful for her kind words, but she didn't feel strong *or* brave right now. She felt sad and weak. "The thing is, something felt different today when I saw that baby," Molly explained further.

"Different how?" her mother asked.

"I'm not sure I understand it, but I kind felt like I wanted to…" Molly trailed off, trying to think of the right words for how she had felt earlier. Sighing, she finished, "like I wanted to hold her…"

Laura smiled, squeezing her daughter's hands back. "Sweetheart, I think that is probably because you are starting to heal that place deep down in your heart where the *mother* in you has been hiding to protect herself."

"I'm not a *mother*, mom, I was *supposed* to be, and I wanted *so much* to be, but there's a good chance that my dream of motherhood left the day my daughter did," Molly replied, tears falling again.

"Oh, sweetheart, that's not true! Hannah made you a mother the day she was created inside of you! You gave her the *perfect* life… you loved her from the first moment you knew of her until the last moment she was with you. That's the most special gift you could ever give her, and she gave you the precious gift of motherhood. Nobody can ever take that from you… not now, now ever! You will forever be that sweet little angel's mother, until the day you get to hold her in your arms again."

"Oh, mom, thank you for saying that," Molly said through her tears. "I never really thought of it that way."

Molly and her mom sat together for a while, just listening to the birds outside the window, both letting their gentle tears fall. Laura grieved for the loss of granddaughter, but also for her daughter and what she had gone through. She wished like everything that she could take the pain away from her and give her the happiness that she'd had back when she was filled with dreams instead of regrets.

"Mom, there's something else I have been meaning to tell you," Molly said, interrupting her mother's thoughts. "I filed the divorce papers a couple of weeks ago. I've been dragging my feet on telling you guys because I don't want you to be disappointed in me. I'm sorry I couldn't make my marriage work. I tried… I really did! I just can't do it anymore."

Laura picked up a towel and started to fold it, looking for the right words that would tell her daughter that she was happy about that decision. She didn't want to sound overzealous, but she *did* want her to know that she was fully supported.

"Sweetheart, your father and I could never be disappointed in you. You were raised with your head on straight, and you know very well that your father would have straightened it for you if you hadn't!" she said, laughing.

Molly laughed for the first time since arriving at her parent's house. "Thanks a lot," she joked.

"Well, it's true I suppose. Also… we fully support any decision you make when it comes to your marriage with Waylon. You know we love him, and we always will, in a way. But… neither your father nor I agree with the way he has been handling everything since you two lost Hannah, and we've seen how miserable he has made everything for you over the last year. If you feel in your heart that your marriage is over and irreparable, then we support that."

"Thank you, Mom. It wasn't an easy decision, but he needs help, and I pray that he'll wake up one day and decide to get it," Molly said, helping her mom fold.

The two women sat together talking and folding until the baskets were empty. Then, they put the laundry away and went into the kitchen to have some fresh cheese curds and sweet tea. There was no snack quite as tasty, as far as Molly was concerned, then squeaky-fresh cheese curds from the nearby cheese factory a few towns away… salty and delicious. Since her dad was still going to be a little while and Molly wanted to wait to say goodbye to him, they decided to take a walk together.

The warm rays of the spring sun bathed the neighborhood in a golden glow as Molly and Laura walked outside for a stroll along the tree-lined streets. The scent of blooming flowers filled the air, creating a serene backdrop for their leisurely late afternoon walk. Molly listened as her mother, a successful semi-retired lawyer at her own private firm, shared anecdotes from her morning at the office, her animated expressions reflecting the humor in her storytelling.

"Molly, you seriously won't believe the client I met today," Laura chuckled, her eyes sparkling with amusement. "He's quite the character. Kept cracking jokes during our entire meeting. I haven't laughed like that in ages."

Molly smiled, enjoying the light-hearted banter. The casual walk offered a welcome respite from the challenges of her own life, particularly the recent turmoil surrounding her divorce. She had thought about telling her mother about everything that had happened with Mia, but she decided to let that rest back where it had happened. Mia had apologized, and it was over now.

Molly's attention shifted as they turned a corner and encountered a familiar sight – Owen and Oliver… and, of course, Buck!

As soon as the dog saw Molly, he took off in a sprint, leaving his owners behind. Molly laughed, bracing herself for impact. This time, though, Buck stopped just before pouncing, allowing Molly to pet his head while his tail wagged furiously.

Molly's mom leaned down to pet Buck's head, asking curiously, "And who might this beautiful creature be, Molly?"

"This is Buck, mom. He is Owen's dog," she said as Owen and Oliver got closer.

"Hey, Molly!" Owen greeted, a wide grin spreading across his face. "Beautiful day for a walk, isn't it?"

Molly returned the greeting, her eyes meeting Owen's. "Mom, this is Owen," she said, addressing her mom. "Owen, this is my mom, Laura."

Owen reached over and shook Laura's outstretched hand, noting the confused look on her face. "Your daughter and I have met several times on walks. You see, my very naughty dog here," he said, pointing at Buck, "seems to really like Molly. He likes to play escape artist and go straight to her when he knows she's around."

There was a hint of awkwardness, a subtle tension in the air as Owen locked eyes with Molly. They had been crossing paths for months on their walks, but today felt different for some reason. Owen shifted his feet as he tried to push the odd feeling in his gut away, confused at the new feelings he was having.

Oliver, the lively five-year-old that he was, tugged at Owen's hand, eager to say hello. Buck's tail was still wagging as he sat calmly now beside the little boy.

"Laura," Owen said, pulling his gaze from Molly long enough to look down at his son, "this is my son, Oliver."

"Hello there, cutie," Laura said, reaching out to pat the little boy on the head. Instead, Oliver reached his hand out, puffing out his chest and making himself appear as though he was a man stuck in a tiny child's body. Laura giggled under her breath, changing direction to give him a shake of the hand. "It's very nice to meet you, Oliver."

"You too, ma'am," Oliver said, smiling up at her.

Buck apparently couldn't contain his excitement any longer, because he jumped up and put his paws on Molly's stomach, licking her face, tail wagging behind him.

"Buck! Get down!" Owen said firmly, pulling the dog off her. "I'm so sorry, Molly...again..." he said, shaking his head, obviously embarrassed.

"That dog sure seems to like you, Mol," her mother said, laughing as she leaned down and ruffled the naughty dog's fir.

"Yeah, he's a charmer alright," Molly replied, her smile masking the complexity of her emotions. In the midst of her divorce, she valued the simplicity of these friendly encounters and saw Owen as a welcome distraction. She had come to really enjoy their meetings in the park, and even looked forward to them when she stopped at the bench to sit awhile. Owen was a witty guy, and she loved how easily he could make her laugh.

Laura observed the interaction between Owen and Molly with a keen mother's eye, sensing the dynamics that appeared to be at play. Knowing her daughter well, she was very perceptive. She prided herself on her ability to read people... It was essential in her line of work, and she couldn't help but notice a subtle chemistry between Molly and Owen right now.

"Daddy, can we go for a walk with Molly and the nice lady?" Oliver asked Owen.

"Uh... I don't know... I guess you'd better ask Molly if that's okay," Owen answered the eager little boy.

"Molly, can we walk with you? Please?" Oliver asked her, his little eyes pleading with her in a way that made her want to scoop him up and hug him.

"Of course you can!" she said. The group all turned to go the same way and off they went, walking in unison as if they'd done it many times before.

They all chatted amicably as they strolled through the tranquil neighborhood, the laughter of Oliver punctuating the conversation. Owen, a master of humor, effortlessly wove jokes into their dialogue, sharing stories of the uniquely amusing teenagers he worked with every day and creating an atmosphere of lightness that seemed to ease the tension that had been in the air previously.

As they reached a fork in the path, Owen and Oliver prepared to head in a different direction. Molly hesitated, realizing that her mother had picked up on the unspoken connection between her and Owen.

The group said their goodbyes, and Owen's eyes lingered on Molly for a few seconds as he turned to walk in the opposite direction with Buck and Oliver.

As they started to walk down the path towards home, Laura discreetly nudged Molly and whispered, "He seems like a nice guy, Molly. And Oliver is adorable."

Molly sighed, conflicted by the uncharted territory of her emotions. "He's just a friend, Mom. We've only bumped into each other a handful of times."

Laura stopped again, gently touching Molly's arm as she offered her a gentle expression. "He seems like a good man, Molly. It's okay to let someone in, you know, when you feel like you're ready to," Laura said, her words carrying the precious weight of maternal understanding.

Molly sighed, her gaze lingering on Owen's retreating figure. The realization that she might be opening her heart to new possibilities dawned upon her. "It's been a long time since I was happy, Mom."

"I know, sweetheart," Laura replied, ever the supportive mother. She smiled knowingly at her daughter. "Sometimes, though, friendships can blossom into something more. Just keep an open heart and mind, okay? You deserve all the happiness that this world has to offer you, Mol."

"I will try, mom," Molly said, suddenly feeling very tired. It had been a *really* long day, and she wished she was closer to home so she could just curl up and go to sleep.

Laura wrapped an arm around Molly's shoulders, offering comfort and support. "Happiness comes in unexpected ways, sweetheart. When it knocks on your door, don't be afraid to let it in. You deserve it."

The duo continued their walk, the spring afternoon unfolding with the promise of new beginnings. Molly, torn between the echoes of the past and the potential of the future, felt a glimmer of hope stirring within her. As the warmth of the sun enveloped them, she considered the possibility that love might find its way back into her life, one footstep at a time.

When they got back to the house, her dad was there, so she said her goodbyes and politely excused herself to head back to Lily's place. She wanted a bubble bath and her comfy bed tonight. The cool evening air wrapped around her as she stepped out of her parent's house, the soft glow of porch lights casting a warm ambiance around her. The visit had been comforting, but as she approached her car, thoughts of the quiet drive home began to fill her mind. Little did she know, her night was about to get more interesting.

As Molly fumbled with her keys, she looked up, and there, at the end of the driveway, was Owen, walking toward her with an uncertain smile. A rush of joy surged through her. Owen, her friend, someone she had started to see through a different lens, was approaching her with an air of… nervousness maybe? That was odd… he was usually so steady and confident around her. Besides, she'd just seen him less than hour before… *"What could he need so badly that he would walk all the way back over here?"* she wondered.

"Hey, Molly," Owen greeted, his eyes conveying a mix of excitement and anxiousness. "I… well, I was wondering if you'd maybe want to catch a movie with me on Friday night? Oliver is staying over at my mom's place, and I thought it might be a nice way for you and I to get to know each other a little better."

Molly's heart danced in her chest. It was a simple invitation, but the weight of its significance hung in the air around her. A movie date with Owen— something that went beyond their casual encounters during walks. She felt a flutter of happiness and a twinge of nervousness at the prospect of taking a step towards a new chapter in her life. Was she ready for this? Was it okay to go on a date when she wasn't officially divorced yet from Waylon? Oh… why not?

A smile spread slowly across Molly's face, genuine and filled with a quiet enthusiasm. "I'd love to, Owen. Friday night sounds great."

Owen visibly relaxed, his shoulders easing as if a weight had been lifted from them. "I'm really glad to hear that! I'll pick you up around six?"

"Sure, that sounds perfect," Molly replied, her voice tinged with a mixture of excitement and uncertainty. "If you don't mind giving me your number, I will text you my address," she said, handing him her unlocked phone so he could type his number into it. Taking it back, she quickly typed Lily's address in, hit send, and then put her phone back in her pocket.

With a shared smile, Owen nodded, said goodbye, and headed back down the driveway. As she got into her car, a whirlwind of emotions engulfed her. The prospect of a date with Owen stirred feelings deep inside of her that she hadn't explored in a long time.

Driving through the quiet streets, Molly found herself caught between anticipation and apprehension. The divorce, though in progress, hadn't reached its finality, and the echoes of her past still lingered. She questioned whether she was ready for this new beginning, whether she could allow herself to open up to the possibility of romance once again.

As she navigated the familiar roads, Molly's mind wandered, grappling with the complexity of her emotions. The scars of her failed marriage were still healing, and the idea of starting anew brought a mix of excitement and fear. She wondered if Owen sensed her hesitancy, if he could see the layers of vulnerability beneath the surface. She'd never really talked about Hannah with Owen... how would he feel about that and the hole that her passing had left in Molly's heart. She wasn't sure she could ever fill that space in again... would that be too much for him to handle?

Arriving at Lily's place, Molly parked her car and sat in silence for a moment. The Friday night date loomed on the horizon, a chance for connection, laughter, and shared experiences. She took a deep breath, acknowledging the uncertainty ahead, and decided to embrace the opportunity and hope for the best. *"Sometimes,"* she remembered her dad telling her multiple times when she was a child, *"the only way to get from one rock to another is to leap."*

Eleven

Chapter 10

Molly paced around her room frantically. She couldn't seem to find a single thing to wear tonight for her date with Owen. Lily sauntered into Molly's room to ask her about dinner but was welcomed by a massive pile of clothes thrown in a pile by the door.

"What in the world is going on in here?" Lily asked, sliding a pile over with her foot so she could walk into the room. "Did you have a war with your closet or something?"

Molly continued to throw pants and shirts out of her closet, completely avoiding Lily's question.

"Uh… Molly? I hate to tell you this, but I'm pretty sure your closet won!" she said, laughing as she crossed the room to where Molly was finally coming out of the closet, frustration painted all over her face.

"I'm going to the movies with Owen in like 30 minutes and I don't have anything to wear!" Molly sank down the wall and onto the floor with a sigh.

"Wait… What? Really?" Lily squealed with delight at Molly's predicament. "Why didn't you tell me?"

"I didn't want to tell anybody because I was trying to decide if I was even going to go, and now that I see this mess, I'm thinking it's a sign that I was right about thinking I should call and cancel!" she said, aggravated as she looked around the room at the mess that her little 'clothing tornado' had created.

Lily laughed, loving the fact that her friend was finally going to jump out there and give this thing with the hot guy from the park a chance. "You know what, Mol? Leave it all to me! You are in my wheelhouse now, girl! Owen isn't going to know what hit him when he sees you tonight!" Lily said with a smile as she cracked her fingers and then entered Molly's closet.

Molly stayed on the floor, her head in her hands, trying to figure out a way to let Owen down easy. This was obviously a mistake.

"Gee, Molly. You seriously need to go shopping for some new clothes!" Lily gave her disapproving gaze. "There's not much to work with that doesn't scream 'I like long naps and eating on a couch by myself!' in this closet!"

"Oh… whatever, Lily! Just pick something for me. It's only a movie… nothing fancy or anything. I'm sure there's gotta be *something* in there that will work!"

After what felt like an eternity, Lily emerged with a royal blue dress, smiling and obviously quite pleased with herself. "Pair this with those cute little slip-ons you have, and he won't know what hit him!" she said, grinning a naughty grin as she laid the dress on the bed. "Now… I need to go get ready for a night out with a friend from my gym, so I'll leave you to do the same," she said as she left in the same flurry she had flown in with.

"Oh… and don't forget those cute little diamond earrings you wore to our girls' night!" she yelled as she hopped down the hallway to her own room.

Molly rolled her eyes. "This is such a mistake!" she said as she grabbed the dress and her undergarments and went into the bathroom to get dressed. She didn't want to be in her robe still when he got there, and at this pace, she was most surely going to be!

* * *

The engine hummed with a steady rhythm as Owen navigated the somewhat familiar streets toward Molly's apartment. The anticipation in his chest felt like a beating drum, the nervous excitement building with each passing block. He had dropped Oliver off at his grandmother's house earlier, a decision made with a mix of practicality and the desire to make this evening special.

Two years had passed since the devastating loss of his wife, and Owen hadn't allowed himself the luxury of pursuing a romantic relationship with *anyone* until now. The idea of dating was both thrilling and terrifying, and the prospect of crossing that line with Molly, a woman he'd really grown to appreciate and enjoy as a friend, added an extra layer of complexity to his emotions.

As he neared Molly's apartment, Owen's palms grew clammy on the steering wheel. He rehearsed possible opening lines in his mind, trying to shake off the nervous jitters that threatened to betray his composure. The fear of ruining their friendship loomed like a shadow over him, but a deeper longing for something more in his life compelled him forward.

Pulling up to her apartment building, Owen took a deep breath, the cool evening air filling his lungs. He parked the car and stared at himself in the rearview mirror, urging the pounding in his heart to slow and his nerves to relax. After a moment of self-reflection, he stepped out of the car, shutting his door behind him.

He had chosen a new pair of blue jeans that fit him well. For a shirt, he'd worn a light blue button-up with long sleeves and an undershirt beneath. He had his favorite cologne on, and he had shaved before he left home. He had never taken so long to decide on a shirt in his entire life, and he'd laughed at the absurdity of it. Now, standing here in front of his truck, he was *sure* he'd chosen the wrong thing. What if she didn't like blue or something?

"This is probably a bad idea, but here goes nothing," he said to himself as he willed his feet to move.

The short walk to Molly's front door felt like a journey through uncharted territory. Owen's hands felt sweaty, and his stomach was in knots. He raised his hand to knock, but hesitation lingered.

What if this changes everything? He thought. *What if we can't go back to being just friends ever again? What if...*

Before Owen could finish that thought, Lily swung the door open, obviously on her way out. Her eyes widened with a friendly grin. "Hey, Owen! Come on in. Molly's just finishing up."

Relief washed over Owen as he stepped into the welcoming warmth of Molly and Lily's apartment. Lily chatted amicably, making small talk to ease the tension, but Owen's focus was on the anticipation of seeing Molly.

And then, she appeared.

Molly descended the staircase, her shy smile illuminated by the soft glow of the apartment lights. Owen's breath caught in his throat at the sight of her. She wore a simple blue dress that accentuated her grace and hugged her curves perfectly. Her hair fell gently around her shoulders, and her eyes sparkled with a mixture of nerves and excitement.

"Hi, Owen," Molly greeted, her voice a soft melody that resonated in the room.

"Hi," Was all Owen could choke out, deciding a literal frog must have climbed into his throat at some point between his car and the apartment door. His voice carried a warmth that mirrored the emotions swirling within him.

Lily excused herself to head out, chuckling at their reactions to one another as she left them alone. Behind Owen's back, she gave a theatrical thumbs up, waving in front of her face to signal he was what she would call *smokin' hot*. Then, she disappeared into the dusk of the spring evening.

Owen and Molly exchanged a few words, their nerves palpable, but overshadowed by the shared anticipation of the evening ahead. Owen offered his arm, and they left the apartment together, stepping into the cool night.

The drive to the movies was filled with a quiet tension, the air thick with unspoken words. Molly gazed out of the window, her mind racing with conflicting emotions. Owen stole glances at her, struck by her beauty and the enigmatic allure that had drawn him to her in the first place. When they arrived, he scooted around his truck to open her door for her, a pleasant reminder to her that chivalry was still alive in some men.

As they entered the movie theater, the atmosphere shifted. The darkness of the cinema provided a cloak of anonymity, and the scent of buttered popcorn filled the air. Owen and Molly settled into their seats, the tension easing as they shared lighthearted banter.

Molly was amazed at how easily conversation came between them. It was as if they'd known each other for years, not months. She enjoyed his amusing stories about teaching, and he seemed to be fascinated with her business and the hard work she'd done to bring it to fruition. Overall, they were both having a wonderful time.

As the movie started, they settled into their seats, sharing the popcorn they'd poured excessive amounts of butter onto as they watched the movie together. The connection between them deepened naturally as they lost themselves in the on-screen world, and the nervous energy began to dissipate.

About halfway through the movie, Owen felt Molly shiver. Without a second thought, he extended his hand toward hers. "My hands are warm… you can use them to warm yours if you're cold," he offered.

Molly nodded, and Owen gently enveloped her hands in his, offering warmth. The simple touch ignited a spark between them, a subtle recognition of something deeper. After a few moments, Molly relaxed her hand, allowing their fingers to slowly become intertwined, and the world outside the movie theater suddenly ceased to exist.

As their hands melted into one another, a current surged through them both. The physical contact was electric, stirring emotions that neither could fully comprehend. Owen stole glances at Molly, captivated by the way her eyes sparkled in the dim light as she watched the movie on the huge screen.

The movie played on, but the real drama unfolded between Owen and Molly. It was a silent conversation of glances, a dance of fingers interlaced, and an unspoken acknowledgment that something had shifted between them.

When the credits rolled and the lights flickered on, Owen reluctantly let go of Molly's hand. The reality of the outside world crept back in, but the residue of their shared moment lingered, leaving them both feeling a little breathless. Molly felt a little embarrassed as she found herself with butterflies in her stomach, kind of like the first date she had back in high school. She was a grown woman who had been married, for crying out loud!

As they followed the crowd out of the theater, the night air carried a newfound tension. Owen drove Molly back to her apartment, the silence in the car heavy with unspoken emotions. He parked his truck, and when he turned to her, Molly's eyes met his with a mix of vulnerability and desire.

They lingered in the truck, the moment filled with anticipation, but neither knowing what should come next. Owen hesitated, a silent plea in his eyes. Molly, caught in the whirlwind of conflicting emotions, mirrored his uncertainty.

Then, with a mixture of courage and longing, Owen leaned in. Their lips met in a tentative kiss, a fusion of emotions that transcended the spoken word. Molly hesitated at first, the weight of her pending divorce echoing in her mind, and Owen could sense the apprehension in her response to his kiss, so he broke the connection, looking at her nervously, worried that he'd made the wrong move. Then, suddenly, something in her shifted, and before he could search his brain for an answer to what it was, she acted.

With a surge of urgency, Molly pulled Owen closer, deepening the kiss. It was a collision of past wounds and budding desires, a moment of vulnerability and surrender. The world outside completely vanished as they became entangled in the unexpected passion that had blossomed between them.

When they finally broke the kiss, a stunned silence lingered in the car. Owen stared at Molly, his eyes searching for affirmation. Molly, breathless and wide-eyed, met his gaze with a mix of surprise and wonder.

As Owen walked her to the apartment door like a true gentleman, their steps echoed with the unspoken acknowledgment that something irrevocable had happened. When they stood at the threshold, hesitation hung in the air. Then, as if guided by an invisible force, Owen leaned in for one more kiss.

Molly, still processing the whirlwind of emotions, initially hesitated but then surrendered to the magnetic pull between them. The kiss held a promise, a shared acknowledgment that their connection had transformed into something beyond friendship. Something without boundaries or limits, without rules or consequences.

As she stood in the doorway to the apartment and watched Owen get in his truck to leave, Molly touched her lips with her fingers. She could still feel the tingling sensation his kiss had left on them. The world had shifted on its axis, and the unspoken journey they had embarked upon left them breathless and eager for what lay ahead.

The echoes of that first kiss lingered in the air, leaving a trail of emotions that neither could fully comprehend but were still undeniably ready to explore.

* * *

The ornate glass door of Berg, Bailey & Tarmon LLC swung open with a jarring creak, revealing Waylon's looming figure. His eyes, bloodshot and filled with frustration, scanned the plush surroundings of the prestigious law firm. His lawyer, Joe Berg, looked up from his polished mahogany desk, a furrow forming on his brow at the sight of Waylon's disheveled appearance.

"Waylon, come on in," Joe said, gesturing to the leather chair in front of his desk. The immaculate office seemed to amplify Waylon's internal turmoil as he slumped into the seat.

"What's this all about, Joe?" Waylon growled, the lingering scent of alcohol trailing behind him like a heavy, stagnant cloud.

"Good morning, Waylon. I asked you to come so we can talk about your upcoming divorce proceedings. Molly's lawyer sent over some paperwork, and we need to respond in a timely manner," Joe explained, his gaze subtly narrowing at the noticeable odor wafting from Waylon.

Waylon scoffed, "I threw all those papers in the fireplace and lit 'em up! I don't want a damn divorce, so why the hell would I sign those papers?"

Joe sighed, his eyes glancing at the clock. "It's a legal process, Waylon. Whether you want it or not, we need to respond. This is why I wanted you to come down here, because you don't ever let me explain this stuff over the phone. As I've tried to tell you before, it only takes one person to file for divorce in this state, not two."

Waylon dropped down into the cushy chair across from Joe's desk, anger etched on his face. "Look… Like I said, I'm not signing anything. I want to fight this, so how do we do that?"

Joe sighed again, glancing at the stack of paperwork on his desk. "Waylon, I'm sorry, but you aren't understanding me. You can't prevent a divorce in Wisconsin just by refusing to sign. It's a no-fault state. It doesn't require both parties to agree for a divorce to be granted."

Waylon's fists clenched, his knuckles turning white. "I don't give a damn about the law. I won't let her walk away from us without a fight!"

Joe looked at him with a mix of concern and exasperation. "Waylon, listen. I understand you're upset, but legally, it's not about fault or who wants or doesn't want the divorce. It's about the process, and it's my job to get you the best results I possibly can."

"I don't care, Joe. I don't want this divorce. I won't let her walk away and take everything I love from me," Waylon snapped.

Joe tried to maintain his calm demeanor. "Waylon, we can discuss your options, but you need to understand the legal implications. It might be better to reach an agreement with Molly rather than dragging this through the courts. You are legally able to get half of the assets, but the two of you need to figure out who will get what."

"An agreement? Do you think this is about *stuff*? It's *her* I want, not stuff!"

"I understand that, Waylon, and I'm truly sorry that your marriage is ending. I can see that it's really upsetting you. The thing is, I have no choice but to send a reply to her lawyer and the courts about how you would like your half of the estate to be handled, so we need to talk about that and make some decisions about what you do and do not want to keep," Joe said, trying to explain things to Waylon in a way that he could comprehend. He could tell that Waylon was miserable, and that he was not handling all this very well.

"She can have whatever the hell she wants. I don't want any of it," Waylon spat, his voice filled with bitterness.

Joe nodded, recognizing the resistance. "I understand that you're angry, but you really need to think more clearly about this. Once the court date has passed, it will be very difficult to try to make any changes to the court commissioner's decisions. The biggest asset to consider is the house… what do you want to do about the house, Waylon?"

Waylon's eyes narrowed. "Tell her she can do whatever the hell she wants with it. I don't care. I don't want it."

"Okay, I'll convey that to her lawyer. And what about the bills and assets?" Joe asked, maintaining a professional demeanor.

"Split the bills. If I can keep my retirement as is, she can take the rest. I don't give a damn," Waylon replied curtly.

Joe sighed, realizing that this was the best he was going to get from Waylon in his current state. "I'll handle the negotiations, Waylon. You don't need to worry about it. But please, try to calm down. This is a difficult time for *both* of you."

Waylon stood abruptly, the chair scraping against the floor. "I'm done here. Tell her whatever you want. I just want this over with."

With that, Waylon slammed the door behind him, leaving the high-end law office in tense silence. He stormed out, his thoughts a tempest of anger and confusion. The drive to the house was a blur, the engine roaring with his frustration and anger.

Arriving at the home that once held the echoes of laughter and shared dreams, Waylon stomped through the rooms, recklessly packing his belongings into some boxes he had in the garage. The familiar surroundings now felt foreign, each item a painful reminder of a life that was slipping away.

He threw his suitcases into the back of his truck, the metallic thud echoing his sense of loss. The once warm and inviting home now stood cold and indifferent. Waylon revved the engine and sped away from the place that would never again be his sanctuary or his home.

Waylon drove until he saw an old run-down hotel on the outskirts of town. The hotel seemed to mirror Waylon's emotional state. He checked in with a bitter sense of defeat, the flickering neon sign above the entrance casting an eerie glow. The room, dimly lit and smelling of stale mothballs, became his temporary refuge.

He sank onto the worn-out bed, cracking open a bottle of whiskey. The liquid burned down his throat, a futile attempt to drown out the pain and confusion swirling within him. How had everything come to this? The woman he loved, the life they built together, slipping through his fingers like sand. His eyes filled with tears, and he swiped at them with the back of his hands. This isn't how things were supposed to go... how had he gotten here?

The harsh reality of the divorce settled over him, the weight of the paperwork and legalities a suffocating burden. He questioned how Molly could do this to him, how their shared history could unravel so swiftly. The whiskey provided a fleeting escape, but the bitterness lingered.

As Waylon sat alone in the dim room, the ghosts of his past haunting him, he wondered if he could ever find peace amid the wreckage of his broken marriage. The remnants of their life together echoed in the silent walls of the hotel, a stark reminder that the road ahead was filled with uncertainties and painful farewells.

"Why, Molly? Why?" he cried as he took another drink. Before long, he passed out on the bed, giving in to the darkness that was consuming him from the inside out.

***

Molly was sitting in her office trying to get some paperwork finished up and some invoices emailed out when her phone rang. Looking at the caller id she saw that it was her lawyer's office calling. She picked it up quickly.

"Hello, this is Molly," she said nervously.

"Hello, Molly. This is Nancy Finn. Do you have a few minutes to go over a few things quickly?" Nancy asked her.

"Yes, I have time. Is everything okay?" she asked hesitantly.

"Yes, everything is fine. I just wanted to go over the information I just received from Waylon's lawyer. It appears that he is refusing to sign the divorce papers. His lawyer, Joe, says he was very distraught at his office yesterday," Nancy explained.

"I see. Waylon has been drinking a lot, and I know he's very angry at me for leaving. Will this cause any issues with the divorce proceedings?"

"No. As I told you before, he doesn't have to agree to the divorce or sign anything now. His lawyer did, however, respond to the issue of assets and debts. Waylon has apparently agreed to let you do whatever you want with the house. He said he doesn't want it and that he's moved out. His lawyer says that the standard 50/50 split will be fine once you figure out what you want to do with it," Nancy explained. "Have you thought about what you'd like to do with the house at all?"

Molly thought for a moment. She hadn't really gotten that far ahead, to be honest. She knew she didn't plan to go back to the house, and obviously Waylon had decided he didn't want to live there either, but now what?

"Do I have some time to think about the house stuff?" she asked her lawyer.

"Of course! We have a couple of weeks to decide and file the proper forms with the court. I'll also need you to send me your financial information so I can get that information entered. Everything must be in at least 30 days prior to your court date, so you only have about two and a half weeks left to get it filed.

"Okay… I'll talk to my friend's husband and try to figure out the best plan. He's a realtor, so he'll know my options. Thank you again for calling, Nancy," Molly said, hanging up the phone. She had a few things to do before closing for the night, and she still wanted to get a walk in before heading home. She had a lot to figure out, and she had no idea where to start.

By the time she turned the key to lock the front door of The Sweet Sprinkle, the warm glow of the streetlights in the city were starting to spill onto the sidewalk, casting a golden hue over the cobblestone path. She'd walked to work that morning, so she headed down the path towards the park.

With a deep breath, Molly allowed her mind to wander as she listened to the sounds of a town preparing to close their doors for another day. The park beckoned with its winding trails and the promise of solitude. The setting sun painted the sky in hues of orange and pink as Molly strolled along the familiar paths. The park had always been her refuge, a sanctuary where she could find solace amidst the chaos of life, and today was no different.

As she reached she and Hannah's special bench, nestled beneath the sprawling branches of an old oak tree, Molly took a seat. The rustling leaves above provided a gentle soundtrack as she gazed out at the serene landscape. Her thoughts, however, were far from tranquil.

The house she shared with Waylon loomed over her like a shadow. The impending divorce had cast a heavy cloud over their once-happy home. The decision about what to do with the house weighed on Molly's heart, its walls echoing with the memories of dreams that had crumbled, especially the haunting image of her infant daughter's empty room.

Molly couldn't bear to walk past that room every day, the ghost of unfulfilled dreams lingering in the air. The thought of selling the house felt like abandoning a part of her past, but staying meant drowning in a sea of memories that grew more painful with each passing day.

"I'm not sure what to do, Hannah. I miss you so much, but it hurts too much to see your room each and every day. I need to find a way to move forward, and I can't do that there," she said softly, speaking into the spring air by the tree she had chosen as Hannah's special place.

Molly watched as a little bird flew down from a branch, landing on the ground only a few feet in front of her. It walked around a little, chirping and singing a spring song. It was as if the bird was trying to comfort her, and she oddly felt a little better. She watched for a few minutes, until the bird flew off, joining the others in the tree. She hadn't seen the beautiful little butterfly lately, but this adorable bird was just as sweet.

Lost in her thoughts, Molly quietly decided to talk to Jeff the next day. He always stopped on Fridays to eat lunch with Mia, so she'd pull him aside and chat with him after they ate. Jeff would know how to navigate the labyrinth of housing decisions. The realization struck her, and a sense of relief washed over her. As hard as this was all going to be, she knew she was doing the right thing.

Twelve

Chapter 11

Claire's office exuded a sense of calm as Molly settled into the plush chair. As usual, the soothing colors and soft lighting provided a safe space for her to unravel everything going on inside her mind and her heart. Claire welcomed Molly with a warm smile.

"How have you been since our last session, Molly?" Claire inquired, her gentle voice inviting Molly to share her thoughts.

Molly took a deep breath before responding. "The nightmares about Hannah—they've stopped."

"Really?" Claire asked. "That's so good to hear, Molly."

"Yeah… I am *definitely* getting more sleep now that I'm not constantly scared to fall asleep for fear of the nightmares coming again. Also… I'm not feeling as sad anymore, or at least not as often."

"I'm happy to hear that as well," Claire said, smiling.

"The problem is that I feel like guilt has taken its place," Molly admitted, frustration evident in her tone.

"What do you mean guilt has taken its place?" Claire asked, curious where Molly was going with that line.

"Well, I just mean that instead of feeling sad, I feel guilty."

"Can you explain what you feel guilty for?" Claire asked her.

"I can try… I guess I feel guilty for not being sad all the time, for moving on, in a way."

Claire nodded, understanding the intricacies of grief in a way that Molly did not. "I know we've touched on this before, but guilt is a common emotion, Molly. It often accompanies the process of healing. How about we explore the feelings you're having together… Why do you think you feel guilty for not being consumed by sadness as much as you used to be?"

Molly hesitated before replying, her gaze fixed on a distant point. "I guess it's like, if I'm not constantly mourning Hannah, I feel like it means I'm forgetting her… That I didn't love her enough or something. It's just this constant battle in my head, you know?"

Claire listened attentively, offering a reassuring presence. "Molly, grief doesn't have a timeline or a set of rules. It's okay to find moments of joy amidst the pain. It doesn't diminish your love for Hannah. In fact, as we talked about before, I believe she would want you to find happiness."

Molly took in those words, a contemplative expression crossing her face. The therapist's validation seemed to lift a weight off her shoulders.

As the session progressed, Molly's conversation shifted to a new presence in her life—Owen. The mention of his name brought a subtle warmth to her eyes. She spoke about their chance encounters in the park, the laughter of his little boy, Oliver, and the budding connection between them.

"It's like there's this mix of emotions inside of me. I never thought I'd feel this way again, especially after Hannah. Owen is wonderful, and Oliver—he's adorable. But, still, there's this lingering and daunting fear, you know?"

"What is it that you're afraid of, Molly?" Claire inquired.

"I guess I'm afraid of getting too attached, of letting someone into my heart again."

Claire nodded, offering a smile. "It's natural to feel apprehensive, especially after what you've been through. Opening yourself up to new connections can be both exhilarating and terrifying. What specifically scares you about getting attached to Owen and Oliver?"

Molly contemplated the question, her fingers tracing invisible patterns on her lap. "I guess it's the fear of loss, of investing *so much* of myself into something and then having it taken away. I really don't think I could bear that pain again. Losing Hannah nearly broke me!"

Claire offered a thoughtful response, "It sounds like a protective mechanism, Molly. You're guarding yourself from the possibility of more heartache. Let me ask you this… What steps can you take to navigate these fears while still allowing yourself to embrace the joy Owen and Oliver bring into your life?"

As Molly pondered the question, she began to share and unfold her recent experiences—the first date with Owen, the shared laughter during the movie, and the unexpected kiss that had ignited a cascade of emotions.

Claire listened without judgment, allowing Molly the space to express the intricate tapestry of her feelings. "It seems like you're in a delicate dance between fear and the desire for connection. It's okay to take it one step at a time, Molly. I'd like you to do a little homework for me before our next session. I'd like you to make a list of some ways you can think of to calm your fears. On one side of the list, place your fears. On the other side of the list, write at least 3 ways to you could cope with that fear. I want you to think of ways that would allow you to feel positive emotions without the weight of expectation stopping you."

"Okay, I think I can do that," Molly said, making a mental note of her homework.

As the session neared its end, Molly was starting to feel a newfound clarity. The knots of guilt and fear had begun to loosen, making room for the possibility of both grief and joy to coexist.

As she walked Molly back out of her office to the waiting room, Claire added, "I want you to remember, Molly, it's okay to mourn Hannah and cry for the dreams you had for her. But it's also permissible to move forward."

Leaving the therapist's office, Molly carried a sense of acceptance within her. The journey ahead was uncertain, but the acknowledgment of her feelings and the permission to navigate the complexities of love and loss at her own pace felt like a gentle guide toward healing.

As she got in her car and closed the door, she decided she needed to get her mind off things for a little bit, and she knew exactly who she wanted to do that with. She pushed the buttons and messaged the man who was quickly becoming her favorite person to talk to… Owen.

Hey! Any chance you and the crew would like to go for a walk today? I could use some fresh air.

It didn't take long for her phone to light up with a reply.

Definitely! Do you want to meet at my place or at the park by your shoppe?

Molly thought for a moment. Although she really liked walking in her parent's neighborhood, she'd rather not have them see her walking with Owen and Oliver just yet. She wasn't ready for all the questions… she didn't really even know the answers yet if she was being honest.

We can meet at the one in town here if that's okay.

Sounds great… see you in about 20 minutes!

Molly looked in the rearview mirror. She looked tired, but there was a smile on her face that she hadn't even realized had been there. She really loved spending time with Owen, and now she found herself wondering about the cute little boy she had met. If he was half as funny as his father, this would be a wonderful distraction.

As she neared the park and found a place to park her car, she found herself excited. She really did enjoy her time with Owen.

"It's just a walk, Molly, calm down!" she said to herself in the mirror.

She wasn't sure how Owen did it, but as she saw him drive up in his truck, she felt butterflies in her belly. Suddenly, she realized she may like this guy a little more than she realized…

"Is that really so bad?" she asked herself as she got out of her car.

Laughing, she thought, *"I really needed to figure my you-know-what out before someone catches me talking to myself!"*

✳ ✳ ✳

The soft glow of the setting sun cast a warm embrace over the park as Owen, Molly, and Oliver strolled along the winding paths. Buck bounded ahead, his tail wagging in exuberance. The air was filled with the sounds of laughter, the distant hum of children playing, and the occasional bark of other dogs in the vicinity.

"Molly, can I walk by you?" Oliver asked in a voice that literally melted Molly into a puddle on the ground.

"Of course you can, Oliver!" she replied, smiling as he bounced over by her, an excited Buck in tow.

"Oh… I see how it is… now *neither one* of you wants to hang out with me whenever Molly is around!" Owen teased, laughing as Molly poked him in the shoulder over Oliver's head.

"It's not *my* fault that I'm more fun than you!" Molly teased back.

As they walked, Molly couldn't help but marvel at the simple joy of the evening. Oliver's infectious laughter echoed through the air when he decided he was bored walking by them and ran ahead instead, Buck gleefully chasing after him. Owen walked beside Molly, their shoulders brushing occasionally. It was moments like these that Molly found solace in—the uncomplicated beauty of shared laughter with a man who had become a wonderful friend… and possibly more.

Yet, beneath the surface, Molly carried a weight that lingered in the recesses of her thoughts. She stole glances at Owen, contemplating whether it was time to share the painful chapter of her past… Hannah's story. Molly wrestled with the fear of unveiling her vulnerability, uncertain of how Owen would handle hearing about the painful memory of Hannah's birth and subsequent death. Still, she knew he had experienced an incredible loss himself, and she knew that if anyone would understand grief's effects on the heart, it was probably Owen.

The sun dipped below the horizon, casting long shadows across the park. Owen sensed Molly's contemplation, his perceptive gaze meeting hers. He squeezed her hand gently, a silent reassurance that she could confide in him.

They found a quiet spot in the park, a bench beneath a beautiful weeping willow tree. Oliver, bubbling with energy, asked if he could play a little longer. Owen nodded, giving Molly a knowing look before turning his attention back to his son. "Go ahead and play on the swings, Oliver. Molly and I will watch!"

Oliver excitedly ran over to the playground equipment just a stone's throw from the bench his dad and Molly had just sat down at. Buck followed, watching his best friend play.

Molly took a deep breath, the cool evening air filling her lungs. She turned to Owen, her eyes reflecting a mix of emotions. "Owen, there's something I need to tell you."

He looked at her with unwavering support. "You can tell me anything, Molly."

A heaviness settled in the pit of her stomach as she mustered the courage to speak. "Before things go any further between us, there's something you should know. It's about my past, about something that is really hard for me to talk about."

Owen sat calmly beside her, his eyes urging her to continue. "You don't have to tell me if you're not ready, but I'm here for you, whatever it is."

She nodded, grateful for his understanding. "A year and a half ago, I lost my baby girl, Hannah. She was stillborn. It's been a pain I've carried with me every day since, and I didn't know how to share it with others or how to push past it myself. I'm in therapy, and it is helping a lot, but it's still really hard. I feel like I'm one tear away from a sobbing mess every moment of my life now, and I hate that."

Owen's eyes softened with empathy. "I'm so sorry, Molly. I can't imagine the pain you've been through."

Molly felt a lump forming in her throat, but Owen's reassuring presence encouraged her to press on. "I just wanted you to know, Owen. I don't want to hide anything from you, especially if we are going to allow whatever is happening between us to go any further."

He gently cupped her face, his eyes locked onto hers. "Thank you for sharing that with me, Molly. You're incredibly strong, and I am always happy to listen when you need an ear."

They sat in companionable silence for a while, the weight of Molly's revelation lingering in the air. As they talked, Owen sensed her internal struggle, the fear of judgment and the vulnerability that came with opening up about such a deeply personal experience.

Suddenly, their peaceful moment was shattered by an unexpected intrusion. Waylon sauntered toward them, an unmistakable scent of alcohol surrounding him. Molly's eyes widened in disbelief, a surge of anger coursing through her veins. She'd seen that look on his face before, knew he was angry. Anger and drunkenness didn't make for a very good combination. The hairs on the back of her neck stood on end, warning her that he was about to confront them.

"What the hell are you doing here?" Waylon demanded in a drawl that came from too much alcohol, his gaze shifting between Molly and Owen.

Owen, his protective instincts kicking in, stood between Molly and Waylon. "Excuse me? I think you need to continue on home, man."

"Owen… this is my soon-to-be ex-husband, Waylon, and he's obviously been drinking," Molly informed him, both embarrassed and angry.

"You need to leave… now!" Owen said, trying to get the man to leave before Oliver realized anything was going on.

Waylon scoffed, a cynical smile playing on his lips. "Well, well, well. Looks like my little soon-to-be ex-wife has found herself a new man. What are you doing with this guy, Molly? Trying to replace me?"

Molly's jaw clenched, her frustration bubbling to the surface. "Waylon, this is none of your business. We are just here enjoying the evening, not for your drunken antics."

Waylon sneered, unfazed by Molly's words. Suddenly, Oliver yelled from the top of the playground equipment, "Daddy… watch this!" He then slid down the swirly slide, excited as ran back to do it again.

"Great job, buddy!" Owen said, never taking his eyes off Waylon.

A vengeful understanding passed over Waylon's face as he watched the boy playing. "Oh, I see. You found yourself a daddy to play with! You're pathetic, Molly."

Owen, attempting to keep his composure, stepped forward. "You need to leave, Waylon. This isn't the time or the place, and I won't ask you again."

Waylon shot Owen a disdainful look but, realizing the futility of the situation, turned and walked away, muttering under his breath.

Oliver, sensing the tension now, approached Molly with a puzzled expression. "Is everything okay, Molly?"

She ruffled his hair, forcing a smile. "Everything's fine, sweetie. How about we head back to the vehicles, okay?"

As Oliver and Buck led the way, Owen and Molly trailed behind, the encounter with Waylon lingering in the air. Once they got back to the cars, Owen put Oliver into his car seat and then walked over to Molly's car.

"Molly, would you like to come by the house for a while? I would really like to finish the conversation we were having before we got interrupted, and maybe about Waylon some as well."

"Um… I guess that would be fine. I really am sorry about Waylon, Owen," she apologized.

Owen helped Molly close her door, telling her to follow him to his house. Molly took the ride to try to settle down after Waylon's little escapade in the park. Before she knew it, they were pulling into Owen's driveway. Owen carried Oliver into the house, holding the door open for Molly.

"I'm going to go put this little guy down to bed quickly and then I'll be right out," Owen said, slipping his shoes off on the mat by the door. "You can have a seat wherever you'd like, and I'll be right back."

"Molly, can you read me my bedtime story tonight?" Oliver asked her, his little dimples showing as he flashed her his best smile.

"Um… I guess I can if you really want me to, and if it's okay with your daddy," she answered, not sure how she felt about being asked to read.

"Of course it's okay… if you want to. Otherwise, I can read to him if you prefer not to. I understand either way," Owen said, knowing, after their talk in the park earlier, that it probably brought up some difficult feelings for her.

"It's fine," she said, still unsure. "Oliver, do you want to pick the book and then we'll read it once your dad tucks you in?" she asked the little boy.

"Yeah!" he responded, jumping like a rabbit all the way to the bookcase by his bed. He looked through the books carefully, as if it was the most important choice of his life. Molly giggled under her breath at his goofy antics. Finally, he chose a book and then jumped into bed. Owen tucked him in and gave him a kiss and a hug, then left the room quietly.

"I'll be in the living room when you are finished," he said to Molly before disappearing down the hall.

Molly sat in the chair next to Oliver's bed and read him an adorable story about a bunny and his mommy. Tears threatened to fill her eyes at the precious feelings she was having as she read and watched the little boy slowly dozing off to sleep. As she looked up from the book after reading the final page, she saw that he was asleep. She sat for a few minutes, just watching the boy sleep. He was so sweet and so happy… she'd give anything to feel that innocent once again. She gently kissed his forehead, put the book back on the shelf, and left his room, closing the door quietly behind her.

She found Owen on the couch in the living room, so she went over to join him. By the time she got there, the tears that had threatened earlier had filled her eyes.

As she sat down by Owen, he saw the tears in her eyes, and he smiled at her with understanding. "Oh, Molly… are you okay? I'm sorry… maybe I should have just told Oliver that I was going to read to him…"

Tears fell down Molly's cheeks as she shook her head. "No, I was happy to read to him… It's just that I had dreams of rocking Hannah to sleep every night, reading to her as she grew. Instead, I lost her, and it still hurts knowing that so many dreams were lost with her."

Owen wrapped his arm around her shoulders, offering a comforting presence. "Molly, it's okay to feel that pain. You've been through so much, and it's okay to mourn the dreams you had for Hannah. Believe me… I know how much the ghosts of the past can haunt you in the present."

"I just miss her so much," Molly said, finally succumbing to the tears and the sorrow she felt so deeply in her heart. She had been unable to talk about this and *feel* like this with Waylon for so long… he would get frustrated and walk away because he didn't want to feel it anymore, but that meant that she'd had to bury those feelings or feel them all alone.

Owen held her close, his arms providing a refuge for the sorrow that had lingered within her for far too long. Molly pressed her face into his chest, sobbing as he held her. She felt safe and cared about, and that was something she'd been missing for so long.

When the tears finally subsided, Molly looked into Owen's eyes, a vulnerability laid bare. "I don't know what to say, Owen. I never thought I could share this pain with someone else."

Owen, his gaze unwavering, simply nodded. "You don't have to say anything, Molly. I'm here for you, and I'll listen as long as you need."

The room was bathed in the warm glow of a single lamp, casting a soft ambiance as Molly and Owen cuddled on the sofa, wrapped in the cocoon of shared stories and the blossoming connection between them. The air held a palpable tenderness as they navigated the delicate landscape of Molly's memories.

Sitting up a little, Molly took a deep breath, her gaze drifting to a distant point as she began to share the tender recollections of Hannah's story. "When I found out I was pregnant, it was like the universe had granted me the most precious gift. I had dreamed of becoming a mother for as long as I could remember," she began.

Owen, his eyes fixed on Molly, listened with an empathetic understanding, inviting her to unravel the layers of her past. Molly continued, her voice a gentle melody that resonated with the joy of recalled anticipation.

"I remember feeling Hannah's first kicks. Those tiny flutters that reassured me she was growing strong and healthy inside me. The dreams I had for her were vivid and full of hope—rocking her to sleep, reading bedtime stories, the sound of her laughter filling our home… There were so many things I couldn't wait to do with her."

Owen's expression reflected the compassion he felt for Molly. He reached for her hand, a silent gesture of support, encouraging her to delve into the depths of her memories.

As Molly spoke, the room seemed to hold its breath, absorbing the weight of the emotions she carried. "The day Hannah was born started like any other. The sun was shining, and the air held a sense of excitement. My contractions began, and I remember the mix of nerves and exhilaration as we rushed to the hospital."

Owen's grip on Molly's hand tightened, a subtle acknowledgment of the emotional terrain she was navigating. Molly continued, her voice tinged with both sorrow and a poignant reverence for the memories she was reliving.

"The labor was intense, but the thought of holding my daughter in my arms fueled me. Owen," she continued, "the love and support I felt from Waylon and the medical team—they were beacons of strength during those trying hours. He wasn't like he is now… he was kind and supportive, and we were so *unbelievably happy* about becoming parents."

Owen nodded, his eyes unwavering, allowing Molly to lead the narrative at her own pace. She took a moment, collecting herself before continuing with the story etched on her heart.

"The room felt charged with anticipation as the moment approached. When Hannah was born, the room fell silent. It was a silence that echoed with the absence of the cries that should have filled the air. The joyous announcement that parents long to hear was replaced by an aching hollowness. The doctor handed her to a nurse who ran with her to an incubator. The room became a haven of chaos… nurses and doctors frantically trying to work on her. I was so scared, Owen!" she said, tears falling.

"I'm sure you were, Molly. I can't even imagine how that felt," Owen offered, the first words he'd spoken since she started recounting Hannah's story.

Molly's eyes glistened with tears, and Owen remained a steadfast presence beside her. She continued, her voice steady, though the emotions beneath it were tumultuous.

"After what felt like hours, they stopped. Waylon was frantic. Neither of us knew what was happening. Then, the doctor told us that she was gone. They didn't know what had happened, but they were unable to revive her. My heart dropped out of my chest. I felt numb. Then, a nurse wrapped her up and handed her to me—tiny, delicate, and so achingly beautiful. I held her close, waiting for that reassuring cry, but there was nothing. She was still and silent, nestled in my arms like a sleeping angel. The world collapsed around me as the reality sank in—my precious baby girl was gone."

Owen's heart ached for Molly, and he squeezed her hand, offering a silent anchor amidst the storm of emotions. Molly drew a shuddering breath, her memories shared for the first time in the presence of another.

"I felt an indescribable emptiness, Owen. The dreams I had nurtured for her—the lullabies I had planned to sing, the bedtime stories that would remain unread—all shattered in an instant. Holding her, lifeless, was a pain I wouldn't wish on anyone."

Tears streamed down Molly's face, and Owen reached for her, pulling her into a tender embrace. In that vulnerable moment, words were inadequate, and Owen simply held her as she allowed the depths of her sorrow to surface.

The room, once filled with the echoes of Molly's memories, held a solemn stillness. Eventually, Molly pulled away, her eyes searching Owen's for understanding. "I've carried that pain for so long, Owen. The grief of losing Hannah, the dreams left unfulfilled—it's been a heavy burden."

Owen, his eyes mirroring Molly's sorrow, spoke with a gentle sincerity. "You don't have to carry it alone, Molly. I'm here for you, anytime you need to share or cry or even just sit in silence and remember. A lesson I had to learn after my wife, Tara, passed away was that while pain is part of you, it doesn't define you."

Molly nodded, sincere gratitude shimmering in her tearful eyes. "It's just so hard, Owen. Even after all this time, the ache remains. The dreams that were lost, the milestones we never reached—they haunt me."

Owen wiped away Molly's tears with a gentle touch, his voice a soothing balm. "Grief doesn't have a definite end time, Molly. It's okay to mourn, to grieve for the dreams you had for Hannah. And it's okay to find moments of joy amidst the pain. I'm still learning that lesson myself… trust me."

Molly leaned into Owen's embrace, finding solace in his words. In that shared space of vulnerability, they confronted the pain of the past and the promise of a future built on understanding and empathy… something Molly had so desperately wanted to have with Waylon before he'd turned to drinking instead of her.

They fell into a comfortable silence, the weight of the past shedding with each shared tear. Eventually, Molly's sobs gave way to a sense of quiet and calm. Owen continued to hold her, offering a haven for her battered heart.

In that hushed moment, Molly felt something change within her. She had allowed herself to release the pent-up grief, and in doing so, she had unknowingly opened a door to the possibility of healing deep within her heart. Her eyes closed as she curled up in the safety and warmth of Owen's embrace, his arms providing a solitude she hadn't felt since losing Hannah. Her breathing slowed and became smooth and rhythmic as she fell asleep on his chest.

Owen sat, holding Molly as she slept. He couldn't imagine the pain she'd been through, and it made him want to find a way to take it all away for her. He knew firsthand the pain that loss could bring, and he didn't wish it on anyone. Filled with emotion, he thought of Tara. He missed her and thought of her every single day, every time he looked at his sweet little boy. Oliver looked just like his mother, and he was thankful that he'd always have a piece of her with him. Tears filled his eyes as he closed them to drift off to sleep. Together, they slept, kindred spirits finding comfort in one another's embrace.

Thirteen

Chapter 12

The golden rays of the morning sun filtered through the curtains, casting a yellow glow in Owen's living room. Molly stirred, her surroundings a haze of confusion as she gradually awoke. The scent of Owen's cologne lingered in the air, and as her eyes fluttered open, she found herself in an unfamiliar position.

For a moment, Molly was disoriented, unsure of where she was. Then, the events of the previous night flooded back—an intimate, shared conversation, the weight of confessions, and the solace she had found in Owen's presence. She slowly realized that she was nestled on Owen's chest, his form providing a makeshift bed on the sofa.

As her awareness settled, Molly couldn't help but study Owen's peaceful features. He slept soundly, with the lines of stress that usually etched his face smoothed in repose. Her fingers traced the curve of his cheekbone, marveling at the quiet strength and vulnerability she saw in him. His shirt was unbuttoned slightly at the top, revealing the chest hairs beneath. A shiver passed through her as she let her mind wander to the rest of the man under that shirt. Scolding herself for thinking like that, she looked around the room. She hadn't really seen it in the darkness the evening before.

Owen's living area was bathed in a serene stillness, broken only by the rhythmic cadence of Owen's breathing. The walls were painted a soft blue color that matched well with the rest of the décor. It appeared that Owen liked things to be more modern than country, and she liked that. It made his house look clean and tidy, and although Molly was sometimes a bit on the disorderly side, she appreciated a man that kept a tidy ship.

Molly shifted, realizing she was a bit stiff from lying on Owen's chest all night. The scent of his cologne enveloped her, a comforting fragrance that whispered promises of safety and warmth. She lay down, covering herself up with a throw that was over the edge of the sofa, and laid her head on Owen's lap, placing a small throw pillow between her head and his lap, with her body stretched out on the sofa. She closed her eyes, surrendering once more to sleep, lulled by the steady beat of the large chime clock on the wall behind the sofa. In that quiet moment, the weight of her grief seemed momentarily lifted.

* * *

Owen stirred awake, opening his eyes and meeting the soft morning light filtering through the curtains. He looked down to find Molly asleep on his lap, her hands resting under her chin and on his...

"Holy crap!" Her right hand was basically cupping his manhood, and the bulge was growing by the second as he watched her face next to it. *"Crap! Crap! Think of a grandma... think of a grandma... Crap!"*

It wasn't working. Now what? He looked at her for a moment and realized that if he wasn't so concerned with controlling his body parts before she woke up, he'd have sincerely enjoyed watching her sleep.

He tried to shift her, but that wasn't going to work. Instead, he tried to think of as many un-sexy things as he could... *great aunt Gertrude, burnt cookies, high school, cows...* nothing was working! What was he going to do?

Suddenly, as he looked down at her, a tender smile touched Owen's lips, replacing the panic he was feeling with compassion and love as he observed her peaceful expression. In the stillness of the morning, he marveled at the vulnerability she had shared with him the night before, the raw honesty that had forged a connection between them.

As Owen considered the delicate balance of emotions, he couldn't deny the undercurrent of desire that stirred within him. Molly, still sleeping, had unwittingly become an intimate presence in his arms. He shifted slightly, again trying to disentangle himself without waking her. However, as he gently moved her hand, a sudden awareness prickled through him. Molly's touch, innocent as it was, sent a surge of desire coursing through him. Even with her hand out of the way it didn't help.

"Damnit... I made it worse!" he thought to himself. Now, instead of her hand on his bits, they were right next to her face! She shifted in her sleep, a smile on her face. He watched as she absentmindedly moved her head, pushing her face into his zipper area. *"Oh... my..."* He tried to shift his thoughts again, attempting to redirect his focus to more neutral territory.

"Uncle John in his overalls... rusty cars... pimples... Buck..." Nope, still wasn't working! Boy, he was in big trouble here!

Unfortunately, the proximity of her warmth, the scent of her body on his, and the memory of her vulnerability the night before proved an intoxicating combination.

Just as Owen was about to try to move her head some so he could slip the pillow back under it, Molly stirred awake, pushing herself up into a sitting position. Her eyes met his, a soft smile gracing her lips as she greeted him with a sleepy "Good morning."

Owen, doing his best to conceal his erection now that she was no longer laying on it, returned the greeting. Molly, in the midst of stretching and waking up fully, noticed Owen's blushing face and obvious discomfort. Her gaze traveled down to where he was now holding a pillow, and she blushed, realizing the unintended consequence of her sleeping position.

"Oh… I'm so sorry," Molly murmured, her cheeks tinted with embarrassment. "I didn't mean to… you know."

Owen, attempting to alleviate the tension with humor, said, "No problem…

I just hope you prefer a firm pillow to a soft one…"

She looked at him for a second before laughing hysterically. He felt like a total idiot. *"Really, doofus, that's all you could come up with?"* he thought, annoyed with himself. Oh well, at least she was laughing… she was beautiful when she laughed.

Owen started to join her in laughter, but the moment took an unexpected turn as Oliver burst into the room with boundless energy. He bounced onto Owen's lap, oblivious to the subtle nuances in the air.

"Dad, can we have pancakes for breakfast?" Oliver asked, his eyes filled with the innocence of a child.

Owen, seizing the opportunity to shift the focus, suggested, "How about we all make pancakes together? Molly, would you like to join us for breakfast?"

Molly smiled, grateful for the reprieve. "I'd love to."

They moved to the kitchen, the prospect of pancakes providing a light-hearted diversion. Oliver eagerly enlisted Molly's help in building something out of Legos before breakfast. The simple joy of the moment, filled with Oliver's silly conversation and the camaraderie in the kitchen, lifted the residual tension.

As Owen expertly flipped pancakes on the griddle, Molly marveled at the newfound ease settling over them. The fragrant aroma of breakfast filled the air, and for a brief moment, the three of them gathering around the table felt like a family.

As they enjoyed their pancakes together, Molly couldn't help but savor the normalcy of the scene. The laughter, the shared meal, the easy banter—it was a picture of domesticity that she hadn't allowed herself to envision in a long time. Smiling, she deciding to embrace the simplicity of the moment rather than dissect the complexities of her emotions. As they indulged in pancakes and conversation, the morning unfolded in a tapestry of shared laughter.

Oliver, oblivious to the adult dynamics in the room, reveled in the company of his dad and Molly. He even persuaded Molly to build a Lego fortress with him after breakfast, the joyous laughter echoing through the living room.

As Molly played with Legos, she found herself immersed in Oliver's imaginative world, the weight of her past momentarily set aside. After breakfast was cleaned up and the fortress was built, Molly and Owen sat together on the sofa, watching Oliver plow it over with a truck.

Molly's phone rang and she grabbed it from the stand near the sofa. Seeing that it was Jeff's number, she politely excused herself to the other room and answered.

"Hey, Jeff."

"Hey, Mol. How's it going?" he asked.

"I'm good, how about you?" she asked, knowing what he was about to say.

"I'm good. I'm just calling to see if you've made a final decision about the house. I know you told me the other day that you are pretty sure you want to just sell it, but I wanted to be sure before I officially start the process of listing it."

"I appreciate that, Jeff. Yes, I am ready to put it on the market. What do you need from me to move forward?" she asked.

"Honestly, I have all the specs from before you guys moved in there, so all that needs to be done is staging and photos. Do you think you'll have time in the next week or so to pack everything up so I can send cleaners and stagers in the week after next? Is that too soon?" he asked, knowing this was probably a lot for her all at once.

"That's fine… I will head over there today and see what I'm working with and then I can let you know. I'm sure I can find a moving company to load everything up and store it for now, until I find my own place," she replied, feeling overwhelmed suddenly.

"Ok… you just let me know if you need any help, okay?" he said, always willing to lend a hand to a friend.

"Will do, Jeff! Have a great weekend, and say hi to Mia for me, okay?"

"Ok. Bye," he said as he disconnected the call.

After ending the call, Molly walked back into the living room where Oliver and Owen were re-building the fortress on the floor.

"What's wrong?" Owen asked, standing to go to her when he saw the concern on her face.

"Jeff just called, he asked if I would have time in the next week to pack up the stuff in my house so he can put it on the market," she said, a sick feeling starting to rumble in her belly. She was okay with packing her things, but she felt nauseous at the thought of packing up Hannah's precious space, all the tiny clothes and shoes and books…

"Molly," Owen interrupted softly, "are you okay? Do you want me to come with you?"

"Um… Yeah, if you don't mind doing that… Are you sure?" Molly looked up at Owen with so much sadness in her eyes that it made him want to scoop her up and hold her until it was gone.

"Of course I will." Owen, having gone through this with Tara's things only a couple of years ago, knew exactly what was going through Molly's head right now. There was no way he was letting her go through that alone. "I'll just call my mom quick and see if we can drop Oliver off this morning and then we can head over there, okay?"

Molly wasn't sure what to say to him. She was so thankful that he was such a kind man, and she was relieved she wouldn't have to go there alone.

Molly freshened up while Owen called his mother. Then, they headed over there to drop Oliver off to play for a while. After that, they drove off to Molly's old house. Molly was nervous all the way there. She wasn't ready to face what was in Hannah's room, but she had to if she wanted to move on. Hannah was in Heaven now, and she wasn't coming back. As much as she loved her and missed her, she knew that it was not to be. It was time that she faced this head-on.

As Molly and Owen arrived at the house, the memories came flooding back. Molly tried to take a deep breath, to steady herself, as she walked up to the door. She could hear the familiar creak of the door as Owen opened it, and she stepped inside. The house smelled the same way it had when she'd left, only it was so silent in there that she felt like she was trespassing in someone else's home. Hannah's room was just down the hall, and Molly's heart was pounding in her chest as she led Owen to it.

Tears were filling Molly's eyes, threatening to spill over and down her cheeks, but she knew she had to be strong. She opened the door slightly, grabbing tightly to Owen's arm. Inside was Hannah's crib, the little toys they had gotten for her, Molly's rocking chair… it was just the way she'd left it.

Molly could feel the lump in her throat growing as she looked around the room. It was like a snapshot of a life that was never given a chance to begin. She could see the tiny yellow duck that Hannah's grandmother had given her. It was sitting on the dresser, untouched since the day of her baby shower when she had put it in that very spot. The light was dim, as if the room itself was in mourning.

Molly felt as if she was intruding on something sacred, something that should have been left alone. But she knew she had to do this, for her own peace of mind. She took a deep breath and walked over to the crib. It was still made up with a tiny pink blanket, the one that they had bought for Hannah's homecoming.

Molly's hand trembled as she reached out to touch the blanket. It was soft and delicate, like the life that had been taken away so soon. Molly picked the blanket up, sat down on the rocking chair near the crib, and cradled it in her arms, tears streaming down her face. She couldn't hold them back any longer, the grief was too much. She clutched the blanket to her chest, as if it could bring Hannah back. Owen knelt on the ground in front of her, one hand on her knee and the other cupping her face in it. He wished he knew how to help her right now. It killed him to see her so heartbroken.

"I'm right here, Molly. Just let it out," he said softly.

That was all the encouragement she needed. She fell forward into his arms, sitting on his lap and crying. Her body ached; her heart felt like it was leaving her body. She sobbed until there was nothing left, then she pulled herself back together. Owen lifted her as if she was a child, setting her back in the chair. He got up and crossed the room to grab a Kleenex he had seen just outside the bedroom door on a stand in the hallway. He came back to Molly, giving it to her to blow her nose.

"Thank you, Owen," she said, her voice shaking.

"We don't have to do this today, Molly. If you want, we can take a break and come back tomorrow after you are feeling a little better. It's up to you."

"No… I need to do this now, Owen. Would you mind going into the closet out in the hallway and grabbing a couple of empty totes? We keep a stack in there in case we need to put anything in the attic."

"No problem," he said, following her instructions. He came back a minute later with four clear totes, removing their lids and placing them against the wall.

With trembling hands, Molly picked up the first tote and began to put the items inside. There were baby clothes that had never been worn, a rattle that had never been used, and a tiny pair of shoes that would never be filled. She gently folded the clothes, placing them in the tote ever so carefully, as if they'd break if she wasn't gentle enough. Her heart ached, but she knew it was time for her to do this. She couldn't put it off any longer.

As she packed each item, a memory of what could have been came rushing back. She could see Hannah crawling on the floor, playing with the toys. She could hear her laugh, a sound that would now be forever silent. Molly took a deep breath, trying to hold back the sobs that threatened to break free.

Molly turned to the last item in the box, a tiny pink dress with a matching bow. It was the outfit they had chosen for Hannah's Christening. She held the dress to her chest, feeling the soft fabric against her skin. Then, ever so gently, she placed it in the tote, motioning for Owen to cover it and place it on the stack with the others.

The room was silent, except for the sound of Molly's heart breaking. She closed her eyes, trying to imagine a world where Hannah was here, where everything had turned out differently. She stood up and looked around the room one last time. She knew she couldn't stay here any longer, couldn't keep replaying the what ifs in her head. With a final glance at Hannah's crib, Molly turned and walked out.

As she closed the door behind her, she felt as though a weight had been lifted from her shoulders. She knew she had done the right thing… she'd come back on the day the movers came and she'd bring those boxes to her parents' house for safe keeping. For now, though, it was time to move forward, letting the past rest. For the first time in over a year, she felt peace entering her heart again.

Owen put her hand into his and walked her out of the house and to the truck. Stopping to help her in, he placed an emotional kiss on her lips. It was quick and sweet, and filled with a promise of unconditional support and love… something her heart needed more than anything at that moment.

Still… If she needed it so badly, then why did it scare her so much?

* * *

The evening sun dipped below the horizon, casting an amber glow over the city as Molly wearily made her way home from work. The day had been long, and all she craved was a quiet sanctuary within the familiar walls of she and Lily's apartment. However, as she approached the door, she could hear a male voice that was unfamiliar to her.

Opening the door cautiously, Molly was met with the sight of Lily engrossed in conversation with a man she had never seen before. Awkwardness hung in the air, and Molly offered a quick nod before retreating to her room, yearning for solitude.

Inside her room, Molly weighed her options. She didn't want to intrude on Lily's evening, and the thought of feeling like a third wheel in her own home was unappealing. An idea struck her, and she pulled out her phone, typing a message to Owen.

Hey, do you and Oliver want to grab some ice cream? I need to get out for a bit.

Almost instantly, Owen's response came through. *Sure, we'd love that. Meet you in 10?*

As Molly made her way to the agreed-upon meeting spot, the warm May breeze and the prospect of ice cream lifted her spirits. She couldn't shake the awkward encounter at home, but the thought of spending time with Owen and Oliver provided a welcome distraction.

The trio found themselves at a cute little local ice cream parlor, indulging in sweet treats and laughter that transcended the lingering discomfort from earlier. Owen had ordered mint chip, while she had gone with the traditional cookies and cream. Oliver, on the other hand, had cotton candy with sprinkles. They were enjoying their ice cream when Owen's phone rang, disrupting the light-hearted atmosphere.

"Huh… I wonder why Grandma is calling at this hour," he said, shrugging as he answered the call.

"Hey mom," he said, smiling as he tried to steal a scoop of Oliver's ice cream.

Within seconds, though, his expression shifted as he listened to the voice on the other end.

"Owen, sweetie, it's your father. He's had a heart attack. He is at St. Anna's over on the opposite side of the city… you know the one I'm talking about?" she asked.

"Um… yes, I know. I'm not sure I'm the best person to come down there though, mom," he said, his voice thick.

"Honey, you need to come over here now please. It's important that you be here. Message that nice neighbor of yours and see if she can take Oliver for you. I'll meet you at the hospital. Okay?"

"Okay, mom. I'll be there as soon as I can."

The weight of the situation hung in the air as Owen quietly shared the news with Molly, careful to make sure Oliver didn't hear him. The conflicting emotions, the unresolved history between father and son, now underscored by the fragility of life, left Owen grappling with a myriad of feelings.

Owen messaged his neighbor, and she agreed to take care of Oliver for the night. Turning to Molly, Owen hesitated before asking, "Molly, would you mind coming with me to the hospital?"

Without hesitation, Molly agreed, recognizing the gravity of the situation. They tossed what was left of their ice cream and loaded Oliver up in the truck, bringing him swiftly back to Owen's place. They grabbed a few things for him and dropped him off at the neighbor's house. Then, they headed across town to the hospital.

When they arrived at St. Anna's Hospital, Owen's mother greeted them, her eyes reflecting a mix of worry and relief. She explained that his father would need bypass surgery the following day and emphasized the importance of Owen being there.

Owen accompanied his mother, Cheryl, and stepfather, Joe, down the hall to the Critical Care Unit to see his father, leaving Molly to wait in the hallway. The nurse, a sympathetic presence, approached Owen, providing details about the upcoming surgery and the subsequent need for care and recovery. His father would have to go to a nursing facility after his surgery for a while. He needed help with his daily tasks until he could get back on his own two feet again.

Returning to the hallway, Owen's conflicted expression spoke volumes. Molly could sense the emotional turmoil, the regret that lingered from their recent argument still fresh. Owen steeled himself, determined to face his father.

As they entered the room, a palpable tension hung in the air. Owen's father, a grizzled man with a stubborn demeanor, was curt and dismissive. "Took you long enough," he grumbled, eyeing Owen with a mixture of annoyance and vulnerability.

Then, his eyes fell on Molly, standing quietly in the doorway. Something shifted within him as he invited her into the room. Molly approached, a kind smile on her lips. She introduced herself and offered words of comfort, a warmth that softened the edges of the strained father-son dynamic.

As Molly spoke with Owen's father, a realization dawned on him. He saw the way Owen looked at her, the tenderness in his gaze, and a spark of understanding ignited. It didn't take a genius to see that his son had finally fallen in love again. It was about damn time! Now, he just needed him to take over the farm, especially after all of this mess. He wasn't sure how long it would be before he could do chores again… wasn't sure what he'd do.

Owen, observing the interaction, felt a swirl of emotions. Molly's presence seemed to diffuse the tension, offering a bridge between past grievances and the possibility of healing. How in the world did she do that? How did she get his crotchety old man of a dad to act… nice!? She must be a magician or something!

After a brief conversation, Owen announced his need for rest, promising to return the following day. As they left the hospital room, Owen thanked Molly for being there, a gratitude that resonated in his eyes.

In the quiet hallway, Molly turned to Owen, her eyes reflecting a depth of understanding. "I know I don't know everything about your sordid past with your father, but I do know one thing's for sure… Life's too short, Owen. We've both learned that lesson the hard way. Forgiveness might be the key to unlocking the connection you need with your father, and you know very well that *you're* going to have to be the one that takes the first step."

Owen pondered her words, the weight of their truth settling on his shoulders. Maybe Molly was right. Perhaps it was time to let go of the lingering resentment, to mend the fractures that time had created. There had to be a way to help his dad to understand his side… to know how much he loved teaching. It wasn't just a job to him… it was his way of making a different in the lives of as many kids as he could in his lifetime. It was his passion, just like farming was for his father.

With Lily's apartment occupied and the night unfolding with unexpected turns, Molly decided to crash on Owen's couch. Owen, appreciating Molly's supportive presence, assured her that it was okay to let Oliver stay at the neighbor's house until morning.

"How about we watch a movie?" Owen asked her after grabbing a pillow and a throw for her to cover up with.

"As long as you don't care if I start snoring in the middle of it," she answered, smiling.

"Absolutely not… snore away!" he said, laughing.

Owen turned the television on and found an old movie that was on. He sat down and pulled Molly into his arms to snuggle in. She melted in, fitting as though she was made for his arms. He loved the way she felt against his body, and he found his body was reacting to her closeness. He hoped she wouldn't notice.

As the movie played on, Owen found himself struggling to concentrate. He wanted to kiss her, but he was afraid she wasn't ready for that. He knew her mind was in overdrive, and he didn't want to risk her making a decision that she'd regret later. He cared about her way too much for that.

Molly shifted, raising her head some so that she was looking at him. Her eyes looked sleepy, but there was something else in their gaze…. Something that looked like… need maybe? Was he just imagining that because he wanted so badly to see it?

Owen smiled, a smirk that held multiple meanings. He would give anything to know what was in that beautiful mind of hers right now.

"Do you not like this movie?" he asked her, curious why she was looking at him instead of the screen.

"Yeah, it's fine. I was just thinking, I guess."

"Oh boy… is that a good kind of thinking, or a bad kind of thinking?" he asked her, teasing.

She smiled. "It's this kind," she said as she shifted again, only this time so she could get close enough to take his face in her hand and kiss him. The kiss was sweet at first, an exploration of tastes. Quickly, though, it turned to something more. Owen opened his mouth slightly to allow her to enter, and it was all the invitation she needed. Their mouths began an erotic dance of curiosity… neither able to tell where their mouth ended, and the others began.

"Molly…" Owen mumbled, pulling away slightly. "Are you sure? I know you…"

"Owen," she interrupted, "I'm sure."

Owen was fighting the battle of his life between the need to have Molly in the most intimate way possible and the need to protect her and keep things from going any further than she was ready for. He was falling in love with her, and it scared him to death. He wanted to make love to her more than anything, but he knew tonight wasn't the time. He wanted their first time together to be special and perfect. He told himself as they kissed that he would stop things before it got that far. For now, though, he had the most beautiful women in the world in his arms, and he was damn sure going to enjoy it!

Owen pulled away for a moment, only to look her deep in the eyes, move his hands onto her face to cup her cheeks, and bring her mouth to his, slowly and sensually. He kissed her deeply, as though his life depended upon her taste. Their tongues touched and licked and explored. He ran his tongue along hers, making her shake with excitement. When he pulled away this time, it was only to move down her chin, kissing his way over her neck, stopping to nuzzle at the tender area just below.

Owen's breath was hot and wet, and she could hardly handle the feelings it was igniting in her belly. What was it about Owen that made her feel so good and so safe? She wasn't sure what it was, but she was surely *not* going to worry about it now. Instead, she let her head fall back, allowing him access to her neck and chest.

Owen put his hands around her waist, slowly lifting her shirt from her body. She allowed it to go over her head, exposing her entire upper body. He looked at her again, taking her in. She shivered with anticipation, loving the way he was gazing at her. He had passion in his eyes, and she felt completely undone by them. Desire filled her in return as she reached over and pulled his shirt over his head. She ran her hands down his muscular chest, her nails making a gentle trail behind them. She shivered again.

Molly leaned forward, following the trail with her mouth, placing kisses and nibbles along the path. Owen groaned lightly, causing a reaction in her midsection. She stopped at his right nipple, looking up at him for a moment before taking it in her mouth. He gasped, the moan becoming louder. She had never felt so much power. Before she could think, he pulled her mouth from his nipple and put it on his own.

Reaching around her body, he unhooked her bra, allowing her breasts to hang as the bra fell away from her body. He pulled the straps down, throwing it onto the floor, and then he pulled away to gaze at her bare breasts. This time, it was her turn to moan. Good God… he hadn't even touched her yet and she was almost there! What was it about him looking at her body with such need in his eyes that was driving her so wild?

Owen pulled her onto his lap, her legs on either side of his, her middle snug against his throbbing erection. Her breasts were almost even with his face now, allowing him perfect and easy access. He leaned forward, taking a nipple into his mouth, and her head fell back, pure ecstasy filling her entire body. She shuddered, pleasure coursing through her, as he nibbled and suckled at her breasts. He ran his tongue over them both, making her feel like she was going to explode.

"Owen," she said in a husky voice. "I want you so badly…"

"I want you, too, Molly. Can you feel how much I want you back?" he answered.

She could feel his erection between her legs, causing a need she had no idea she'd had until now. She shook her head, wanting to see him and touch him and everything that came next. Her brain kept telling her she needed to slow down, but her body was screaming at her to continue.

Owen knew things were going to get out of hand if he didn't find a way to put the brakes on, and fast. As much as he wanted her, he also knew she was emotional right now from everything she was going through with her divorce and cleaning out Hannah's room. He didn't want her to regret anything in the morning… what kind of man would he be if he took advantage of her vulnerability? Nope… he wasn't going to be that man! The problem was that she felt so good in his arms!

"Molly, I want you, and I intend to have you when you are ready, but right now I think we better slow this down a bit," he said, his low voice heavy with need.

Molly lifted her eyes to his, conveying her agreement with a nod. Then, she kissed him, deep and filled with meaning. Pulling away, she grinned mischievously as she said, "That doesn't mean we can't have a little fun though, right?"

That look in her eyes… how could he possibly say no to that? He slowly laid her on the couch on her back so he could have better access to her body. He wasn't about to leave her like this… leaning over her, he kissed her again on the mouth, his hand touching her breasts, cupping and pinching at the nipples. She was going wild, and he loved that he was making her feel so good.

Slowly, he moved his hand down her body, causing her to shiver with excitement. Reaching the elastic of her leggings, he slid beneath, moving his fingers closer to her hot center. As he reached his destination, her body moved into his, her moans becoming louder. He smiled at her, looking into her eyes, as his fingers touched the tiny rosebud in the center of her body. She closed her eyes, not sure she could hold on much longer, but wanting it to last forever. He rubbed the sensitive spot, driving her wild.

Molly's body finally gave in to the throws of love as precious release took over, causing every nerve ending in her body to scream out in joy. As she calmed and her breathing slowed again, he smiled at her, loving the happiness on her face. He moved his hand away, putting it on her back as he pulled her into him so they could lay together on the sofa, her breasts still exposed. He placed a gentle kiss on her lips before she lay her face on his chest. Molly, obviously exhausted from the experience, quickly fell asleep.

As he watched her sleep, Owen couldn't imagine any place he'd rather be at this very moment, or any person he'd rather be holding. A quiet revelation snuck up on him, crashing into him like a meteor… he was falling in love with her. The realization both thrilled him and terrified him all at once. He hadn't felt this way since Tara, and he honestly hadn't thought he ever would again. Smiling, Owen closed his eyes and joined her in the depths of slumber.

Fourteen

Chapter 13

The morning sun painted the room in soft hues of spring warmth as Molly and Owen lay entwined in each other's arms, the afterglow of their first sexual encounter lingering in the air.

The intimacy they'd shared with one another had bonded them together, creating a newfound closeness that felt both comforting and exhilarating.

As they snuggled beneath the cozy blanket, Molly's thoughts meandered towards the practicalities of her life. With her house on the market and Lily's apartment potentially becoming available, she felt the need to carve out a space of her own. The realization struck her, giving her a clearer sense of direction. She knew it was time for her to move forward, and she couldn't do that under Lily's foot all the time. Knowing what she needed to do next and wanting to share that with Owen, she turned her body some so she could talk to him. She knew he'd understand, and she'd need his help with her next steps.

"Owen," she began, her voice a gentle murmur against the morning quiet, "I'm thinking of asking Jeff to help me find a condo in the city, near my shoppe. I want to have my own place now that the house is on the market, and I want to give Lily her apartment back. I'm kind of hoping that my house will sell fast so I can use some of the money from the equity in the house to pay for the apartment and some of the things I'll need. Do you think that will work, or should I wait until the house sells?"

Owen's response was a warm smile, an understanding acknowledgment of Molly's desire for independence, especially after everything she'd been through lately. "That sounds like a great idea, Molly. Having your own space is important. I'm sure Jeff can definitely help you find something perfect."

"I don't need anything fancy… just something that will help me get a fresh start," she said, smiling. She felt refreshed, like even more weight had been lifted from her shoulders. She was making so many big decisions lately… decisions that were for *her*… not Waylon, or her shoppe, or her friends. Just *her*, and it felt good.

"Sounds good to me! You know what else sounds good to me?" he asked with a smirk.

"No, what?"

"Coffee!" he said, laughing.

"I completely agree!" she said, reciprocating his excitement for the hot morning mood-lifter. She rarely did anything before her coffee was sitting in her stomach.

They disentangled themselves from the blanket, the prospect of coffee luring them towards the kitchen. Molly put the shirt she'd been wearing the night before back on, and Owen threw his shirt back on as well. Then, he headed to the kitchen to make a pot of coffee while Molly headed to the bathroom to freshen up.

By the time she came out from the bathroom, Owen was filling two cups with the steaming hot liquid. He carried them into the living room, meeting her at the sofa. As they settled into the soft cushions, a steaming cup of coffee in hand, the atmosphere was light, filled with shared laughter and easy companionship.

Owen, as he sipped his coffee, found his thoughts drifting towards Molly in a way that surpassed the realms of friendship. The depth of his feelings took him by surprise, and he mulled over the implications. He hadn't felt this away about any woman other than his late wife, Tara, and he was struggling with so many feelings inside his heart that it was hard to sort them out. He felt excited about the new possibility of a life with Molly, but, at the same time, he felt scared about the possibility of losing her like he had with Tara.

As Molly enjoyed the warmth of the coffee, Owen's gaze settled on her, and a realization dawned—their connection was evolving into something deeper. He considered the possibilities, and a spontaneous idea took root in his mind.

"I'm not sure what's going on in that handsome head of yours," Molly said, grinning at him, "but it must be pretty big because I'm pretty sure I see actual smoke coming out your left ear…" Owen hadn't realized that she'd been staring at him.

"Sorry about that… I was just thinking about what you said before about moving," he began, his voice a tender undertone, "It gave me an idea…"

"Oh yeah? And what idea would that be?" Molly asked, teasing him.

"Well… What if you considered moving in here, with me and Oliver instead? I know he adores you, and I think that after last night there's probably no question in your mind about how much I like you too!" he teased.

Molly's heart skipped a beat at the unexpected proposition. The notion of taking their connection to such a level felt both exhilarating and overwhelming. She grappled with conflicting emotions, her mind racing with thoughts of the impending divorce and the desire to tread cautiously.

"Owen," she hesitated, her eyes reflecting a mix of emotions, "I appreciate the offer, I really do. But I need some time to think about it. My divorce isn't final until next week, and I want to make sure we're both ready for something that serious."

Owen nodded, his understanding evident. "Take all the time you need, Molly. I just want what's best for all of us."

They finished their coffee, the atmosphere shifting to a more contemplative one. The weight of Owen's suggestion lingered in the air as they discussed inconsequential matters—school pranks, childhood memories, and the mundane details of their lives.

Owen prepared a simple breakfast of eggs and toast, attempting to infuse a sense of normalcy into the morning. However, Molly found herself struggling to concentrate, her mind tethered to the complex web of emotions winding themselves around her heart.

After breakfast, Molly decided she needed some space to gather her thoughts. She asked Owen to take her back to the apartment, and as they arrived, a sense of unease settled between them. She gave him a quick kiss, a gesture tainted with an underlying tension, and slipped back inside before they could delve into the unspoken complexities.

Alone in her room, Molly laid down, her thoughts swirling in a tumultuous sea. The weight of recent events pressed upon her, and she grappled with the consequences of her choices. The intimacy with Owen, the impending divorce, and the offer to move in—all these factors converged, creating a storm of confusion.

She couldn't shake the nagging feeling of guilt that clung to her. Four more days until her divorce was final, and here she was, entangled in a web of emotions with a man she was undeniably falling for. What kind of woman was she, anyway? She knew her marriage to Waylon had been over for a while, but she wasn't a cheater! She couldn't wait until Wednesday, until the divorce became final, and she could put that part of her life behind her. Until then, though, she didn't feel right making any major decisions.

As she lay there, the fear of making a mistake gnawed at her, and she questioned the wisdom of allowing herself to be vulnerable amid so much uncertainty. Molly found herself caught in a spiral of conflicting emotions. She couldn't escape the sense of guilt that accompanied her every thought. The closeness with Owen felt right, yet the timing felt undeniably wrong.

* * *

The sterile scent of the hospital greeted Owen as he stepped off the elevator onto the cardiac wing. His heart thrummed in his chest, matching the rhythm of the monitors that beeped in the background. He clenched and unclenched his fists, his emotions churning like a tempest inside him. A long night of tossing and turning had definitely not helped with his current mood.

It had been too long since he last visited his father at the farm, and he knew that. He'd let his emotions get the best of him, and because of that, their relationship was strained, to say the least, fractured by years of disagreements and stubbornness. He had known his father had wanted him to take over the family farm since he was a little boy, to carry on the legacy that had been passed down from generation to generation. Still, Owen had always had *other* dreams, ones that didn't involve the endless toil of tending to the crops and livestock.

As he made his way down the corridor lined with identical doors, Owen couldn't shake the guilt that gnawed at him. His mother had pleaded with them both to set aside their differences, to find common ground, but they had remained obstinate, locked in a stalemate of pride and resentment.

Pushing open the door to his father's room, Owen found him lying in the hospital bed, looking smaller and frailer than he remembered him looking the night before. Tubes and wires snaked from his body, tethering him to machines that monitored his every heartbeat. Despite their rocky relationship, Owen couldn't deny the pang of sorrow that gripped his heart at the sight of his father in such a vulnerable state.

Chuck West's eyes flickered open as his son entered the room, and a flicker of surprise crossed his face before it hardened into a mask of stoicism. "Well, it's about time," he greeted gruffly, his voice raspy with fatigue.

"Dad, nice to see you too," Owen replied, his own voice tight with emotion. He approached the bed, unsure of what to say or how to break the ice that had formed between them.

Chuck gestured for Owen to take a seat in the chair beside the bed, and Owen complied, sinking down into the worn upholstery. For a long moment, they sat in silence, the tension between them palpable.

"Where's that pretty girl you had yesterday?" Chuck finally asked.

"She had some orders to deliver from her cupcake shop today," Owen replied.

"Huh. A business lady, huh?"

"Yep."

"She looked like she had good sense in that pretty head of hers. Maybe she can share some of that with you," Chuck mumbled with a grunt as he motioned towards his son.

Owen ignored him. His father was crotchety and old, and he was tired of arguing with him. It never got him anywhere anyway. He sat up a little in his seat, looking at his dad. There was something in his eyes, something he'd never seen before. If he was right, he could swear it was fear. His dad had never shown fear in all his 64 years of life… he was too damned stubborn to be afraid! Still, Owen could swear he saw the hint of it now, and it softened his demeanor some.

Finally, Owen cleared his throat, summoning the courage to speak. "Look, I know we haven't seen eye to eye lately… or ever, really," he began hesitantly.

"And I suppose you blame me for that, don't you?" Chuck blurted back at him.

Owen swallowed hard. His dad was definitely not making this any easier for him. Still… he wasn't going to fight with him.

"But…" Owen continued, "I want you to know that I respect you, and everything you've done for me since I was little."

There is was. He'd gotten through it. *"I wonder what the old man has to say about that one,"* he thought.

Chuck's brow furrowed in confusion, his features softening slightly at Owen's words. "What's your angle here, anyway?" he asked, not quite sure what to think about Owen's change in demeanor.

"No angle. I'm just trying to tell you I'm done fighting with you. Life's already short enough… I'm tired of spending it arguing with you."

Chuck chewed on that for a bit, obviously not sure what to think of all of this. After what felt like an eternity, he sighed a sigh that it seemed he'd been holding onto for years.

"I've always wanted what's best for you, son," he admitted gruffly. "I just can't figure out, for the life of me, why you wouldn't want to carry on the family legacy and take over the farm, Owen."

Owen shook his head, a sad smile tugging at the corners of his lips. "I know you don't understand, Dad, but I'd really like to try to help you if you'll *actually listen* to me for once."

Chuck looked at his son, realizing that he had no fight left in his weak body.

Instead, he nodded at him, gesturing for him to continue and to attempt to plead his case.

"I really do appreciate everything you've done for me… for us. But… farming is *your* love… teaching and coaching are *mine*. It's where I belong, just the same way that farming has always been for you."

There was a flicker of understanding in Chuck's eyes as he listened to Owen's words. A long night of thinking about life and the decisions he'd made over the years had given him a little more clarity about this whole situation with the two of them.

"I suppose I can't fault you for following your heart," he conceded reluctantly. "Even if I think it's the wrong decision, and even if it means breaking with a longstanding West family tradition."

Relief, mixed with a little confusion, flooded through Owen at his father's admission, the weight of years of expectation and disappointment beginning to lift from his shoulders.

"Thank you, Dad," he murmured gratefully. "I just want you to understand… to accept me for who I am."

Owen realized that this was the best he was going to get from his father at this point. Truth be told, it was more than he had ever thought would be possible, so he considered that a victory in their fight against the constant arguing and discontent.

Surprising Owen even further, Chuck reached out a trembling hand, clasping Owen's in a gesture of reconciliation. "I may not always agree with your choices, son," he admitted gruffly. "But I'll always be proud of you. And I'll always love you."

Tears pricked at the corners of Owen's eyes as he squeezed his father's hand, his heart overflowing with years of unshared emotion. "I love you too, Dad," he whispered hoarsely.

For a few moments, the two men sat together, tears being shed in unison. There wasn't much else either one could say. Owen decided an apology was in order. Even though his father had been to blame for most of their arguing, he realized now that he, too, had taken part in the process, and that he could have ended this ridiculous feud a long time ago if he had just tried harder.

"I'm sorry for all the years we've wasted allowing fighting and stubbornness to get in the way of spending time together."

Chuck nodded, his gaze softening with regret. "Me too, son. Me too."

As they sat together in the quiet of the hospital room, the air heavy with newly spoken apologies and unshed tears, Owen felt a sense of peace settle over him. For the first time in years, he allowed himself to hope that maybe, just maybe, they could find a way to mend their fractured relationship. He had missed his dad.

Their moment of reconciliation was interrupted by the arrival of a nurse, bustling into the room to prepare his father for surgery. He was going to have a double bypass surgery on his heart, so they needed to get him ready and into the pre-op area. Owen watched in silence as they wheeled his father out of the room, a knot of anxiety tightening in his chest.

Before they disappeared from view, Owen called out, his voice thick with emotion. "I'll be here waiting for you when you get back, Dad," he said. "I love you."

Chuck turned to look at him, a rugged smile tugging at the corners of his lips. "I love you too, son," he replied quietly, his voice barely above a whisper. Then, he turned his attention to the nurses pushing him out the doorway.

"Okay, ladies… let's get this here ticker a-tickin' again!" he told her, giving his best flirty grin to the closest nurse. She laughed and continued down the hall with him.

As the door swung shut behind them, Owen sank back into the chair, his thoughts swirling with memories of the past and hopes for the future. For the first time in years, he allowed himself to believe that maybe, just maybe, there was still a chance for them to reconcile, to rebuild what had been broken. Now, his dad just needed to pull through this heart scare so they could at least see where it could go from here.

As he sat there, alone in the quiet of the hospital room, Owen made a silent vow to himself. He would forgive his father, right here and right now. It was time to let go of the past and embrace the future with an open heart. Life was way too short for grudges and regrets, and he refused to let their stubbornness stand in the way of any more time they had together.

∗ ∗ ∗

Molly stood behind The Sweet Sprinkle's granite-topped island, her hands moving deftly as she piped pink swirls of frosting onto a tray of freshly baked cupcakes. The bright spring sun streamed in through the windows, casting streaks of natural light over the shop, the still air filled with the sweet scent of vanilla, almond and sugar. There was music playing softly over the speakers throughout the shoppe, the playlist of choice today coming from Molly's favorite Pandora station.

While Molly piped the tops of 5 dozen cupcakes, Mia bustled around the kitchen, her brow furrowed with concentration as she worked on rolling out a batch of fondant for a cake that she was preparing for a 50th birthday party the following day.

"I still can't believe you're selling the house, Mol," she said, her voice a mixture of reminiscence and frustration. "It just seems so final."

Molly sighed heavily, her exhaustion growing by the minute with this recurring line of conversation with Mia.

"I know," she admitted softly. "But it's time, Mia. I need to move on with my life, and that means letting go of the past. The house has too many memories within its walls, and too much sadness for me. I wish you could try to understand that."

Mia frowned, her hands pausing in their work as she turned to face Molly. "I get that you don't want to keep reliving some of those memories, Mol, but what if you change your mind down the road somewhere?" she protested. "What if you want to move back into the house someday?"

Molly shook her head stubbornly, her mind made up. "I won't," she insisted firmly.

"I'm telling you, Mol… if you sell that house, you'll regret it one day!"

"I've made my decision, Mia. I need to let go of the past and start fresh, and I need you to respect my decision to do that."

Before Mia could respond, the bell above the door chimed, and Jeff walked into the shop, a coffee in one hand and a for sale sign in the other.

"Hey, ladies," he greeted cheerfully, his voice filled with warmth. As soon as he saw the looks on both of their faces, his smile faded. "What's going on in *here?*"

Mia shot Molly a pointed look, her frustration evident in her expression. "Molly refuses to listen to me about not selling the house," she announced, her voice tinged with annoyance. "I think she's making a *big* mistake."

Jeff frowned, his brow furrowing with concern. "Hey, now," he said gently, stepping between the two women. "Let's not fight about this, okay?"

"Don't get in the middle of this, Jeff! It's not your fight. All I'm asking is that Molly listen to me on this. She's obviously not thinking clearly!"

"I'm done arguing with you about this, Mia. This is my decision, not yours! If it's a mistake, then it's my mistake!"

"Okay, okay…" Jeff interrupted, moving to stand closer to his wife. Giving her a smile, he calmy said, "Honey, let's give Molly some space to figure her own life out, okay? We talked about this before… you can have your opinion, but it's her decision. Your job is to support her, not argue with her. You two are way too close to let this get in the middle of your friendship, right?"

Mia rolled her eyes at her husband, clearly annoyed that he had a point. "Fine."

Jeff knew that was the best he was going to get at this point, so he turned his attention to Molly. "Molly, would you be able to run over to the house sometime before Saturday to grab the last of your things? I've got it all staged for an open house starting at 10am on Saturday. I'd be happy to come help you if you need me to, just let me know."

Molly nodded, her heart sinking at the reminder of the task ahead. "Thanks, Jeff," she murmured, forcing a smile despite the unease that gnawed at her insides. "I'll make sure to swing by on Thursday sometime. I'm off that entire morning for therapy and running errands, so I should be able to get it done fairly quickly. I only have a few boxes left, so I should be able to grab them myself."

Jeff shot her a reassuring smile before turning to leave, first giving his wife a kiss, then walking towards the door. His footsteps echoed against the tiled floor as he made his way to the entrance.

"I'll see you ladies later… try to get along while I'm gone, please," he called out over his shoulder, an uncomfortable laugh escaping his mouth. "I've got to get some flyers printed for a showing I have in town tomorrow."

Mia and Molly said their goodbyes, watching him leave in the same confident fashion he had entered in. Jeff was forever the businessman, always airing a sense of confidence and professionalism.

Once he was gone, Mia turned to face Molly, her expression a mixture of defeat and damaged pride. "I'm sorry, Molly," she said softly, her voice tinged with regret. "I didn't mean to come down on you like that. I just… I don't know. This whole divorce thing with you and Waylon, it just feels like it all happened so fast."

Molly sighed heavily, her heart aching at the reminder of the ending of her marriage to Waylon. "I know, Mia," she murmured softly. "But I didn't have a choice. I had to do what was best for me… for *us*."

Mia nodded, her eyes brimming with forced understanding. "I know," she whispered, reaching out to grasp Molly's hand in hers. "I'm sorry, Molly. I just want what's best for you, you know?"

Molly squeezed her hand reassuringly, a small smile playing at the corners of her lips. "I know, Mia," she said softly. "And I appreciate it. But I need you to trust me on this."

With a sense of resolution, the two women returned to their work, their conversation turning to lighter topics as they focused on the task at hand. They laughed and joked together as they worked on decorating the fairy cupcakes before turning their attention to the birthday cake.

As they put the finishing touches on the cake, Mia glanced up at Molly, her eyes twinkling with mischief. "Can you believe we're making a cake that looks like a freaking toilet?" she asked with a grin. "I never thought I'd see the day."

Molly laughed, her heart light with the warmth of their friendship. "I know," she agreed, her voice filled with amusement. "It's definitely not our usual style!"

The two women laughed, imagining the poor woman whose birthday it was about to be surprised by not only a party but also a cake shaped like a toilet!

On the top, they piped the message her family asked for: *Happy Birthday, Britt ... now you're old as shit!*

At 4:00, Molly headed out from the shop, needing to run home and shower so she could get ready for a meeting with her lawyer to make the last preparations for court the following day. She was dreading the whole thing, and she hadn't planned on the argument between her and Mia that morning to make the day even harder. She said goodbye to Mia, thanking her in advance or closing the shop so she didn't have to come back after her meeting.

On the way home, her mind continued to race. She knew she was doing the right thing, but it still hurt… she felt the despair deep inside her heart. Her marriage was about to be over… permanently. She had never planned to be a woman walking into a divorce. She was raised to believe that marriage was forever, and she didn't believe in divorce.

Still, she now found herself in a very different position, and it was hard to stomach. She loved Waylon and probably always would, but maybe sometimes love just wasn't enough… she knew from experience that love could only heal two broken hearts if *both* people were willing and able to share that love.

Unfortunately, Waylon had decided to bury everything in alcohol instead of walking the journey with her. If only things had been different… if only…

Fifteen

Chapter 14

The soft glow of dawn filtered through the curtains as Owen roused Oliver from his slumber. With a gentle shake and a tender smile, he coaxed the little boy awake, his heart swelling with love at the sight of his tousled hair and sleepy eyes.

"Time to rise and shine, buddy," Owen murmured, his voice warm with affection as he pulled back the covers and helped Oliver sit up in bed.

Oliver yawned and stretched, rubbing his eyes as he blinked away the remnants of sleep. "Morning, Dad," he mumbled, his voice still thick with drowsiness.

"Good morning, champ," Owen replied, pressing a kiss to his son's forehead before picking him up so he could sit on his lap. This was Owen's favorite time with his boy… Oliver was always cuddly in the mornings, and he loved everything about having his son in his arms. After a bear hug, he sat him down on the floor and began their morning routine. Owen was a man of simplicity and structure. He had a routine down, and he knew the importance of sticking to it so they could get out the door on time each day. As a single father, he knew it was much easier to be disciplined than it was to be chaotic.

Together, they navigated the familiar rituals of breakfast and getting ready for the hours ahead, their laughter and chatter filling the cozy kitchen with the promise of a good day.

As they sat at the table, munching on toast and cereal, Owen couldn't help but feel a twinge of anxiety gnawing at his insides. Thoughts of Molly lingered at the forefront of his mind, casting a shadow over the morning's festivities.

"Dad," Oliver chimed in, breaking the comfortable silence that had settled between them. "When is Molly coming over to play again?"

Owen's heart did a little "happy dance" at the mention of Molly's name, a rush of conflicting emotions flooding through him. How could he explain to his son the tangled web of feelings that had ensnared his heart?

"I'm sure she'll stop by again soon, buddy," Owen replied, his voice tinged with uncertainty. "We'll have to see what her schedule looks like."

Oliver nodded, seemingly satisfied with the answer. "I love Molly. She's so nice," he added before returning his attention to his breakfast.

Owen, on the other hand, couldn't shake the uneasy feeling that lingered in the pit of his stomach, a nagging sense of doubt that whispered of impending heartache.

"Is anything exciting going on at school today?" he asked Oliver as he finished up his toast.

"Nope! Just coloring and recess!" the little boy answered matter-of-factly.

Owen laughed. "Well, if that's all you do every day at that school, then I think I'd better have a chat with the teacher and tell her you need some more learning time and a little less playing time!" he said, making Oliver give him a shocked look.

"Sorry, Dad, but you can't call her. She told us yesterday that she is sick to death of her *instant graham* making her phone ding all the time so she's going to get rid of it!" he said, causing Owen to erupt in laughter.

"Is that so?" he asked.

"Yep! She doesn't like that instant graham stuff. She told us that it hurts her IQ... whatever that is," he explained.

"I think you mean Instagram, Oliver, and I'm guessing she's partly right!" he said, laughing harder now. Oliver always had a way of making him feel better.

"Okay, pal. Time to brush our teeth and head for school!"

"*Ahh...*" Oliver complained, enjoying his time with his dad.

They put their dishes into the dishwasher and then finished getting ready to head out the door to school. While Oliver was getting his jacket on, he decided to message Molly quick and see if they could go for supper tonight so they could talk about everything that had happened the other night, as well as what the future held for them.

Good morning! I hope you slept well. I was wondering if you would like to have supper with me tonight... I miss you. I know you have a big day today with court and all, so I wanted to tell you good luck and that I will be thinking about you. I hope to see you later.

He put the phone in his pocket and put his shoes on. As much as he longed to explore the possibility of a future with Molly, Owen couldn't shake the fear that gripped him, the fear of losing her like he had lost Tara. The thought of subjecting Oliver to another loss, another wave of heartache, filled him with a bone-deep dread that threatened to consume him whole.

As they drove the short distance to drop Oliver off, Owen's thoughts turned once more to Molly and the delicate dance they were engaged in. Ever since Tara's passing two years ago, Owen had struggled to navigate the treacherous waters of grief and loneliness, seeking solace in the familiar routines of fatherhood and work. Before now, he hadn't even considered dating or moving on with another woman.

But Molly had become a beacon of light in the darkness, a friend and confidante who had helped him find his way back to happiness and hope. And in recent days, Owen had come to realize that his feelings for her ran deeper than mere friendship, blossoming into something more profound and enduring. The other night had been a big deal for him, and he guessed it had been for her as well.

As they arrived at Oliver's school and climbed out of the truck, Owen's mind whirled with thoughts of Molly and the unanswered questions that lingered between them. He stole glances at his phone, hoping for a message from her, a sign that she was thinking of him too. But the screen remained stubbornly blank, devoid of any messages or missed calls.

"I guess I really messed this one up," he mumbled to himself. With every hour that went by without a response, he felt his chances of moving on with Molly slipping away…

* * *

Molly's heart hammered in her chest as she stepped out of her car at the courthouse, her nerves frayed, and her stomach tied in knots. The weight of the impending divorce hung heavy in the air, a tangible reminder of the life she was leaving behind today.

She glanced around the parking lot, her eyes scanning the crowd for any sign of Waylon. She hadn't seen him in weeks, not since that day in the park with Owen and Oliver. Not seeing him anywhere, she made her way toward the doors. As she got closer, she spotted him lurking in the shadows of the lot closest to the building, dark bags under his eyes and a frown on his face. She felt a shiver of apprehension run down her spine as she hurried past, her steps quickening with each passing moment. The last thing she needed right now was to have to talk to Waylon.

"Molly, wait!" Waylon's voice cut through the air like a knife, halting her in her tracks. She turned to face him, her heart pounding in her chest as she braced herself for what was to come.

"What do you want, Waylon?" she asked, her voice tinged with bitterness. "I really don't think now's the best time to talk. We are cutting it close on time already."

Waylon took a step closer, his fists clenched at his sides as he struggled to find the right words. "I just… I can't believe you're doing this, Molly," he said, his voice cracking with emotion. "Throwing away everything we had because… just because of a disagreement on kids!"

Molly felt a surge of anger rise within her at his words, her hands clenching her purse tightly. "It's not just about that, Waylon, and you know it!" she snapped, her voice trembling with pent-up frustration. "It's about your drinking and your refusal to get help… it's about everything."

Waylon's face darkened with rage at her words, his eyes blazing with fury. "And what about that teacher guy I saw you with at the park?" he demanded, his voice rising to a fever pitch. "Are you cheating on me, Molly? Is that what this is about?"

Molly's heart lurched in her chest at the accusation, her mind reeling with disbelief. "How dare you accuse me of that, Waylon?" she spat, her voice thick with anger. "I would never cheat on you. But maybe if you had been paying attention, you would have noticed that you were hurting me repeatedly with your distance and your inability to ask for help in dealing with Hannah's death! I needed you *so badly*, Waylon, and you weren't there!"

With a final, scathing glare, Molly turned on her heel and stormed into the courthouse, her emotions in turmoil as she struggled to regain her composure. She felt a pang of guilt at the harshness of her words, but she knew that she couldn't continue living in a loveless marriage, trapped in a cycle of pain and regret.

Inside the courtroom, Molly took her seat beside her lawyer, her hands trembling with nerves as she waited for the proceedings to begin. Waylon entered soon after, his face flushed with anger as he glared daggers at her from across the room.

The court commissioner took his seat at the front of the room, his gaze sweeping over the assembled parties with a sense of weary resignation. "Mr. and Mrs. Walker, have you both had a chance to review the filed financial statements and the marital settlement agreements?" he asked, his voice tinged with impatience.

Waylon shifted uncomfortably in his seat, his eyes darting nervously around the room. "This wasn't my idea," he muttered under his breath.

His lawyer turned to him, quietly urging him to simply answer yes or no.

Instead, he rudely added, "I don't want a divorce. I want to stay married… she's the one who is wrecking everything we built!"

The court commissioner sighed heavily, his patience wearing thin. "Mr. Walker, I understand that this is a difficult time for both of you," he said, his tone firm but compassionate. "But disrupting these proceedings will only prolong the inevitable. I suggest you let your lawyer handle this before I have to hold you in contempt."

Defeated, Waylon sank back into his seat, his shoulders slumped with defeat. "Fine," he muttered, his voice barely above a whisper. "Let's just get this over with then."

"Again, I will ask if you agree that the documents are factual and reflect your wishes moving forward?" the commissioner stated, clearly getting more annoyed by the minute with Waylon's antics.

"Yes," Waylon answered curtly.

Molly's heart ached as she watched him, torn between the guilt of ending their marriage and the knowledge that it was the right thing to do. She had loved Waylon once, with all her heart, but their love had withered and died, poisoned by resentment and regret.

"I agree as well," Molly said quietly.

As the court proceedings dragged on, Molly felt a mixture of relief and sadness. She was officially closing one chapter of her life, a chapter she had planned to last for her entire lifetime, and it hurt. It hurt to see Waylon, the man she'd been head-over-heels in love with for so many years, so angry and so different than the man she'd known and loved.

Finally, the court commissioner announced their divorce as final, and tapped his gavel to end the proceedings. She numbly thanked her lawyer with a grateful smile, lingering in the courtroom until she was sure that Waylon had left.

As she stepped out into the cool evening air, Molly felt tears falling down her cheeks. She was finally done with this whole court mess, and now she had more decisions to make, but first, she was going to let herself grieve the loss of her marriage and all the dreams she had once had for she and Waylon's life together. She never could have imagined just a year and a half ago when she was holding her baby girl in her arms as she said goodbye, that she'd be standing here saying farewell to her marriage as well. Life had taken so many wrong turns that she wasn't even sure she knew which way was right anymore. Maybe happiness just wasn't meant to be for her.

* * *

Owen's day passed in a blur of lessons and arguing with teenagers, but his thoughts were consumed by Molly and the uncertainty that shrouded their relationship. He checked his phone over and over, never seeing a returned message from her. With each passing hour, his anxiety grew, a relentless drumbeat that echoed in the recesses of his mind. Had he completely screwed everything up by asking her to move in with them? What the hell was he thinking just spitting it out at her like that?

Owen sat in his chair, his mind miles away, absentmindedly tapping his pen against the surface of the desk, lost in thought as he waited for his next class to begin.

The sound of laughter and chatter from the hallway snapped him back to reality, and he glanced up just in time to see a group of students filing into the classroom, their backpacks slung over their shoulders and their faces filled with excitement over the closely approaching end of the day.

"Hey, Mr. West!" one of the students called out cheerfully, flashing him a bright smile as she took her seat at the front of the room.

"Good afternoon, everyone," Owen replied with a smile, feeling a sense of warmth spread through him at the sight of his students. This was a group of tenth graders, and they were his favorite group of the day. "Please take your seats, and we'll get started."

As the students settled into their seats, Owen rose from his desk and made his way to the front of the room, his mind racing with thoughts of Molly and the unanswered messages that still lingered between them. He did his best to push the thoughts aside, focusing instead on the task at hand.

"Today, we're going to be diving into the fascinating world of Henry VIII and his six wives," he announced, his voice filled with enthusiasm as he began to lecture. "Now, who can tell me the name of Henry's first wife?"

Jay, the class clown of the group, raised his hand.

"Yes, Jay, what was her name?" Owen asked skeptically, knowing he was about to get a smart-ass answer.

"I believe it was Eileen Dover!" he said, causing an eruption of laughter from the group.

Shaking his head, Owen laughed. "Seriously? That was the best one you could come up with?"

After the laughter subsided, Lettie, a girl in the front row, raised her hand. After a nod from Owen, she triumphantly called out, "Katherine of Aragon!" a wide grin spreading across her face as she waited for the teacher's response.

"Correct!" Owen exclaimed, nodding in approval as he made his way through the lesson. "Now, can anyone tell me why Henry decided to divorce Katherine?"

As the students eagerly jumped in with their answers, Owen couldn't help but feel a sense of satisfaction at the lively discussion that ensued. He loved seeing his students engaged and excited about history, and he relished the opportunity to share his passion with them.

As the lesson ended, Owen couldn't resist the urge to inject a bit of humor into the proceedings.

"And now… a little history joke," he announced with a mischievous twinkle in his eye. "Why did Henry VIII have so many wives?"

The students exchanged puzzled looks before one brave soul ventured a guess. "Because he couldn't make a decision without his mother there to help?" she suggested tentatively, a grin spreading across her face as the rest of the class erupted into laughter.

"Close, but not quite," Owen replied with a chuckle. "It was because he liked to chop and change!"

The students groaned in mock dismay, but Owen could see the spark of amusement in their eyes as they turned back to their textbooks.

"Alright, enough goofing around," he said with a grin. "Let's get down to business. I want you to read chapter 14 in your textbooks and complete the odd questions at the end of the chapter. And no complaining!"

There was a collective groan from the students, but they quickly got to work, their pencils scratching against the paper as they diligently worked through the assignment. Owen watched them with a sense of satisfaction, feeling grateful for the distraction that their energy provided.

As he settled back at his desk, Owen couldn't help but sneak a glance at his phone, hoping against hope for a message from Molly. But once again, the screen remained stubbornly blank, and Owen felt a pang of disappointment wash over him. Sighing heavily, he forced himself to focus on teaching, turning his attention back to his students with a renewed sense of determination. Several of them were talking and goofing around instead of doing their reading.

"Alright, everyone," he called out, earning their silence after a few seconds. "Let's see who can finish those questions first. And remember, contrary to popular belief, you don't need your mouths open to make your pens work!"

The students laughed, their voices filling the air with joy and camaraderie as they threw themselves into their work. Owen watched them with a sense of pride, and he couldn't help but feel a glimmer of hope stir within him. Maybe, just maybe, everything was going to be okay after all… maybe he just needed to go about this a different way.

As the final bell of the school day rang and the students stormed out of the building, Owen decided what he was going to do. He couldn't bear another moment of uncertainty, another day of wondering if she was mad or sad or hurt or just ignoring him… He needed to see Molly, to talk to her, to lay his heart out in the open in the hopes of finding some semblance of clarity in terms of their future together.

With a sense of determination coursing through his veins, Owen made his way to Molly and Lily's apartment, his heart pounding in his chest as he thought about all the things he wanted to say to her. He knew he may risk losing her by telling her how he felt about her, but he also knew that for his own peace of mind, it was now or never. He had to know if she was in this for the long haul like he was or if he had misunderstood her feelings the other night. He couldn't risk hurting Oliver if she wasn't completely in like he was. He had to know, and he was going to find out, one way or the other.

* * *

Molly sat on the plush sofa in Lily's apartment, her mind swirling with thoughts and emotions. She had barely touched the cup of tea that Lily had made for her, her thoughts consumed by the events of the day and the weight of the decisions that lay ahead.

"So, how did court go?" Lily asked, breaking the silence that hung heavy in the air. She perched herself on the arm of the sofa, her eyes filled with concern as she studied Molly's face.

Molly sighed heavily, her shoulders slumping with exhaustion. "It was… intense," she admitted, her voice tinged with uncertainty. "Waylon actually tried to stop the proceedings at one point."

Lily's eyes widened in surprise, her brow furrowing with concern. "Are you okay?" she asked, reaching out to grasp Molly's hand in hers. "Do you want to talk about it?"

Molly shook her head, her mind still reeling from the confrontation with Waylon. "Not really," she murmured, her voice barely above a whisper. "I just want to forget about it and move on with my life."

Lily nodded sympathetically, her heart aching for her friend. "I understand," she said softly. "But you can't keep running from your problems, Molly. Eventually, you're going to have to face them head-on."

Molly's heart sunk as she contemplated Lily's words, a surge of panic rising within her at the thought of all the decisions she still had to make. She knew she needed to talk to Owen about the other night, to explain her feelings and her absence the last few days, but the thought of facing him, of admitting the depth of her emotions and fears, filled her with a paralyzing sense of dread.

As if on cue, a sharp knock echoed through the apartment, the sound reverberating through the air like a thunderclap. Molly's heart leaped into her throat at the sound, her mind racing with a million thoughts.

She glanced towards the window, her pulse quickening as she caught sight of Owen's truck in the parking area. Panic seized her heart as she realized she wasn't ready to face him, at least not yet… not until she had figured everything out in her head.

"Lily, what do I do?" she whispered, her voice trembling with fear. "I can't talk to him right now. I'm not ready."

Lily's eyes widened in surprise, her brow furrowing with concern. "Molly, you can't just hide from him forever," she admonished gently. "You need to talk to him, to figure things out."

Molly shook her head stubbornly, her mind racing with fear and uncertainty. "I can't, Lily," she whispered hoarsely. "I just can't… not right now."

Lily sighed heavily, her heart aching for her friend. "Okay, Mol," she said softly, her voice tinged with resignation. "I'll handle it. You stay here."

With a sense of unease, Lily made her way to the door, her heart heavy with the weight of her friend's burdens. She took a deep breath to steady herself before swinging the door open, her eyes meeting Owen's with a mixture of sympathy and regret.

"Hey, Owen," she said, forcing a smile despite the unease that gnawed at her insides.

"Hey, Lily. Is Molly here?" he asked, his eyes searching past her to try to see inside, hopeful he'd see Molly come into sight.

"I'm sorry, Owen, but she's not. She went shopping with her mom this afternoon."

Owen's shoulders slumped with disappointment at Lily's words, his heart sinking like a stone in his chest. "Oh," he murmured, his voice tinged with sadness. "I just wanted to talk to her. It's… it's nothing important."

Lily's heart ached at the despondent look on Owen's face, her resolve waning with each passing moment. "I'm sorry, Owen," she said softly, reaching out to place a comforting hand on his shoulder. "But maybe she can call you later after she gets back. I'll make sure she gets your message."

Owen nodded; his expression resigned as he turned to leave. "Thanks, Lily," he said quietly, his voice heavy with disappointment. "I appreciate it."

As she watched him walk away, Lily felt a pang of guilt twist in her chest. She knew she should have told him the truth, should have confronted Molly about her feelings and forced her to face her fears head-on. Still, the thought of adding to her friend's burden was too much to bear, and so she remained silent, her heart heavy with the weight of her own indecision.

Returning to the apartment, Lily found Molly still sitting on the sofa, her face pale and drawn with exhaustion. "He's gone," she said softly, her voice tinged with regret. "But we need to talk, Molly. About Owen and Oliver, and especially about why you're hiding from him like a frightened child."

Molly's heart constricted with guilt at Lily's words, her eyes brimming with unshed tears. "I'm sorry, Lily," she whispered, her voice thick with emotion. "I just… I don't know how to deal with all of this. It's too much."

Lily reached out to grasp Molly's hand in hers, her heart aching for her friend's pain. "I know, Mol," she murmured softly. "But you can't keep hiding from all of this. Owen seems like such a great guy, and I really do think he'd understand that you need some time to disassemble the chaos in your head and heart right now."

Molly nodded, her resolve wavering as she struggled to come to terms with her emotions. "I know," she whispered hoarsely. "But I'm just so scared, Lily. What if I'm not ready? What if I mess everything up?"

Lily squeezed her hand reassuringly, her eyes filled with sympathy. "You won't mess anything up, Molly," she said softly. "But you need to talk to him, to tell him how you feel. Otherwise, I'm afraid you'll never find the answers you're looking for."

Molly nodded at her with the weight of her own indecision weighing down upon her heart. "I know," she whispered, her voice barely above a whisper. "I'll talk to him. I promise."

As Lily rose to leave, Molly's phone buzzed with a message from her mom.

"Hey, sweetie," it read. *"Your dad and I were wondering if you wanted to stop by for supper tonight."*

With a sense of relief, Molly felt a smile tug at the corners of her lips. Maybe her mother could provide some clarity, some perspective on the tangled mess of emotions that swirled within her. Maybe she could help Molly find the courage to face her fears, to confront her feelings head-on.

"I'd love to… I just have to clean up quick and then I'll head over." Molly replied, happy to have a mother that somehow seemed to always know when she needed her.

"Okay," her mother responded, *"See you in a bit!"*

Taking a deep breath to steady herself, Molly rose to her feet and made her way to the bathroom. There, she splashed some cool water on her face. As she looked up and into the mirror, she saw the reflection of a young woman with eyes that were sad. She saw a version of herself that she wasn't sure she recognized. She was used to sadness, but not this look... she looked lost... Molly wasn't sure what to do.

Snowflake jumped up on the countertop, rubbing her soft fur against Molly's arm as if to comfort her.

"Hey, Snow. *You* don't care if I look like a train wreck, do you?" Molly asked her, petting her long soft fur.

Snowflake meowed and then jumped back down, running to the entry to enjoy the food Lily had placed in her dish for her.

Sighing, she headed towards the front door, her heart heavy with the weight of the decisions that lay ahead. As she stepped out into the cool evening air, she couldn't shake the feeling that maybe she needed to stop worrying so much and try to trust her own instincts a little bit.

"*Will I ever be happy again?*" she wondered as she climbed into her car. She was starting to think that maybe Waylon wasn't the one standing in the way of her happiness... maybe, just maybe, it was her.

* * *

Owen felt as though he was watching himself go through the motions from a distance as he made himself a frozen pizza, his mind consumed by thoughts of Molly and the unanswered questions that lingered between them. He couldn't shake the feeling that he had blown everything, that his impulsive decision to ask her to move in with him and Oliver had pushed her away for good.

As he sat in the kitchen staring blankly out the window, Owen's mind raced with thoughts of Molly, of the warmth of her smile and the sparkle in her eyes. He knew he had feelings for her, deeper and more profound than he had felt since his late wife, but he also knew that he couldn't force her to feel the same way.

His phone buzzed with a call from his mother, her voice warm and familiar as she greeted him on the other end of the line.

"Hey, Mom," he said, forcing a smile despite the heaviness in his heart. "What's up?"

His mother's voice was tinged with concern as she spoke, her maternal instincts kicking in at the sound of his voice. *"Is everything okay, Owen?"* she asked, her voice soft with worry. *"You sound... off."*

Owen sighed heavily, his resolve crumbling as he confessed his fears to his mother. "It's Molly," he admitted reluctantly, his voice tinged with regret. "I went ahead and blurted out that she should move in here since she wants to move out of the place she's in now, but I don't think she was ready for that. I think I scared her off for good."

His mother's voice was gentle as she spoke, her words filled with wisdom and compassion. *"Oh, Owen,"* she murmured softly. *"You can't force someone to feel something they're not ready to feel. You need to give her space, time to figure things out on her own terms."*

Owen sat a quietly for a moment, listening carefully to his mother's words. "I know, Mom," he whispered, "but it's hard. I care about her so much, and I just want her to be happy… for *all* of us to be happy *together*."

His mother's voice was soothing as she spoke, her words a balm to his wounded heart. *"I know, Owen,"* she said softly. *"But sometimes, the best thing you can do for someone you care about is to give them the space they need to find their own happiness. Trust me, she'll come around when she's ready."*

Feeling a cautious sense of relief wash over him, Owen thanked his mother for her advice before ending the call and sinking down onto the sofa with a heavy sigh. He knew she was right, knew that he needed to give Molly the space she needed, but the thought of waiting, of not knowing what the future held, filled him with a sense of unease that hated.

"Oh, on a different topic, your father is getting out of the hospital tomorrow... they want to transfer him to an assisted living center for a week or so while he recovers from surgery, especially since there's nobody home with him on the farm. He is refusing to go by ambulance transfer... imagine that... so I was wondering if maybe you could pick him up and take him? It should only take a couple of hours, but not

sure if you can get off school at this short of a notice or not..."

"Um… yeah, that should be fine. I've got a lot of time built up. I'll hop on the absentee app and get that done quick when we're finished on the phone. What time do I need to be there?"

"The nurse said any time after ten o'clock is fine."

"Okay, I'll plan on ten or so then. Thank you for calling and for helping me see things a little clearer, mom. As always, it is very much appreciated," he said as they exchanged goodbyes, and he hung up the phone.

Owen rose to his feet and made his way to the kitchen. He knew he had to give Molly some time and space, but he also knew that he couldn't give up hope, couldn't stop fighting for the chance at happiness that he knew they both deserved.

"Well, Buck," he said as he let the dog in from doing his business outside. "I guess I have to be patient."

Buck looked up at his owner with adoration, his head tilting as though he was trying to figure out what he was saying. Walking over to the cupboard at the end of the island, he whined and shook his tail. He knew it was treat time, and there was no way he was going to let Owen leave without giving him his bone.

"What? Do you want one of these or something?" he asked Buck, teasing him a little.

Buck barked his "yes" and then sat nicely, waiting for Owen to give him his treat.

Owen handed him the treat and petted him on the head before heading towards the door. "See ya' later, Bucky boy!" he said, earning a hearty bark from Buck.

As he walked to the door to put his shoes on so he could go pick Oliver up from the birthday party, Owen couldn't shake the feeling that maybe, just maybe, everything was going to work out… somehow. His mom was right… he just needed to give Molly the space she needed, to wait for her to come to him when she was ready.

Molly's love was worth fighting for… worth waiting for, and he refused to give up hope that they would find their way back to each other again… he just hoped it wouldn't take too long. Every day without her felt like an eternity.

169

Sixteen

Chapter 15

Molly's hands tightened around the steering wheel as she navigated the familiar streets toward her parents' house. The soft auburn hues of the setting sun painted the sky in streaks of pink, red and orange, casting a warm glow over the town she'd loved since she was a little girl. Dayton Hills was a small farming town, with rural family farms as well as a friendly and tidy town filled with single family homes. Still, despite the picturesque scene outside, turmoil brewed within Molly's heart.

She was still trying to make peace with the fact that her divorce was now finalized, marking the end of a chapter she had longed to close, still never imagined even a year ago would end as it had. With it came a sense of liberation, a newfound freedom to explore the depths of her heart, but as she drove, her thoughts lingered on the next steps. Should she stay with Lily or find a condo of her own? To make the matter even more complicated, there was the proposition from Owen that she move in with him and Oliver. The more she thought about the options, the more confused she got. She just couldn't decide which made the most sense, and which would cause the least amount of stress right now, because she wasn't sure how much more she could take.

Their relationship had moved forward quickly the other night, a tender connection forged amidst the rubble of the broken dreams she'd shared with him in the days leading to their night of passion. Owen's warmth and understanding of loss and grief had resonated deep within her, thawing the ice that had been chiseled on her heart after losing Hannah. His gentle affection had breathed new life into her weary soul, and yet, beneath the surface of their budding romance, doubts lingered like shadows in the corners of her mind. As much as she wanted to push them aside and jump feet first into Owen's arms, something inside of her kept pulling her back.

The prospect of Owen having a son gnawed at her insides, a reminder of the complexities of their relationship. Could she embrace motherhood again, knowing the pain of loss all too well? She wasn't even positive she wanted to have another child, let alone a child who came alongside a certain handsome, funny and kind teacher that she just so happened to have a schoolgirl-like crush on. The thought of navigating the delicate balance of parenthood filled her with equal parts longing and trepidation.

Lost in her thoughts, Molly approached the last stoplight before turning onto her parents' street. She was thankful it was green as her stomach was starting to rumble with hunger as she thought about the amazing homemade meal awaiting her at her parents' table. Her mother was such a wonderful cook… something she had definitely inherited. She had learned to love baking from a very young age, her mother always letting her help in the kitchen. Some of her favorite memories had been made in that familiar and warm place.

Molly squinted as a red glow bathed the intersection in an eerie light, a moment frozen in time before chaos descended.

A truck's blaring horn shattered the silence, followed by the deafening screech of tires. Instinct took over as Molly's foot slammed on the brakes, but it was too late. The world erupted into chaos as metal collided with metal, the bone-jarring force of the impact sending her car careening into the intersection. Glass shattered with an ear-splitting crash as metal twisted and groaned.

Time felt as though it had slowed to a crawl as Molly's car spun out of control, a whirlwind of shattered glass and twisted metal. The sickening lurch of her stomach accompanied each rotation, her body tossed like a leaf blowing in the wind. Pain tore through her body, every nerve feeling as though it was ablaze with agony. The acrid scent of burning rubber filled the air, mingling with the metallic tang of blood she could taste on her tongue.

And then, with a final agonizing lurch, everything fell silent.

Molly could hear nothing but the sound of her own breathing, the thud of her speeding heartbeat a thankful indication that she was still alive. She closed her eyes, feeling achingly tired and too scared to move. She lost all track of time as she fought to stay conscious amidst the chaos all around her.

A heavy, suffocating haze of smoke began to fill the air in front of her car, causing Molly to panic. She tried to move her arm, but the pain was unbearable. She knew instantly that she was stuck, and she felt a type of fear she'd never felt before. Was this how she was going to die?

Molly struggled to make sense of the world around her, her mind a jumble of fragmented thoughts and fractured memories. Panic continued to claw at the edges of her consciousness, threatening to drag her under into the abyss of despair. Confusion fogged her mind. Was she all alone? Had she done something wrong? What happened? She could feel a wet trail of blood spilling down her face from her head, still in too much pain to reach her hand up and touch it. How was she going to get out of here if she couldn't move?

Suddenly, she thought she could hear the distant wail of sirens, a mere whisper against the cacophony of chaos that was surrounding her, a beacon of hope in the darkness. Molly closed her eyes and tried to calm herself down. They were going to get her out… they had to!

As she focused on breathing, pain seared through her belly. She was too scared to look down, feeling dizzy each time she tried to move her head. Instead, she kept her eyes closed, not wanting to see the destruction and smoke all around her. Voices got closer and closer, shouting commands to one another, muffled and distant as if coming from another world.

Hands reached out to her, gentle yet urgent as paramedics and firefighters worked to free her from the wreckage. The sound of metal being torn away echoed in her ears, a symphony of destruction that threatened to overwhelm her senses. The voices around her murmured words of reassurance, their soothing tones a balm to her broken body and shattered thoughts.

Through the haze of pain and confusion, Molly opened her eyes, catching glimpses of the world outside. Flashing lights painted the night sky in hues of red and blue, casting eerie shadows across the scene. Faces hovered above her, their expressions a mixture of concern and determination.

And then, as if from a great distance, she felt herself being cradled by several paramedics' hands and lifted from the wreckage. She looked up as they pulled her out, catching a glimpse of twisted metal and shattered glass. She was placed on a stretcher as the cool night air kissed her skin. The movement made her stomach lurch, so she closed her eyes again as she was rolled towards the waiting ambulance, the sound of her own ragged breathing echoing in her ears.

As darkness closed in around her, Molly felt herself slipping further and further away. She clung to consciousness with all her strength, afraid of what lied in waiting for her on the other side. Still, despite her fear, she found solace in the knowledge that she was not alone. She looked into the eyes of the paramedic that was talking to her, still unable to make out the words they were saying. She was surrounded by strangers who had now become her lifeline.

Molly's pain dulled to a distant ache as exhaustion claimed her, pulling her down into the dark depths of sleep.

* * *

"Honey, what time did Molly message that she was leaving Lily's place?" Molly's dad asked her mother as he glanced at his watch. "It seems like she should be here by now, doesn't it?"

James Flynn was typically a patient man, but he wasn't a fan of his daughter being late for something. His body was tense as he walked to the window, nervously looking out. He had always taught Molly to be punctual, and she usually was, so it made him uneasy when she was late.

Laura peeked at her phone in one hand while she was stirring the soup with the other. "Uh… it looks like it was 5:15," she said, setting the phone back down to take the soup from the burner so it wouldn't scorch. "It's been about an hour… that's odd. Why don't you message her quick and see how much longer she'll be."

He scoffed. "You women and your messaging!" he said, clearly annoyed with the idea of typing something out that he could just call and say over the phone. "I'll just call her quick."

James looked through his recent calls and found his daughter's name. He pushed the button and put the phone up to his ear, waiting to give Molly a talk about punctuality. It would all be in good humor, of course, but he didn't like when she worried them like that.

After several rings, the phone went to voicemail.

"Huh… that's odd. She didn't answer," he said, clearly getting worried now. "I'll try again."

He hit redial and placed the phone to his ear again, impatiently waiting for his daughter to answer. This time, the phone was answered, and he heard a women's voice on the other end.

"Hello?"

"Molly, where in the world are you? Your mother and I were getting worried!"

"Hello, sir. My name is Clara, and I am a nurse at the Stanson Medical Center Trauma Center. Who, may I ask, am I speaking to?"

Molly's dad turned white as a ghost. Trauma center? What the heck was going on?

"My name is James Flynn… The Stanson Trauma center? Why do you have my daughter's phone?" He walked into the kitchen and sat at the table, gesturing for his wife to join him. Placing the phone on the table, he hit the speaker button so they could both figure out what was going on together. "Did something happen?"

"Sir, your daughter Molly has been in an accident. She was brought here via ambulance and is being assessed by the trauma doctors now. I cannot share

information about her condition over the phone, but if you are able to safely come down here, the doctors should be able to update you as they are able. Is that possible?"

Molly's parents sat together at the table, neither sure what to do. How had this happened?

"*Sir?*" the nurse said, waking both from their confusion.

"Um... yes, sorry. We will be there in about 20 minutes. Thank you for letting us know."

"*No problem,*" Clara replied. After a few seconds, she added, *"Sir... She is stable right now, so please drive safely and we will talk to you soon."*

"Okay," he said, hitting the call end button. As soon as the phone was disconnected, Laura fell into her husband's arms and sobbed. Her baby girl was lying in a hospital bed, and she had no idea what had happened or how badly she was hurt. Pulling herself together, she turned the oven off, removed the rolls, and went to freshen up quickly so they could head to the hospital.

As James and Laura got closer to the intersection just south of their home, they could see the bright red and blue lights all over the place. Laura's stomach felt sick as they inched closer and closer to the wreckage. A police officer was directing traffic. Laura could see what her daughter's car was once lying in pieces on the pavement and a smashed truck nearby. Tears flowed as she imagined how scared Molly must have been.

James followed the path the police office directed him to drive in as he passed the site of the accident. He felt a mixture of fear, anger, and dread as he saw what was left of his baby girl's car. He knew the nurse had said she was alive, but how could she be? There was nothing left of her car! He didn't have time to look at the other vehicle, but he guessed it was probably just as bad as Molly's.

James focused on driving, looking away from the wreck. He had to be strong and concentrate on Molly now, for Laura and Molly's sakes. Still, he was petrified that his little girl was not going to look like herself anymore after that crash... if she even made it through. Tears flowed down his cheeks as he reached over to hold his wife's hand, giving it a comforting squeeze.

Molly was tough... she was going to get through this! He knew that in his heart. She was a fighter, and he knew she'd fight her way back to them.

Afterall, he'd taught her to never give up, and he wasn't about to let her quit now.

* * *

Molly slowly opened her eyes, unsure of where she was or what was happening. Looking around, she found herself surrounded by the sterile white walls of a hospital room. The steady beep of machines filled the air, a reminder of the fragility of life. She tried to move, but pain flared through her body like wildfire, forcing her to remain still.

Voices murmured nearby, their words a distant buzz in her ears. She strained to make out their meaning, but her mind felt foggy and distant, as if wrapped in cotton wool. She closed her eyes again, trying to clear the haze. Consciousness returned in fragments, a haze of pain and confusion clouding Molly's senses. She blinked against the harsh glare of fluorescent lights, her surroundings swimming into focus like a mirage.

And then, like a ray of sunshine breaking through the clouds, she heard her name being called. She slowly reopened her eyes, turning towards the sound, her heart pounding in her chest.

"Mom..."

The word escaped her lips in a hoarse whisper, a plea for reassurance amidst the chaos. And then, like a lifeline cast into the abyss, familiar faces materialized at her side.

Tears welled in Molly's eyes as she met her mother's gaze, her heart overflowing with gratitude.

Her mother's worried eyes met hers, a silent exchange of love and relief. Lily's voice trembled with emotion as she reached for Lily's hand, a lifeline in the storm.

And then, amidst the tumult, Owen's presence filled the void, his touch a balm to her fractured soul. She clung to him, her heart pounding in rhythm with his own, a silent symphony of shared fear and hope.

"Molly," her he whispered, his voice thick with emotion. "Thank God you're okay."

"Owen," she choked out through tears that were now flowing down her cheeks. "I…" she trailed off, pain searing though her head.

"It's okay," he said, wiping the tears from her face as they fell. "You rest now, we'll talk later."

Molly closed her eyes, feeling safe knowing he was next to her. Hours blurred into eternity as she drifted in and out of consciousness, each moment a delicate balance between life and the unknown. Pain pulsed through her body, a constant reminder of the nightmare she had lived through.

* * *

Owen sat at Molly's bedside in the dimly lit hospital room, his heart heavy with worry. The rhythmic beeping of the machines filled the silence, a stark reminder of the fragility of life. He reached out to gently brush a strand of hair away from her face, his fingers lingering against her skin.

She lay still, her face pale against the crisp white sheets, her chest rising and falling in shallow breaths. She had small cuts all over her face, all cleaned up and bandaged now, but still a bruised and bloody reminder of the fact that he'd almost lost her just hours before. He wanted to gently press his lips to each wound, taking away the pain and scars with a mere magical kiss. *"If only it were that easy,"* he thought.

Owen's gaze softened as he watched her, his mind flooded with recollections of their recent times together… stolen moments here and there that added up to treasured memories. He had never thought he'd again know a love like this, a love that consumed him with every beat of his heart. When his wife had passed away, he felt as though his heart had shattered, and there was no way he would ever have room to love another woman like that again… not if there was a chance that she'd leave him too. He wasn't sure then if he would be able to handle that… and he still wasn't sure. All he knew for sure was that he was in love with Molly, and he'd almost lost her.

As he sat there, watching over her in the quiet stillness of the hospital room, a gnawing fear gripped his chest. The accident had shaken him to the core, a stark reminder of how quickly life could be snatched away. He couldn't bear the thought of losing her, not after they had finally given in to the feelings between them and started to explore where it might take them.

His thoughts drifted to his first wife, Tara, a ghost that still haunted the corners of his mind. Her memory lingered like a shadow, a constant reminder of the pain he had endured. He had loved her with every fiber of his being, only to have her torn away from him in the cruelest of ways.

And now, with Molly lying before him, her life hanging in the balance, Owen couldn't shake the feeling of déjà vu. He couldn't bear to lose her too, to endure the agony of another heartbreak. As the hours stretched on, Owen's thoughts were consumed by the weight of his love for her. He longed to tell her how he felt, to pour out his heart and soul and beg her to stay with him forever. But the words caught in his throat, trapped by the fear of rejection.

Suddenly, as if in response to his silent plea, Molly stirred beside him. Her eyelids fluttered open, revealing eyes clouded with confusion and pain. Owen's heart leaped in his chest as he reached out to gently squeeze her hand.

"It's okay… you're going to be okay. Just take a deep breath and try to calm down," Owen said, gently trying to help her calm down as she became agitated.

She blinked up at him, her gaze searching his face as if trying to piece together the fragments of reality. Owen could see the fear and uncertainty etched in her features, a mirror of his own inner turmoil.

Her mother and father continued to hover nearby, their faces etched with relief as they watched Molly awaken again. Lily stood off to the side, her eyes red-rimmed with tears, a silent testament to the depth of her love for her best friend.

As Molly's gaze swept over the room, her eyes widened in realization. She struggled to sit up, wincing in pain as she shifted against the pillows. Owen moved to help her, his arms encircling her as he gently supported her weight.

"What happened?" she whispered, her voice hoarse with disuse.

Her parents exchanged a look, their expressions grave.

"Maybe we should talk about that later, darling," her father said, giving her hand a squeeze. "Right now, we just want you to get lots of rest so you can get out of here and back home to recover."

Molly frowned, readjusting herself in the bed again. She finally was starting to feel a little clearer, and she needed to know what had happened. She looked down as she felt a shooting pain go down her leg, seeing a brace on her right leg.

Seeing what she was looking at and realizing they still hadn't talked to her about her injuries, Molly's mother said, "Sweetheart, your knee is very badly bruised from the dash smashing into it. By the grace of God, the doctors say there are no fractures there… just badly bruised. It will be very sore for a while, but you should be back on your feet in no time."

Owen's voice was calm and steady… far from the terror he was feeling inside. Still, no reason to upset her any further. Right now, she needed him to be strong, so she didn't panic any more than she already was.

"You have bruising and some cuts on your face from the airbag and the broken glass, and the doctors had to do surgery when you first got here to repair your spleen. Apparently, the seatbelt tightened so hard against your body that it caused damage that had to be fixed. They said the surgery went really well and that you will be back to yourself in a few weeks."

Molly nodded, not sure she could speak even if she wanted to. This was all just too much for her to sort through in her groggy mind. Just thinking about it was making her head pound again.

Owen, seeing her wince from the pain in her head said, "You also have a pretty nice concussion from the air bag and all the jerking around during the crash. They said to let them know if you have a headache so they can give you something for the pain," he continued, concern written all over his face. "Do you want me to go get them?"

"I'll go get them," Molly heard her dad say from the foot of her bed as he turned to head out the door of her room.

Molly turned to her Mom, attempting to smile at her. "Thank you for being here, Mom," she whispered as loudly as she could muster up.

"Oh, sweetheart, there's no place I'd rather be. I'm so sorry this happened," her mother said, tears filling her eyes. Molly could see the exhaustion and fear in her mother's eyes and wished she could take it away.

"How? What happened, Mom?" she asked, needing to know how this had happened. It had all been so fast in the car. Bright lights, crashing sounds, pain, silence, then sirens and more chaos all around her. She just needed to know so she could get some of the fuzziness out of her head.

Molly watched her mother and Owen exchange an odd look, and it worried her.

"What is going on," she asked again.

Molly's dad moved next to her mom, sitting on the edge of her bed and taking her hand. His eyes looked weary, and she hated that she had scared them so badly.

"Mol, I will tell you what we know, but I need you to promise me you'll try to stay calm." Her father said, concern written all over his face. "Can you do that for me?

Molly nodded, getting more and more nervous as her father spoke. *"What in the world had happened?"* she thought to herself. *"Did I run a stop light or something?"*

Molly was desperately trying to remember, but everything still felt so foggy in her brain. No matter how hard she tried, she couldn't seem to make sense of the pieces in her mind.

"It was Waylon," her father explained, his voice heavy with sorrow. "He was drunk and ran a red light. He hit the front end of your car, sending you spiraling through the intersection."

Molly's breath caught in her throat, her hands trembling as she clutched the blankets tightly. Owen watched as Molly's face paled, her eyes brimming with tears as the truth sank in. He could see the pain and devastation written across her face, a rawness that tore at his heart.

"He's badly injured," her mother added, her voice trembling with emotion. "Broken bones, cuts and bruises… The doctor said he's lucky to be alive," Her voice caught in her throat as she added, "and so are you."

The mention of Molly's ex-husband's name sent a shiver down Owen's spine. He had heard her speak of Waylon before, knew of the struggles they had faced in their marriage. But he had never imagined it would come to this, that Waylon's demons would lead to such destruction.

Molly turned her head away, allowing the tears to fall. She couldn't believe this was happening. How could Waylon have let his drinking go this far? She didn't even recognize him anymore. He was no longer the man she had loved with her whole heart. It killed her that losing their precious little girl had driven him to become someone other than himself. There had been so many moments that she had felt like she didn't want to go on living, like she couldn't breathe without her little girl. Still, she'd found her way through that devastation, and she couldn't understand how he could have gone the completely opposite direction.

Seeing that Molly needed some time to process what they had said, her father rose from the bed, leaning down to kiss her on the forehead. "Sweetheart, we are going to go get something to eat from the cafeteria and give you some time to rest, okay?"

Molly nodded at him, reaching out to squeeze his hand. She knew that Waylon had been loved by her parents like a son, and that they were devastated too.

As Molly's parents left the room to give them privacy, Owen remained by her side, his heart heavy with unspoken words. He longed to comfort her, to ease the pain that weighed so heavily on her soul. And yet, he couldn't find the courage to speak the words that burned in his chest.

"Molly," he began, his voice steady despite the turmoil raging within him. "I've been sitting here trying to figure out how to tell you all the things that have been flashing through my head over the last couple of days. I was terrified I was going to lose you. I need you to know... I love you."

Tears welled in Molly's eyes as she met his gaze, her heartache laid bare for all to see. In that moment, surrounded by the wreckage of their shattered reality, Owen knew that he was going to do everything he had to do to have Molly in he and Oliver's lives. He prayed silently as he sat there, holding her hand, that his love would be enough to heal her broken heart and light the way forward into the unknown.

Seventeen

Chapter 16

Molly slowly opened her eyes, trying to figure out where she was as the dreamy world she'd been in for the last few hours dissipated. She could smell the faint aroma of floral-scented hand sanitizer, reminding her quickly that she was in a hospital. Her eyes slowly focused in on the stark white walls of the sterile room. She tried to lift her head, quickly wincing with pain as she dropped it back to the pillow gently. The dull ache of her injuries was a painful reminder of the chaos that had unfolded in the days prior.

Looking around, Molly realized she was alone. She gingerly moved her head to the left, seeing a nurse sitting just outside her room. She appeared to be typing something on the computer, and seeing Molly look her direction, got up and entered the room.

"I'm happy to see you are awake, Molly. My name is Felicity, and I took over for Tara at 3:00," the auburn-haired nurse said in a voice that Molly thought had a hint of a southern accent to it.

"Hello," Molly said, doing her best to smile back.

"Can you tell me if you have any pain anywhere?" she asked in a soft voice.

Molly felt like she was broken literally *everywhere*. Her entire body was screaming at her. "Honestly, I'm not sure where to start," she said with a half-hearted chuckle.

The nurse smiled back at her. "I'd imagine that's true. I will go ahead and grab your pain medication for you. The doctor ordered it to be given every six hours as needed and you haven't had anything in close to seven, so you can definitely have some more at this point."

"That sounds good," Molly said, feeling as though her head was going to explode.

"Okay, I'll be right back," she said as she left the room.

The events of the accident replayed in Molly's mind like a broken record, each moment etched into her memory with painful clarity. She knew she needed to go see Waylon, to be sure he was okay. Even though they were divorced now, she would forever hold a special place in her heart for him. He was her first love, and she could never forget that. As mad as she was at him for everything that had happened, a part of her felt sorry for him too. She wished she could go back and change the way things had happened with Hannah, but she knew she couldn't. What she could do, however, was make sure he was okay.

When the nurse returned, she entered some information into her computer, scanned Molly's bracelet, and then sterilized the IV port so she could put the medication directly into Molly's IV.

"Molly, the doctor said that we need to get you up and walking as soon as possible to help avoid any blood clots from forming due to lying in bed so long. When you feel that you need to use the restroom, please let me know and we will go ahead and get you up and moving, okay?"

Molly knew she was going to get sleepy again from the medicine, so she needed to go see Waylon now if she was going to go. With a deep breath, she turned to her nurse, her voice soft yet resolute.

"I actually do need to use the restroom soon," she said, "and I would also like to go see my ex-husband, Waylon, if that is okay," she said, her words echoing in the stillness of the room. "Would you be able to wheel me to the room he's in?"

The nurse's brow furrowed in concern, her eyes searching Molly's face for any sign of hesitation. All she found was a steely determination, a quiet strength that belied the turmoil raging within.

"Are you sure?" the nurse asked, her voice tinged with concern. "You've been through an awful lot, and I would imagine you are very sore. Moving around too much right now might not be the best idea for you."

Molly nodded, her gaze unwavering. "Yes, I'm sure," she said. "I know it will be painful, and I promise I will lay back down as soon as I get back and rest again, but I need to see him. Please…"

"Okay, just give me a minute to go get some help getting you from the bed to the chair," she said as she left the room to go find a wheelchair and some help.

Before long, nurse Felicity returned with another nurse to help her lift and guide Molly into the chair. Each movement made the muscles in Molly's body scream at her. She gasped at the pain in her stomach, carefully putting her hand over it to support the bandages as she sat up.

"Maybe we should wait, Molly," Felicity said, worry on her face.

Molly took a breath to settle herself again. "No, it's okay. I just didn't realize how tender my stomach was until trying to sit up, that's all. I'll be okay."

Felicity and the other nurse exchanged glances before proceeding to help Molly to her feet so they could walk with her to her private bathroom in her room.

Molly felt like every step was a mile, but she made it, determined to prove that she could handle being up and around.

After using the restroom, the nurses returned to help her back out into her room and shift her into the chair. With gentle hands, one of the nurses covered her with a blanket so she wouldn't get cold, while the other nurse unhooked Molly's monitors from the machines and re-hooked them to a portable one that could hang on her chair. Then, Felicity moved Molly's IV bags to the hanger up above her in the special wheelchair. When they were all set, she thanked the other for her help as she left the room again.

"Okie dokie… are you ready to go, Molly?" she asked her, checking all the monitors to make sure Molly was still doing okay.

"Yes, let's go," Molly replied. She felt a little dizzy, but better than she had before. She knew she had to control that somehow so she could go see Waylon.

If not, they'd make her go back to bed.

Slowly, Felicity guided her through the long thin corridors of the hospital. The journey felt endless, each passing moment stretching into eternity as they drew closer to their destination. Molly could hear a constant background noise of beeping monitors, muffled voices, tapping footsteps, and the distant sound of sirens coming into the ER area. She was never a fan of hospitals, and this was *definitely* not helping.

Finally, they arrived at the ICU, a quiet sanctuary of beeping monitors and hushed whispers. The nurse pushed Molly into room 1437, a small room in the corner of the ICU. Molly's heart pounded in her chest as she took in the sight before her.

There Waylon lay, his once vibrant spirit reduced to a mere shadow of its former self. Wires and tubes snaked across his body like tendrils of despair, connecting him to a maze of machines that monitored his every breath. His right leg was in some sort of contraption that was bending and straightening it, and it was bandaged up from his toes to his hip. His right arm was casted, obviously broken. He had bandages on his face and head, and a tube in his mouth breathing for him. He looked lucky to be alive, and she thanked God that he was.

Molly's breath caught in her throat as she gazed upon him, her heart breaking at the sight of his frail form. She placed her hand to her mouth as the tears began to flow down her face. Waylon had become a stranger to her, a ghost from a past she could scarcely remember.

Still, amidst the wreckage of their shattered dreams, there was a glimmer of the man she had once loved. She saw it in the lines of his face, the way his chest rose and fell with each labored breath.

With trembling hands, Molly reached out to him, her fingers brushing against his cool, clammy skin. She felt a surge of emotion welling within her, a flood of memories and regrets that threatened to overwhelm her.

"I'm so sorry, Waylon," she whispered, her voice choked with tears. "I wish things had gone differently."

But Waylon remained silent, his eyes closed to the world around him. He was lost in a world of his own making, a prisoner of his own demons.

Molly squeezed his hand, her heart heavy with the weight of their shared pain. She wanted to shake him, to scream at him for what he had done. But deep down, she knew that anger would only breed more sorrow.

Instead, she chose forgiveness, a beacon of light in the darkness that threatened to consume them both. Closing her eyes, she forgave him for the accident, for the pain he had caused, for the shattered dreams that lay scattered at their feet. She knew that for them to move past this, she'd need to let go of the hurt and the anger.

"I love you, Waylon," she whispered, her voice barely a whisper in the silence of the room. "And I forgive you."

Tears continued to stream down Molly's cheeks as she spoke the simple words, her heart aching with the weight of her confession. She prayed that somehow, someway, he would find the strength to overcome his demons and emerge from the darkness into the light.

As Molly nodded to Felicity, the kind nurse moved the wheelchair back from the bed and towards the doorway. Looking up through wet eyes, she saw a young doctor enter Waylon's room. He introduced himself to her as Dr. Williamson, and the grave look on his face had her worried. He had been overseeing Waylon's care since the accident. To Molly's surprise, he already knew who she was, and he gave her a quick update on Waylon's condition since she was still listed as his next of kin in his medical record.

Dr. Williamson explained that Waylon's injuries were very extensive and would require several surgeries to repair. Right now, they were trying to get his vitals steady so that he could handle surgery. He had several broken bones and had hit his head very hard during the crash. The doctor calmly explained that he was unsure of possible brain damage at this point. They were hoping to have a neurologic exam completed very soon to try to assess any permanent affects.

"As of now, Waylon has not woken up, Molly. We are hopeful that he will, but I can't promise you that that will happen," Dr. Williamson said with compassion.

Molly could see that he cared and that he was frustrated, and she appreciated that he was doing his best to explain everything in a way that she could understand.

"I don't want to sugarcoat this… it's very bad, and we aren't sure yet that he will make it through this, but we are hopeful. We are doing everything we can for him. The next 48 hours will tell us a lot, so we will continue to take good care of him and hope for a turn-around, okay?"

Molly knew that the road ahead would be long and fraught with uncertainty for Waylon. He was still in critical condition, his fate hanging in the balance with each passing moment, and she needed to get some rest so she could go home as soon as possible. The hospital made her feel nervous and she wanted to be in her own bed.

With a heavy heart, Molly asked Felicity to wheel her back to her room, her body trembling with exhaustion and grief. She sank back into her bed, the weight of the world pressing down on her weary shoulders. Felicity and another nurse helped transfer her monitors and IV bags and got her all tucked back in as comfortably as she could be.

As Molly lay there thinking about everything that had happened recently, she began to feel tired, her eyes getting heavier with each passing moment. As she drifted off to sleep, her dreams were haunted by visions of what could have been, of the life she and Waylon had once dreamed of together, of her precious baby girl lying lifeless in her arms.

Still, amidst the shadows of regret and despair, Molly could feel a glimmer of hope, a promise of redemption that lingered on the horizon. If only she could grasp it and hold on with her whole heart… if only…

* * *

The next 3 days felt like a blur to Molly. Her body felt as though it had been drug along the road by her car rather than tossed around inside it. Every muscle ached and every bone felt broken. She had awoken this morning to the news that she was being released later today. She couldn't wait to get out of the hospital and into a normal bed.

She looked up as the nurse walked into the room, closely followed by a kind-eyed woman carrying her breakfast. She was only eating soft foods still due to the pain in her jaw from the airbag, but at least she didn't have to continue the liquid diet she was on the first couple of days! Her stomach groaned at the smell of oatmeal and coffee as the woman sat her tray near her.

"Good morning, Miss Walker," she said as she smiled at her.

"Good morning," Molly replied, returning a grin. "Thank you very much for bringing my breakfast. I'm super hungry today!"

"I bet you are," the woman replied. "Enjoy your breakfast!"

With that, the woman quickly left the room, on to the next. Molly couldn't wait to dig in. Her stomach had been making noise for the last 30 minutes. Today was the first day she'd really felt hungry, so she decided that must be a good sign.

"Good morning, Molly," her nurse said. "I'm happy to hear you have your appetite back. When you get out of here later, I'd recommend you stick to soft foods for a while. It should help your jaw to not get so sore, and it will also help keep your stools soft since you don't want to get bound up. Bearing down wouldn't feel very good after your surgery."

"Yeah… that's what I figured too," Molly replied. "I remember how much that hurt after I had my Hannah. I don't want to have that happen again."

"Oh… I never knew you had a little girl, Molly! How old is she now?" the nurse, Shelby, asked. She obviously had no way of knowing what had happened to Hannah.

Molly swallowed hard. "Hannah was stillborn almost two years ago."

Seeing the sadness quickly replace the smile on the nurse's face, she added, "Oh, it's okay. I know you didn't know! I'm doing much better with all of it now. It took me a very long time, but I'm in therapy now and it's really helping me learn how to move forward."

"I'm so happy to hear that therapy is helping, and I'm so very sorry about your sweet little girl," Shelby said, squeezing Molly's hand gently.

"Thank you."

Shelby checked Molly's vitals and handed her some Tylenol to take. "The doctor is putting your discharge orders in now, so I'll let you enjoy your breakfast, and then we'll work on getting you unhooked from all these wires and such so you can take a real shower, how does that sound?"

"Oh, my goodness… that sounds amazing!" Molly replied, a genuine smile filling her cheeks.

"I thought that might make you feel better since it's been almost a week since you've had a real shower!"

"Absolutely! I feel disgusting!" Molly said, laughing.

Shelby excused herself from the room to get a few things ready and allow Molly some time to eat her breakfast.

Molly mixed some brown sugar into her oatmeal and then took a spoonful into her mouth, savoring the taste. It had been a long time since she'd had oatmeal, and she'd forgotten how much she loved it.

As she slowly enjoyed her breakfast, she thought about her discussion with nurse Shelby. Usually, when someone asked her about Hannah, she found it really hard to talk about. It gave her a sinking feeling in her stomach, like she may be sick.

This time, though, she hadn't gotten that same feeling. It was odd… she'd actually felt… well, she wasn't quite sure how to define how she'd felt. It hadn't hurt like usual, that's all she knew, and she would take it! She hoped that it meant that she was finally moving in the right direction… in a direction towards happy memories of Hannah instead of painful ones.

"Good morning, beautiful!" Owen said, interrupting her thoughts.

Molly looked at the handsome man who had just walked into her room, not quite sure how she had managed to get so lucky and find him in the park that day. His eyes were soft and sweet, and his personality matched them. She could see the love he had for her written all over his face, and it made her feel so much better every time he came to see her.

She looked down at his hands and saw a stunning bouquet of coral-colored roses with bright greenery intertwined throughout. They were in a vase that had a matching ribbon on it, and there was an adorable teddy bear clutching the vase. He was such a thoughtful man. She knew he had brought them to brighten up the dull white room because she'd told him the day before that they needed a little color in their rooms.

"Good morning, Owen. I'm not sure I'm a picture of beauty, especially right now. You may want to schedule an eye appointment, and soon!" she laughed, wincing at the pain in her midsection when she did.

Seeing her wince, Owen quickly found his way to her side, setting the flowers in the windowsill and then sitting on the bed next to her. He reached up to cup her cheek gently. "Are you okay? Did that hurt?"

She smiled at him softly. "I'm okay, Owen. I'm just sore, that's all."

"Good," he said. "I can't stand seeing you hurting so much. I'd do anything to take your place right now."

Owen leaned down and kissed her sweetly on forehead. "I missed you."

"I think you may have missed… want to try again?" she asked, grinning mischievously.

Owen cocked one eyebrow up, looking at her with confusion. Suddenly, he realized what she meant. Shaking his head he said, "You are a naughty one, aren't you?"

Before she could respond, he had his lips on hers, kissing her with a gentle need that had her wishing she was *anywhere but here.*

Pulling away, Owen looked at her half-eaten breakfast. "Well, it looks like you're eating like a champion today, huh?"

"I'm sure trying. I was super hungry at first, but I don't want to overdo it in case it doesn't sit well or something."

"Ah… I see. That makes sense," he replied. "Has the doctor been in yet this morning?"

"Yep! He was in around 7am and told me that he's springing me from this joint!"

"What?" Owen said, an instant smile filling his face. "Are you serious? That's amazing news, Molly!"

"Yeah… I'm so excited to get out of here. The nurse… her name is Shelby… said she'd help get me unhooked from everything after I finish my breakfast, and then I can take a shower!"

"I'm so happy you get to go home, Molly. I'm sure this place is driving you a little crazy."

"Uh… yeah. Crazy is one word for it," she replied sarcastically. Molly could see that Owen was thinking about something, so she added, "A penny for your thoughts?"

"Huh?" Owen said, pulled from whatever he was thinking about so hard. "What was that, Molly?"

"I said would you mind telling me what you are thinking so hard about?"

"Oh… sorry. I was just wondering where you are planning to go when you leave…" he said, obviously nervous now.

"Well, I guess I will probably go to my parent's house for a couple of weeks. The doctor said I have to take it easy for the next 4-6 weeks in order to let all the internal and external injuries heal up from the accident. Then, I'll be good as new hopefully!"

"I see," he said, clearly disappointed in her answer.

Molly reached over and grabbed Owen's hand, looking into his eyes as she spoke. "Owen, I know you want me to come live with you and Oliver, and I'm not saying that won't happen. I just need some time to figure everything out, and my parents will want me to come there for a while so they can make sure I'm okay. At some point, after I have some time to think, we can sit down and talk about everything, I promise."

Although he looked a bit defeated, Owen nodded his agreement. "I understand, Molly. I just want to be sure you know that I am happy to take care of you too."

"I know that, Owen, and I appreciate it very much," she said, smiling at him. Leaning forward, she kissed him gingerly. "If you can give me a little time with it all, I promise we'll have that conversation and figure all of this out together, okay?"

"Okay. I guess I can wait a little longer… you're definitely worth it," he said, grinning back at her and giving her hand a little squeeze.

Sadie finished up her breakfast while she and Owen talked about Oliver's newest antics. He was such a goofball, and she missed him very much. He'd been there to visit her the day before, and they'd played with his toy cars a little on her table tray. He was a cutie and he seemed to really love Molly. It made things both easier and more complicated all at once.

After she finished eating, the nurse came back in to help get her ready to go. Owen leaned forward to give her a kiss. "I think I'm going to head home and grab a few things before I go get Oliver from my mom's place. Is it okay if we stop by your folks' place later for a visit?"

"Of course you can! I'd love to see Oliver!" she said, grinning from ear-to-ear. This man had a way of making her smile like a child again, and she loved that about him. "You are free to stay while I get ready if you'd like. I don't want you to feel like I'm pushing you out of here."

"As much as I'd like to stay and spend time with you, I know you've got a ton of work to do to get released, so I'll head out." Leaning in close to her ear, he added in a quiet voice, "Plus… I'm not sure I could look away when they get you out of that gown, so it's probably best to go so we can avoid a very awkward moment between you and I and this nurse…"

Molly laughed out loud, grabbing her stomach as the stabbing pain struck. She winced, but still smiled through it at him. "Shame on you, Owen!" she said.

Owen kissed her, laughing as he walked out of the room. He looked back one last time, need and love written all over his expression. She smiled and waved as she watched his beautiful behind walk away. She hated to see him go, but she could watch that hind end all day every day! It was a good thing she'd be at her parents' place and not Owens. She was pretty sure she'd end up hurt and back in the hospital if she was there, because her feelings and his body would get her into some trouble for sure!

"Man… that one's a looker for sure!" Shelby said, smiling at Molly. "And he sure seems to love you. It's written all over his face every time he looks at you."

"Yeah… I'm very lucky. He is definitely a patient man. I just have a lot to figure out in my head before I can fully give him my heart, you know?" she asked, not quite sure what answer she was looking for or why she was talking to a stranger about her love life.

"I absolutely understand that, and I think you are doing the right thing. Give yourself all the time you need. If you two are meant to be together, one week or ten weeks won't matter. My personal opinion is that people tend to leap before learning, and that's not typically a very good idea. Take the time to know him and to know your own heart before you make a decision that affects the rest of your life."

Shelby and Molly talked like old friends while she removed Molly's IV and got her unhooked from all the cords and monitors. Molly felt so much better when they were all off of her. Next, Shelby helped her get to her feet, taking a moment to regain her bearings. She walked with her to the bathroom, Molly taking her time as her muscles ached and screamed at her. In the bathroom, Molly sat on a seat in the shower, removing her gown and preparing to wash. Shelby handed her a washcloth and turned the water on for her, making sure it was the right temperature before excusing herself from the bathroom.

"There's a call button right next to you in the shower, so if you need me just pull the cord. I'll be just outside in the room. The soap and shampoo are on the wall there as well."

"Okay, thank you," Molly answered, loving the feeling as the water flowed over her body. She took her time in the shower, allowing the hot water to soothe her aching joints. She washed her hair and her body, thankful for the opportunity to feel clean again. When she finished up, she shut the water off and grabbed the towel that had been hung for her on the rack by the shower. She toweled off as best she could before calling Shelby back in.

Shelby came into the bathroom with Molly's a fresh gown and helped her back into it. She walked back to the bed with her and helped Molly back into it. Molly felt refreshed and renewed, and a little less pain in her body.

"As soon as your parents get here with your clothes, we can get you dressed and get you on your way home!" Shelby said, smiling. "Have you called them yet?"

"No… I better do that quick. They only live a little way from here, so I'd assume they'd be here in an hour or so. Is that okay?"

"Absolutely! Tell them to take their time. You can just get a little more rest in while you wait for them," Shelby answered. "I'll go fill your mug with fresh ice water and then give you some time to relax."

Molly grabbed her cell phone and called her mom, letting her know she needed some clothes so she could go to their house. Her mom was ecstatic, saying she'd be there within the hour.

Molly sat back in the bed and closed her eyes. She might as well get some rest while she waited. After all, there wasn't much else to do in this place!

* * *

Waylon's mind was a fog of confusion as he slowly drifted back to consciousness. It felt as though he had been trapped in a dark void for an eternity, lost in a sea of oblivion. But now, as he struggled to open his eyes, he was met with the harsh glare of fluorescent lights and the sterile scent of disinfectant.

For a moment, he lay there, disoriented and groggy, trying to make sense of his surroundings. It felt as though he had been pulled from the depths of a nightmare, only to find himself trapped in a waking dream. His entire body felt heavy, like it was attached to the bed somehow. He tried to lift his head but couldn't move. What the hell was going on? Where was he?

Waylon looked all around the room with his eyes, trying desperately to find someone to help him. He could see white walls, machines, tubes, wires, a clock, and emptiness. Nobody was there with him. He couldn't tell whether he was dreaming or awake, his eyes feeling heavy and full. Monitors were beeping a steady rhythm near his head… beep, beep, beep…

He was trying like everything to figure out what was happening and why he was here. His brain felt like thick fog had filled the spaces and was clogging his memory. He tried to move but it was like his body was separated from his brain. He felt nothing… just confusion and heaviness. He closed his eyes, trying to calm down and make sense of what was going on as the room started to spin in circles around him.

Slowly, as he sorted through the jumbled thoughts in his brain, the pieces began to fall into place. Blinding headlights, screeching tires, the sickening crunch of metal. He recalled the chaotic sensation of being thrown forward, the sharp pain that had ripped through his body as everything had gone suddenly dark.

And then, with a stark rush of clarity, it all came flooding back to him. The guilt, the shame, the overwhelming sense of despair that had consumed him prior to the accident. He had caused this – he had been behind the wheel, drunk and reckless, when he had collided head-on with another car.

"Oh shit... I hit someone!" he thought, terrified now for whomever he hit. *"How could I have been so damned stupid? What if I killed them?"*

The realization hit him like a physical blow, sending waves of nausea crashing over him. He tried to cry out, to scream in anguish at the magnitude of his own grave mistake. In the dark, silent room, all that emerged was a hoarse, rasping sound, muffled by the tube that had been inserted into his mouth to help him breathe.

Panic surged through him as he tried to sit up, his heart pounding in his chest as he grappled with the foreign object lodged in his throat. He felt as though he were suffocating, trapped in a nightmare that was apparently impossible to escape from.

And then, summoned by the monitor alarms that were sounding Waylon's distress, the doctor and nurses burst into the room, their faces drawn with concern. They rushed to his side, their voices a soothing chorus in the midst of his chaos.

"Easy now, Waylon," the doctor said, his tone gentle yet firm as he placed a reassuring hand on Waylon's shoulder. "You're safe now. We're here to help you."

Waylon's eyes flickered with fear as he looked up at them, his chest heaving with exertion. He felt like a wild animal caught in a snare, desperate to break free from the confines of his own body.

The nurses moved quickly and efficiently, their hands a blur of motion as they checked his vital signs and adjusted his IV lines. Waylon's blood pressure soared as they worked, his heart racing with a frantic rhythm that echoed in his ears like a drumbeat.

And then, with a deft motion, the doctor reached for the breathing tube, his hands steady as he prepared to remove it.

"Waylon," the doctor said in a steady tone, "I'm going to remove this breathing tube but I need you to calm down first. If you can control your breathing with it out, we will leave it out, but I need you to know that if your lungs aren't ready yet, we will have to sedate you and put it back in.

Waylon's breath caught in his throat as he braced himself for the sensation, his entire body tensing with anticipation. He looked at the young doctor, nodding his agreement, fear remaining in his eyes.

"Okay, this is going to be very uncomfortable for a few seconds, but it will feel much better once it's out. Take a nice deep breath for me and then let it back out slowly," the doctor said as he prepared to remove the tube.

As Waylon breathed out, the doctor pulled with a swift tug. Within seconds, the tube was out, leaving behind a raw, burning sensation in its wake. Waylon coughed violently, gasping for air, his chest heaving as he struggled to fill his lungs with oxygen.

"Easy now, Waylon," the doctor said, his voice a soothing balm amid Waylon's turmoil. "Take slow deep breaths. You're doing great."

After what felt like an eternity, Waylon's breathing steadied and became less labored. Oxygen was placed in his nose to help give him an extra boost for his now-exhausted lungs. As long as they didn't put that tube back in, he was just fine with whatever they did. He closed his eyes, willing his heart to stop beating so hard in his chest. His lungs felt like they were on fire, and he knew he needed to calm down, so they didn't have to work so hard.

When he opened his eyes again, Waylon looked at the doctor. "What..." was all he could hoarsely squeak out, wincing immediately in pain.

"Would you like me to walk you through everything we've done to this point and talk to you a bit about your injuries?" the doctor asked him calmly.

Waylon nodded weakly at the doctor, his throat obviously too raw and sore from the ordeal to speak yet. He felt as though he had been reborn, emerging from the darkness into the harsh light of reality. As he lay there, battered and broken in that hospital bed, he knew that there was no turning back.

The doctor and nurses hovered over him; their faces etched with concern as they explained the extent of his injuries. He had sustained multiple fractures, internal bleeding, and a traumatic brain injury. It would be a long and arduous road to recovery, fraught with pain and uncertainty.

"To be very honest with you, Mr. Walker, we did not know if you were going to ever wake up again," the doctor told him. "It is nothing short of a miracle that you are alive right now, and even more that you are alert and interacting with us."

The young doctor seemed completely shocked that Waylon was even alive, and that added to Waylon's sense of dread about what had happened. Still, there was one thing the doctor had left out. He hadn't told him about the person in the other car. Waylon had to know what had happened to them. He couldn't rest any more until he knew.

Motioning to the nurse in a gesture meant to tell her he needed a pen and paper; Waylon decided it was easiest to talk to them that way. She walked away and promptly came back with a pen and a small red notebook. He had no idea where she'd just found that, but it was no matter. He smiled his best smile at her and then did his best to write his question on the paper.

What happened to the other person?

Waylon looked back up at them, his eyes filled with remorse and regret. They both looked at each other as if they weren't sure whether to tell him.

"Oh God, no! I must have killed someone!" he thought to himself.

Seeing the panic in his eyes, the beautiful nurse quickly added, "Sorry, we just aren't sure if it's our place to tell you about that."

In a moment, the doctor added, "Maybe we should just let you rest for a while and then we can revisit this when you wake up. Does that work?"

Waylon nodded in frustration, suddenly feeling as though his eyes weighed a thousand pounds. Maybe the doc was right… maybe he needed to sleep for a little bit.

As he allowed his eyes to close and his body to drift back off to sleep, he had one last thought: This was obviously his second chance – a chance to atone for his mistakes, to make amends for the lives he had shattered. Now, he just needed to know exactly how 'shattered' he had made someone's life.

With that, Waylon gave up the fight and succumbed to the darkness of sleep.

Eighteen

Chapter 17

Molly had never felt as free and thankful as the moment her face hit the warm spring air for the first time in a week. Her accident was still fresh in her mind, but also felt like it had happened a long time prior. The last week had dragged on for an eternity, and she was happy to finally be leaving the confines of her hospital room and heading to her parents' house.

"Free at last!" she said, smiling as she breathed in the fresh air.

Shelby laughed as she wheeled Molly to the curb in her wheelchair. Her mother was walking next to them pushing a small black cart that had her flowers from Owen on it as well as her other belongings, medications, and tools she'd need for the first few days at home. "I bet it feels good to be outside again," she said as she looked out over the parking lot for Molly's father.

Before long, Molly's dad pulled up in her parents' SUV and parked just in front of the curb where Molly was sitting. He came around the car and started to load the items from the cart into the car as Shelby opened the door to help Molly get inside. Once she was in the seat, she helped her to buckle her belt, careful not to put too much pressure on her midsection.

"That's going to be a little sore for a while, Molly. I recommend you steer clear of cars for the first week or so until that incision heals up a little better.

Then it should feel much better when you put a seatbelt on," Shelby told her after seeing Molly wince when the belt pressed to her stomach.

"I won't be going anywhere for a while, I promise," Molly responded with assurance.

"Okay, well it was sure great to get to know you, Molly. I wish you all the best in your recovery!" she said as she moved back to close the door.

"Thank you very much for everything, Shelby. I really do appreciate how nice everyone here was to me," Molly said, not sure how to express her gratitude to the kind nurse who she had grown to like. The door closed and Molly rolled the window down a little, adding, "And don't forget to stop by the shoppe and try a cupcake on me when I'm back at work!"

"You can count on it!" Shelby replied, turning to push the cart and wheelchair back into the hospital.

"Okie dokie, kiddo," her dad said as he took his place behind the wheel. Her mom got in to the seat behind his and buckled her belt. "Ready to go?"

"I sure am!" Molly said excitedly. She couldn't wait to get out of here and into her own childhood home. She knew she'd heal much faster in the comfort of her own home… and eating her mother's wonderful home-cooked meals was definitely a better thought than the hospital food she'd been living on.

Her mom reached up and placed a hand on Molly's shoulder and Molly took it in hers. "I love you, sweetheart, and we are both so happy you are okay," she said through teary eyes.

"I love you too, Mom," Molly replied.

The ride home was quick and thankfully eventless. Molly hadn't considered the fear that she would have riding in a car again. She felt as though her nerves were shot, and she just wanted the ride to be over. Before she knew it, they were pulling into her parent's driveway. Her dad pulled the car into the garage and parked it in his usual spot. Then, he got out and came around to help Molly out of her seat.

Molly gingerly walked into the house and found a comfortable place on the sofa in the living room. She'd teased her parents when they sold their old sofa and bought one with electric seats, but now she was sure glad they had done that! She sat back and settled in, thanking her mom for the pillows she'd laid there for her to use to get comfortable. Her body still felt as though it had been through a war, but she was trying to get through the days without anything more than over the counter pain medications. She saved the heavier medicines for at night when it was hard to get comfortable and sleep. She hoped to be off those in the next couple of days as well.

As soon as she got comfortable, she heard a familiar meow. She turned her head slowly, seeing Snowflake come running towards her from the kitchen.

"Snowflake!" she said, happy to see her cat after a week without her. She figured she was still at Lily's place, but her mom and dad had obviously brought her here to welcome Molly home. Snowflake purred loudly as Molly pet her soft white fur.

"Now it feels like home," Molly told her mom as she started to feel her eyelids get heavy.

"We're so happy to have you here," her mom replied, leaning over to pet Snowflake on the head gently.

Molly and Snowflake snuggled in, and before long, Molly was asleep.

* * *

Molly's eyelids fluttered open, the early evening light filtering through the curtains and casting an amber glow around the room. Blinking away the remnants of sleep, she shifted on the sofa, the quiet of her parents' home enveloping her like a warm embrace. On the wall she could hear the light ticking of her mother's large grandfather clock. She remembered laying here as a child and sleeping in her father's arms, lulled by the gentle tick tock sound. It felt good to be back, to be surrounded by the familiar comforts of home after the chaos and despair of the hospital.

As she stretched her limbs, a tantalizing aroma wafted into the room, causing her stomach to grumble in anticipation. The scent of homemade bread, warm and inviting, filled the air, mingling with the comforting scent of spices and savory delights. The smell was filled with tender love and care, and it reminded her of all the times her family had gathered around the table, sharing a meal and creating memories with one another.

With a contented sigh, Molly moved the pillows from her side, knowing that she needed to walk to the bathroom, and dreading the process. She pushed the button on the side of the sofa and watched her feet slowly fall to the floor. Carefully, she used the side arm to pull herself up, wincing slightly as she felt the lingering soreness in her muscles from the accident. She had been through *so* much in the past week – the pain, the fear, the uncertainty – but now, as she stood in her mom and dad's cozy living room, she felt a sense of calm wash over her. Taking her first steps forward, she told herself that she'd survived so far, so she could definitely survive a trip to the bathroom.

As she made her way into the kitchen, she found her mother bustling about, her hands busy rolling meatballs for supper. The sight of her brought a smile to Molly's lips, a swell of gratitude filling her heart for the unwavering support and love that her mother had shown her throughout her ordeal.

"Hey, Mom," Molly greeted, her voice soft with emotion as she approached her mother's side. "What smells so amazing?"

Her mother turned, her face lighting up with a warm smile when she saw Molly up and about. "Fresh bread," she replied, her eyes twinkling with affection. "Your favorite."

Molly's heart swelled with warmth at her mother's thoughtfulness. It was moments like these that reminded her of just how lucky she was to have such a loving family by her side, especially in times of need. "I'm just heading to the bathroom quickly… well, slowly actually," she added, laughing gently.

"Do you need any help? I can wash up quick and help if you do."

"No, I think I can get it. I'll yell if I do though," Molly replied.

"Okay, just let me know," her mom said with a concerned smile.

Molly made the short and slow walk to the bathroom. She was thankful that her father had installed a bar to hold onto for her grandmother a few years ago in the bathroom. Her grandma Ruth had stayed with Molly's parents for a short while before her passing. She'd had a very aggressive form of cancer and Molly's dad couldn't stand the thought of her dying in a nursing home somewhere with no family near her, so she'd stayed with them until the very end.

Molly's mom had been in complete agreement with her husband about his mother staying with them. It was one of the things Molly admired most about her parents. They may not always get along, but they always had each other's backs. It was something Molly had always tried to emulate in her own marriage. Unfortunately, hers hadn't gone so well.

Molly sighed as she stood and washed her hands. She looked in the mirror. She hadn't really looked at her own face since the accident, and the sight nearly made her jump. She had small cuts all over her face from the glass, one of them, just above her left eyebrow, had needed 4 stitches. Each cut was starting to heal, and the bruising she had on both eyes and near the cut on her forehead were all starting to turn a purplish-yellow color.

"I look like a nightmare!" she said, tears filling her eyes.

Hearing her crying, her father knocked on the bathroom door. "Honey, are you okay? Do you need some help?"

Molly opened the door, looking into her father's eyes with sadness. "I can't believe Owen called me beautiful. I look like something out of a horror movie!" she cried.

Her father smiled, gently hugging her. She sank into his arms, letting the tears flow. "Sweetheart, Owen is absolutely right. No matter what marks you may have on your face from the accident, you are the most beautiful thing I've ever laid eyes on… besides your mother, of course…"

Molly pulled away, looking up at her dad. She rolled her eyes at him, thinking he was being ridiculous. "You must need *your* eyes checked too!" she said, smirking at him.

Her father laughed. "Nope, just had them checked last week! They are perfectly fine!"

Molly's dad slid to the left so she could get by him to head back to the sofa. He followed her, helping her into the comfy position she had been in before. He covered her with the cozy blanket and leaned down to give her a kiss on the forehead.

"Molly, you will always be beautiful to all those who love you… including

Owen. All you have to do is watch that man look at you when he walks in the room to know that he has been bitten by the darn bug that got me 38 years ago too. That bug is ruthless, I tell you!"

Molly laughed again. Her dad had always had the ability to make her laugh, and she appreciated that now more than ever.

"Thanks, dad," she said, smiling.

"No problem! I just speak the truth. There's a lot of wisdom in this head of mine after all these years! I keep trying to tell your mother that, but she doesn't seem to agree," he said with a perplexed look on his face.

Molly rolled her eyes for the second time in 5 minutes. Her dad had a way of taking her mind off of things when she was sad. He excused himself to head back out to the yard to finish up. "If I don't get the lawn done, your mother won't let me eat supper!" he said as he walked out the front door.

Molly heard her mom laugh in the kitchen. "That man!" she said. "I've been waiting two days for him to finish that lawn up, so he may just be right!"

Molly leaned back in the seat, wishing she knew where her box of books was so she could at least read or something. She was getting really tired of just sitting around all the time. After a little bit, her mom came into the room and sat next to her on the sofa.

"How are you feeling after your nap, sweetheart?" her mom asked with genuine concern written on her aging face.

Molly's mother was still beautiful after all these years. She had a soft peach complexion and wore very little makeup. Her hair was worn long with natural wave all throughout it. It was gray now, with just a hint of the dark brown it used to be. Her eyes were kind and a stunning shade of blue. When she smiled, her entire face seemed to light up.

Molly sighed, feeling a rush of emotions welling up inside her. "I'm okay, Mom," she replied, her voice tinged with uncertainty. "Just a little sore, but I'll manage."

Her mother nodded sympathetically, reaching out to gently brush a strand of hair from Molly's face. "I'm so glad you're home, honey," she said softly. "We've been so worried about you." Tears filled her mother's eyes as she spoke, and for the first time Molly thought about how hard this must have been for her parents.

Molly's throat tightened with emotion as she looked into her mother's eyes, seeing the love and concern shining there. She knew she was lucky to have such a caring family by her side, especially in times like these.

Taking a deep breath, Molly gathered her courage and spoke up. "Mom, there's something I wanted to talk to you about," she began hesitantly. "It's about Owen."

Her mother's expression softened; her eyes filled with understanding. "Sure, sweetheart," she encouraged gently. "You know you can tell me anything."

Molly took a deep breath, steeling herself for the words that were about to spill from her lips. "I… I love him, Mom," she admitted, her voice barely above a whisper. "I'm in love with Owen."

Her mother's eyes widened in surprise, but there was a warmth in her gaze that spoke volumes. "Oh, Molly," she murmured, squeezing her daughter's hand gently. "That's wonderful news, sweetheart."

Molly's smile faltered as she voiced her deepest fears. "I'm just… I'm scared, Mom," she confessed, her voice trembling with emotion. "I'm scared of getting attached to Oliver and then something happening to him. I'm scared that I won't be a good mother. I'm scared that I'll be completely attached to him and then Owen will leave me, or something will happen, and I'll lose him just like I did with Hannah!"

Her mother's fingers tightened on her hand, offering comfort and reassurance. "Oh, honey," she murmured, pressing a kiss to Molly's forehead. "You are going to be an amazing mother to that little boy, Molly. I have no doubt about that."

Molly's eyes filled with tears as she listened to her mother's words of encouragement. It was exactly what she needed to hear – a reminder that she was capable of love and strength, even in the face of her deepest fears.

"Sweetheart, your precious Hannah gave you a gift that no person or distance can ever take away," she said, smiling at her daughter through her own tears.

"What is that?" Molly asked, confused.

"Hannah made you a mother. You may not have your little girl in your arms, but she's in your heart. You became a mother the moment she was created inside of you. You protected and loved her for every moment of her life, and that is such an amazing gift. Not even death can take that away, not if you don't let it."

Molly was crying now. She had never thought of it that way. She missed her little girl every moment of every day.

"Mom, I've never told anyone this, but I talk to Hannah. It was actually something my therapist recommended, but I love it. I go to this little bench in the park near my work, and I sit and talk with her. It feels *so* good to have that time with just her and I. It's special and just between us," she explained, hoping her mom wouldn't' think she was crazy.

"Oh, Molly, I think that's wonderful! What an amazing idea!"

Molly was so happy that her mom understood. Of course she did… she'd always been the one that had been a voice of reason and calm for Molly when she was spiraling or upset.

"The first day I sat there, this beautiful butterfly flew over and sat on my leg. It was like it just wanted to sit there and enjoy the day. It eventually flew off, its beautiful little wings fluttering in the breeze. The crazy thing was that the next time I went there, it came back!"

Molly looked at her mom, expecting to see her laughing, but instead she saw… understanding? How could she possibly think she wasn't nuts or something?

"I see. That's pretty incredible, Molly. I think your little girl was sending you a message that she hears you and enjoys that time with you as much as you do with her," her mom said, smiling at her daughter.

"Do you think so?" Molly asked her, hopefulness written all over her face.

"I do, and I'm really happy that you are making time to have those special moments with Hannah. I also have something to tell *you*, and I think you might find it quite interesting!" she said.

"What?" Molly asked inquisitively.

"Well… the other day, I was in the garden planting the cucumber plants when a beautiful little butterfly landed on a tulip that had just opened near me. It sat there for a long time, just like you described at the park that day.

I wasn't sure why it did that, but I just sat and watched it for a while. Then, just like you said, it fluttered its precious little wings and flew into the air and away. It wasn't until you told me your story just now that I realized the significance of that sweet little creature."

Molly stared at her mom in disbelief. Her little girl was okay, and she had sent a sign to her momma to show her she was there with her. Was that even possible?

"The truth is, sweetheart, that no matter if you believe in those sorts of things or not, it can still be a comfort to you in the times when you are feeling sad. Those times are never going to end, unfortunately, but you really shouldn't wish them away. They are a reminder of the people we lost, and you can't miss someone if you never loved them."

Molly and her mom sat together for a little bit, just enjoying the quiet moment together. They hadn't had time to sit with one another for a long time. Molly had been so busy at The Sweet Sprinkle, and her mom was always running here or there. She made a mental note that she needed to do this more often.

"One more thing I thought of when you were talking earlier was that you should consider talking to your doctor about your concerns with having a baby. I know you aren't at that point right now, but I also know that you have thought about it a lot. Maybe the doctor can help shed some light on the possibilities and the risks of having another baby so that you can put those fears to bed too. I think there are so many worries in that beautiful head of yours that you aren't allowing yourself to find happiness for fear of the sadness that may follow. Am I right?

Molly thought about what her mother was saying. After a bit, she said, "Yeah, I think you may be right. I guess it couldn't hurt to ask." It was a daunting prospect, but Molly knew it was probably the right thing to do.

Just then, there was a knock at the door, and Molly's heart skipped a beat with excitement. Her mother had told her that some people were coming over for supper and she couldn't wait to see them. Her mother went to the door and opened it to welcome their guests.

It took about two seconds for Molly to figure out that it was Lily and Mia.

They both came into the living room in a flurry, each with their arms filled with gifts. Lily had a beautiful bouquet of wildflowers in a vase, and balloons in the opposite hand. Mia, on the other hand, had a gift bag in one hand and a familiar box in the other. Lily sat the flowers on the end table and let the balloons hang off it. Mia came over and sat next to Molly on the sofa, handing her the bright pink box that had a sticker on it that read: The Sweet Sprinkle. It was her favorite cupcake, german chocolate with her specialty coconut buttercream frosting on it! She smiled as her stomach growled.

"Thank you both very much!" she said, smiling at her two best friends in the whole world. She had missed seeing them while she was in the hospital. She remembered them each being there once or twice, but she had been pretty out of it from the pain meds, so her brain was a bit foggy.

As they chatted and laughed together, Molly felt a sense of warmth and gratitude wash over her. She was surrounded by love and support, and she knew they would be there for her through this whole mess.

Before long, there was another knock sounded at the door, and Molly was totally surprised as she watched Owen and Oliver step inside, their faces bright with excitement. Oliver bounded forward, his eyes sparkling with joy. Owen quickly grabbed the little boy before he could jump up into Molly's arms. He knew that would hurt her, but Oliver didn't understand that. He gently placed the boy next to Molly on the sofa.

"Molly has an owie, remember? You can sit by her, but you have to try to sit still and not jump up on her, okay?" he reminded the excited little boy.

Oliver nodded at his daddy, and then snuggled into Molly's side as she put her arm around him.

Molly's heart melted as she hugged the little boy close, feeling a rush of love and affection wash over her. In that moment, she knew with absolute certainty that she was exactly where she was meant to be – with Owen and Oliver by her side.

As they all sat down to supper together, Molly felt a sense of peace settle over her like a comforting blanket. Her mother's mashed potatoes, corn casserole, and Swedish meatballs had never tasted so delicious, and she savored every bite, grateful for the simple pleasures of home and family. She looked around the table, thankful for each and every person at it.

After supper, Owen helped Molly get settled back in on the sofa. Everyone came back to the living room to sit and talk. Before long, Oliver got tired of talking, asking, "Daddy, can we play a game… please?"

Owen smiled at him. "Buddy, I think we'd better get going pretty soon. Molly's had a long day and she's probably getting very tired."

The devastated look on Oliver's face destroyed Molly. She couldn't stand seeing him so sad.

"It's okay, Owen. We can play a game if you can find one that I can do from here," she said, smiling as Oliver jumped up with excitement.

"Thank you, Molly!" he said as he bounced around the room, clearly thrilled with her decision to play with him.

"I think there's a few games in that cabinet just below the T.V. there, Owen. You can go ahead and look through them if you'd like. Maybe there's one in there that Oliver would like."

Owen opened the cabinet door and Oliver immediately grabbed the Zingo game. Molly wasn't sure when her mom had gotten that game, or what it even *was* for that matter, but Oliver obviously knew of it and loved it, so that was good enough for her.

After explaining how to play, they all grabbed their Zingo cards and got ready.

Molly settled herself comfortably on the sofa, a soft cushion supporting her still-recovering body, while the others arranged themselves in a circle on the floor around the game.

Oliver's eyes sparkled with excitement as he eagerly examined the colorful Zingo board he'd chosen. "Are we ready to play, guys?" he asked, bouncing with anticipation.

"Absolutely, buddy!" Owen replied, his voice filled with enthusiasm as he slid the Zingo slider, exposing the first two tiles beneath. "Let's see who can fill their board first!"

Molly watched with a smile as the game got underway, her heart swelling with affection as she observed the joy and camaraderie shared between her friends and Owen's little boy. Despite the aches and pains that still lingered from the accident, she couldn't help but feel a sense of warmth and contentment wash over her.

As the game progressed, laughter filled the room as tiles were matched and boards filled up. Oliver's giggles were infectious and his enthusiasm contagious as he cheered on his teammates each time they yelled "Zingo!" faster than he did.

Molly couldn't help but marvel at the sight before her – Owen's easy smile, Lily and Mia's infectious laughter, and Oliver's boundless energy. It was moments like these that made her realize just how lucky she was to have found her way into their lives… and to have survived the accident so that she could be here right now.

Every now and again, as she watched Owen interact with Oliver, Molly found herself catching glimpses of something deeper – a tenderness in his gaze, a warmth in his smile, each speaking volumes about the love he had for his little boy. With each passing moment, she found herself falling a little more in love with him.

As the game ended, with Lily emerging victorious as the Zingo champion, the group erupted into cheers and applause. Oliver was thrilled with the outcome, his face lighting up with delight as he high fived each of his competitors in turn.

"Great job, everyone!" Owen exclaimed, his eyes shining with pride as he ruffled Oliver's hair affectionately. "That was a lot of fun, but we need to get going now, buddy. You need a bath and Molly needs some rest."

Oliver whined a bit, but he got up and gave Molly a gentle hug before going to the door to put his slip-on shoes back on. Molly's mom handed him a little baggie with treats in it for the next day as she hugged him and helped him get his spring jacket back on.

Molly turned her attention to Owen as he leaned in to kiss her goodnight. It was a simple and gentle kiss, but with it came a surge of emotion welling up inside her.

"I love you," Owen said quietly.

Before she could second guess herself, she motioned for him to come closer.

"I love you, too," she whispered into his ear.

Owen leaned his head onto hers for a moment, the motion intimate and sweet. When he pulled away, she could see tears in his eyes. Oliver was calling his name now, and there were too many eyes and ears near to talk about what had just happened, so he kissed her one more time and then joined his son in the doorway.

As Molly watched him leave, a smile tugging at the corners of her lips, she knew with absolute certainty that everything was going to be okay. As soon as she was feeling better, she was going to move in with Owen and Oliver. The decision made her feel so much better… like a weight had been lifted from her.

The last couple of years had been horrible, and she'd had so many moments where she had wished she'd just go to sleep and wake up with her little girl, but she'd pushed through and she'd persevered, and now she knew that with Owen by her side, she was ready to face whatever the future held.

The difference was that she was no longer alone with her grief and her fears. Now, she and Owen would face the unknown *together*.

Nineteen

Chapter 18

Molly stepped out of her car, the fresh June air in Wisconsin coming alive with the vibrant energy of summer. She had gotten up early today to watch the sun rise over the rolling hills and verdant landscapes of her parent's small town. She'd even taken a short walk before getting ready for her first day back at work. When she'd taken that first breath of air, she found it to be filled with the promise of warmth and renewal.

On her 20-minute drive into the city, the streets all around her were a bustle with activity as locals and visitors alike emerge from their winter hibernation to bask in the long-awaited sunshine.

She looked over towards the park near her shop, wishing she had time to go sit awhile. This morning, the sound of laughter and chatter filled the air, mingling with the cheerful melodies of songbirds perched in the towering trees that lined the sidewalks. She could see a couple of young children being pushed on the swing by their parents. The scene made her wish she was all moved in and ready to start her new adventure with Owen and Oliver. She hadn't wanted to rush it, but today, more than ever, she wished that she could.

The scent of freshly cut grass traveled through the air, carried on the gentle breeze that rustled through the branches. On the other side of her shoppe was a quant flower shop, and she could smell the sweet aroma of blooming flowers – lilacs, roses, and lilies – filling the air with their intoxicating perfume. She needed to remember to stop in there later today to order a bouquet for her mother for her birthday. Her mom absolutely loved orchids, so she was hoping they'd have some there for her to choose from. She made a mental note as she shut her car door.

In early June, Wisconsin was a place of beauty and possibility, where the sights, sounds, and smells of summer came together to create an unforgettable experience for all who were lucky enough to experience it firsthand.

The aroma of freshly baked cupcakes filled the air as Molly stepped back into The Sweet Sprinkle, her heart fluttering with a mixture of nerves and excitement. It had been almost six weeks since she'd been in her beloved cupcake shoppe, and the familiar sights and smells brought a flood of memories rushing back.

As she bustled about the kitchen, whipping up batches of batter and swirling frosting onto delicate cupcakes, Molly couldn't shake the feeling of anticipation that tingled in the pit of her stomach. She knew that today would be different – that today, she would take a step forward, towards healing and happiness. She was hoping to talk to Mia about it, but for some reason she hadn't gotten in yet. She and Jeff must have had a "morning in" as they liked to call it. Mia had messaged her that morning and Mia had said she'd be a bit late but didn't give a reason. Oh well, this gave her some time to herself to get back in the swing of things.

Just as she was placing the finishing touches on a tray of lemon meringue cupcakes, the tinkling of the bell above the door announced the arrival of two familiar faces – Lily and Mia, her faithful friends and co-conspirators in all things sweet.

"Surprise!" Lily exclaimed, her eyes sparkling with mischief as she and Mia swept into the shop, arms laden with balloons and bouquets of flowers. "Welcome back, Molly!"

Molly's heart swelled with gratitude as she embraced her friends, feeling a rush of warmth and affection wash over her. "Thank you, guys," she murmured, her voice choked with emotion. "It's good to be back."

Molly removed her apron and helped the two co-conspirators find a home for the balloons and flowers. Then, they all settled in around a cozy table in the corner, sipping on steaming cups of coffee and nibbling on freshly baked treats. Molly knew the two of them were up to something, but she couldn't quite figure out what. It always made her nervous when those two were actually getting along so well. Plus, they had a funny look on their faces when they looked at each other a little bit ago.

Lily cleared her throat suddenly, wasting no time in getting down to business, as usual.

"So, spill the beans, Molly," Mia demanded, her eyes twinkling with curiosity. "What's the deal with you and Owen?"

Molly's cheeks flushed crimson as she found herself at a loss for words. She had been so focused on her own internal struggles that she hadn't had a chance to tell her friends about the whirlwind romance that had blossomed between her and Owen. Over the last month, he'd been over to see her almost every day, and she and Oliver had read more books together than Molly even knew existed! She'd gone over for supper a few times over the last couple of weeks, and she and Owen had been doing some serious making out. She wasn't about to share that with the "gab twins" over here though!

Taking a deep breath, Molly gathered her thoughts and dove in, sharing the details of her blossoming relationship with Owen and her growing affection for his son, Oliver. She told them about her fears and uncertainties, her hopes and dreams for the future, and the overwhelming sense of happiness that filled her heart whenever she was with them.

Lily and Mia listened intently, their expressions shifting from curiosity to excitement as they took in Molly's words. They both loved her very much, and Molly knew that. She assured them it was all going to be okay, and that she'd gone to see her therapist several times over the last month. She was doing the hard work, and it was definitely paying off.

Molly shifted gears and told them that she had fallen in love with Owen and her desire to move forward with him. They both looked at each other with excitement and joy, and Molly breathed a sigh of relief that she didn't even know she'd been holding in. For some reason, she'd thought that they wouldn't approve.

"I'm so happy for you, Molly," Lily exclaimed, reaching across the table to squeeze her friend's hand. "You deserve all the love and happiness in the world."

Mia nodded in agreement, her eyes shining with tears of joy. "I'm sorry for doubting Owen," she admitted, her voice filled with remorse. "It sounds like he's exactly what you need right now."

"He definitely is," Molly agreed.

"And he's hot as hell!" Lily added, causing the room to fill with the laughter of the three friends.

When they calmed down, Mia put her hand on Molly's. "Molly, I have something I want to tell you, and I'm not quite sure how you're going to feel about it."

Molly could see that Mia was worried, and it made her nervous.

"Mia, I'm sure whatever it is will be just fine. Now let's hear it…" she said, smiling reassuringly at her best friend and business partner.

"Um… well… I wanted you to hear from me first. I'm pregnant…" Mia said with apprehension.

Molly gasped. "Wait… what?" she squealed excitedly. "Why aren't you jumping up and down with joy then?" she asked her.

"Well, I'm really happy but I was really worried about how you might feel about it after everything that happened with Hannah," Mia explained, relief taking the place of fear on her face.

"Oh, Mia. I'm so sorry you were worried about telling me! I am so unbelievably happy for you and Jeff! Seriously! I am fine… I promise!" she said, standing up to hug her friend. "A baby… I can't even believe it!"

Lily stood and hugged the two women too, giggles filling the empty space where tension had been just moments prior. "I *love* being Auntie Lily!" she said.

The three of them sat back down, talking excitedly about Mia's pregnancy. She was due in January, and they had found out while Molly had been in the hospital. She'd wanted to wait until Molly was feeling better to tell her and Lily.

Molly was so happy for her friend. While Mia told them about her hopes and dreams for this pregnancy and this baby, she sat back, quietly thanking Claire for all the help she'd given her over the last six months. She realized in that moment that she'd come farther than she'd even known. She was happy for her friend, and there wasn't even one single feeling of jealousy or sadness. She was nervous for her, and she supposed that came with the territory, but she was happy just the same.

As they talked, the bells above the door rang out once more, and Molly's heart dropped into her stomach as she looked up to see Waylon, in a wheelchair pushed by his friend Lance, in the doorway, his expression filled with defeat.

Instantly, Lily and Mia leaped to their feet, their protective instincts kicking into overdrive as they moved to shield Molly from harm. But to their surprise, Molly held up a hand, silencing their protests.

"It's okay, guys," she said softly, her voice steady with determination. "I'll be fine."

As Waylon approached, his friend by his side, Molly felt a wave of compassion wash over her. Despite everything that had happened between them, she couldn't help but feel a pang of sympathy for the man she had once loved with all her heart.

"Hey, Mol," Waylon murmured, his voice thick with emotion as he wheeled himself closer to her. "I was hoping we could talk for a bit."

Molly hesitated for a moment, her heart pounding in her chest, before nodding silently in agreement. She knew that she needed closure – for herself, for Waylon, and for the memories of the life they had once shared together.

"Sure, Way. Why don't we go for a little walk to the park so we can talk for a bit, is that okay?" she asked him.

"I'd really like that," he replied, the sadness in his voice pulling at her heartstrings.

As they made their way to the park bench outside, Molly felt a sense of heaviness settle over her. This was it – the moment she had been dreading and yet secretly longing for, all at once. Waylon stopped close to the bench and, with help from Lance, got up from the chair and transferred to sit next to her.

"Thank you, Lance. I appreciate the assist," he said, smiling at his friend.

"No problem, Way. I'm going to run over to the bookstore really quick. It's my niece's birthday this weekend and I need a gift. I'll be back in a half hour or so, if that's okay," Lance responded.

"Sounds good," Waylon nodded.

Turning towards Molly, he felt his throat tightening with emotion as he struggled to find the right words to say. "I… I don't even know where to begin, Molly," he admitted, his voice thick with regret. "I'm so sorry for what I did to you – for almost killing you. I hate myself for it, and I don't think I'll ever be able to forgive myself."

Molly reached out a hand, resting it gently on Waylon's arm. "I know, Waylon," she said softly, her voice filled with compassion. "I know you didn't mean for any of this to happen. But the fact remains that it did, and we both have to live with the consequences."

Waylon nodded, his eyes brimming with tears as he looked into Molly's eyes. "I've been going to therapy, Molly," he confessed, his voice barely above a whisper. "I'm trying to understand why I started drinking after we lost Hannah – why I couldn't cope with the pain in a healthy way. I'm learning, Molly, and I'm trying to do better."

Molly's heart ached with sadness as she listened to Waylon's words. She knew how much he had struggled in the wake of their daughter's death – how he had buried his grief in alcohol, unable to face the pain head-on. And while she couldn't condone his actions, she couldn't help but feel a pang of sympathy for the man she had once loved with all her heart.

"I'm proud of you, Waylon," she said quietly, her voice filled with genuine warmth. "I'm proud that you're taking steps to heal – to become the man you were meant to be."

"I just…I want you to know that I still love you – that I'll always love you. And if there's even the slightest chance for us to be together again, I'll do whatever it takes to make things right."

"I appreciate you saying that, Way, but we have both changed a lot since

Hannah passed away, and it's time for us to move on and go in different directions. I hope you can understand that."

Waylon's heart sank as he heard Molly's words, the weight of her rejection crushing him like a ton of bricks. But deep down, he knew that she was right – that their relationship had run its course, and that it was time for both to let go and move on.

With a heavy heart, Waylon reached out to grasp Molly's hand, squeezing it gently in his own. "I wish you nothing but happiness, Molly," he said softly, his voice filled with sincerity. "And I hope that one day, you'll be able to find it."

Molly nodded, her eyes brimming with tears as she leaned forward to press a gentle kiss against Waylon's cheek. "Thank you, Waylon," she whispered, her voice choked with emotion. "And…and I'm proud of you too. I really am."

"I don't deserve your forgiveness, but I'd still like to ask for it," he said, looking at her with despair.

"Waylon," Molly said, letting out the breath she'd been holding in. "I forgave you a long time ago, at the hospital when you were still in a coma. You probably didn't have any idea I was there, but I was. I held your hand, and I told you I loved you and that I forgave you."

Molly's eyes filled with tears as she poured her heart out to the man who she'd once planned to spend the rest of her life with.

Sitting side by side on the weathered wooden bench, Molly and Waylon spoke openly and honestly for the first time in years. He apologized profusely for the pain he had caused her, his voice trembling with emotion as he spoke of his regrets and his struggles to come to terms with his actions.

Molly listened in silence, her heart aching with compassion for the man before her. Despite everything, she couldn't deny the depth of his remorse, or the sincerity of his desire to make amends. As they talked, Molly found herself opening up in ways she never thought possible. She spoke of her own pain and grief, her fears and insecurities, and the difficult journey she had been on since the accident.

For the first time, Waylon allowed himself to be vulnerable – to share his innermost thoughts and feelings with her. If only he had been able to do this before… before their world got turned upside down.

Molly looked at the man who had once held her heart in his hands. He had obviously been doing amazing work in therapy, and she was so thankful for that. Maybe something good could come from this tragic accident, and if so, she'd thank God for it.

Waylon's tears continued to flow, mirroring Molly's. They sat quietly together like that for a few minutes, just listening to the birds and the wind whisper through the trees. Molly looked down and laughed softly as her precious butterfly friend fluttered in and landed on her hand. She slowly lifted it so they could see the beautiful creature.

"Well, would you look at that?" Waylon said, smiling. "I've never seen anything like it."

"I know you'll never believe me, Way, but I think this is a sign from Hannah that we are both going to be okay."

Waylon looked at her with curiosity, then laughed. "I suppose that's possible… or, maybe we are both crazy… one or the other!"

Seconds later, the butterfly fluttered away again, and they were both left in silence.

When Lance returned, Molly hugged Waylon tightly, her heart heavy with emotion. "Goodbye, Waylon," she whispered, her voice thick with tears. "I hope we can be friends again someday."

As she made her way back to The Sweet Sprinkle, Molly felt a sense of lightness wash over her – a weight lifted from her shoulders that she hadn't even realized was there. As she stepped through the door, she knew with absolute certainty that she was ready to move forward, no matter what lie ahead. For now, though, she had a lot of work to get caught up on, so she decided she'd better get back to it!

"Are you okay, Mol?" Mia asked when she walked back into the shop.

"I'm actually good, Mia. We had a really good talk, and I think Waylon's finally on his way towards working through all the grief of losing our Hannah. Maybe this whole mess will have a good outcome for both of us…" Molly said, smiling at her friend.

"Did you hit your head out there or something? You're acting a little too cool and calm about this, Mol." Mia said, frustrated with her friend's ability to just "brush off" what happened.

"No," Molly replied with a giggle. "I just mean that he's going to therapy and he's working through his grief, and that makes me happy. I tried for a year to get him to do that with now luck. Maybe this was the wakeup call he needed."

"Well, I hope so," Mia said. "I know you both went through a horrendous deal when you lost Hannah, and I have no idea what to say to help make that better, although I really wish I did."

Molly hugged her friend. "I know that, and I love you for it," she told her, smiling. "Now," she added, "we'd better get to work on that cake for the Anderson anniversary party tomorrow. They'll be here early in the morning to grab it.

The two friends got to work decorating, piping, making frosting flowers, and writing on the beautiful two-tier white cake with red and lime green accents. She had known the Andersons for quite a few years, and she wanted their cake to be perfect.

Lily popped her head in at lunchtime and ate her sandwich while she chatted the two women up and down about some crazy lady who'd come in to get her beehive fixed up. Lily always had funny stories to tell, and Molly appreciated her humor very much. It was one of the reasons she loved her so much.

Molly worked so hard that she lost track of time, only stopping to look at her phone when it buzzed a notice of a message coming in. She touched it with her pinky, careful not to get frosting all over the screen. It lit up, showing that Owen had sent her a message.

Hey beautiful. I was wondering if you'd like to go out for pizza with me tonight? We can have some good food and talk. Would that work for you? My mom is taking Oliver to the carnival over in Delimar, so we'll have some privacy to chat. Let me know! ~Owen

Molly smiled. Her stomach instantly flipped, and she felt those wonderful butterflies she always felt when Owen walked into a room. She couldn't wait to move in with him and Oliver, to finally get started on the next chapter of her life together with them. She went to the sink and washed her hands so she could message him back.

Grabbing her phone she typed: *Sounds fun to me… I'll run home after work and shower quick and then be ready around 5. See you then!*

The rest of the day went by in a blur. All Molly could think about was being in Owen's arms, smelling his cologne and feeling his heartbeat against hers. He had a way of making her feel like the only person on the planet, and she loved how safe she felt in his arms. At two o'clock, she and Mia locked the shop up and parted ways. Molly had a therapy appointment that afternoon, and she didn't want to be late.

* * *

"Good afternoon, Molly!" the receptionist at Claire's office said when she looked up and saw her enter the office. "It sure is a beautiful day out today, isn't it?"

"Yes, it is for sure," Molly replied, smiling at the kind woman.

"I'll flag you as here so Claire can come get you when she's ready. You can have a seat," she said, typing into the computer as she spoke.

"Sounds good. Thank you," Molly answered, making her way to the semi-comfortable chairs in the waiting room. Molly felt a mix of nerves and excitement bubbling within her. It had been a whirlwind of a week, filled with unexpected twists and turns, and she was eager to share it all with Claire. She had so many things to tell her about during this session.

Molly couldn't wait for her date with Owen tonight either. She and Owen had been 'dating' for the last few weeks, and she was thoroughly enjoying her time getting to know him better. Plus, she got the bonus of hanging out and playing with Oliver. She was amazed at how easily she was adapting to the 'family' life with them.

"Molly, come on in," Claire said in a friendly voice, pulling Molly from her thoughts.

Molly followed Claire into her office, sitting in her usual spot. As Claire welcomed her with a warm smile, Molly took a deep breath, then she began recounting the events of the past few days.

"I guess I'll start with my surprise visit from Waylon the other day at work," Molly said, jumping into the story.

"Really? I'm curious, why did Waylon stop by?" Claire asked curiously.

"Well, he wanted to apologize for driving drunk and almost killing both of us. He told me that he's in therapy now, which I think is fantastic. He also said that he hoped I'd forgive him and that he'd like to try to make things work again between us."

"And what did you tell him?" Claire asked gently, her eyes filled with compassion.

Molly hesitated for a moment before answering. "I told him that I *had* forgiven him," she said quietly. "But I also told him that our marriage is over. It was a difficult conversation, but I knew it was the right thing to do."

Claire nodded understandingly. "It takes a lot of courage to confront the past and move forward," she said. "I'm proud of you for being able to do that, Molly."

A sense of relief washed over Molly as she heard Claire's words of encouragement. It was reassuring to know that she had someone like Claire in her corner, cheering her on every step of the way.

"Thank you," Molly replied, smiling. "It actually wasn't as hard as I thought that it would be. I know how much we have both been through, and I know how much he was hurting. It wasn't the real Waylon that spiraled like that with the liquor. It was the grieving Waylon. It's not as hard to forgive when you think of it that way."

As the conversation turned to her decision to move in with Owen, Molly felt a surge of excitement coursing through her veins. She spoke of her love for Owen and Oliver, and how the thought of starting a new chapter with them filled her with happiness.

"It's like my heart just knows it's the right thing to do," she said, a smile tugging at the corners of her lips. "For the first time in a long time, I feel like I'm allowing myself to be happy again."

Claire smiled warmly at Molly, her eyes shining with pride. "You've come such a long way, Molly," she said. "I truly believe that you deserve all the happiness in the world, but *you* needed to believe that *yourself* as well."

As their session came to an end, Molly felt a renewed sense of hope and optimism coursing through her veins. She knew that there would still be challenges ahead, but she also knew that she was stronger and more resilient than she had ever thought possible.

Leaving Claire's office, Molly felt lighter than she had in months. She couldn't wait to share the news with Owen and to embark on this new journey with him and Oliver by her side. Tonight would be a turning point for their relationship, and she was ready to embrace it with open arms.

* * *

Molly stood by the front window of her parent's house, petting Snowflake when she jumped up into the windowsill and purred at her. "You're so high maintenance, Snow," she said, laughing as the cat looked at her like the entitled creature she was.

Molly re-focused her attention to the driveway, feeling like a schoolgirl waiting for her first date to arrive. She had butterflies in her stomach as she watched for his truck to come down the lane. She laughed at the absurdity of the situation. She was a grown woman for heaven's sake!

"Molly… you need to *calm down* and get your emotions in check, girl!" she mumbled to herself. At this rate, she was going to tackle the poor man down and have her way with him right there in the yard! If he had any sense, he'd run away!

She saw his truck pull into the drive and tried to control her heart before it leapt right out of her chest. How did this man have so much power over her anyway? Watching him walk up to the doorway, as handsome as ever, she decided she was losing her mind. She took a deep breath and answered the door, willing her heart to stop pounding. It didn't listen.

* * *

Owen got down from the truck and walked slowly up the pathway to the house. He was trying to calm his nerves down, having no idea why he even felt them in the first place. He'd been seeing Molly for weeks now, and he couldn't figure out why this night felt so different.

"Calm yourself down, man!" he said to himself. He hadn't felt this nervous since his first date back in high school. He only hoped that this one would go better than that one had… she'd ended up throwing up all over him while they were watching a movie *that* time. Apparently, the flu had hit the school and she'd been the latest victim. It hadn't been the best memory, that's for sure.

Taking a deep breath, he reached up and rang the doorbell, clearing his throat and preparing himself for whoever opened the door. Still, nothing could have prepared him for the way he'd feel when he saw Molly.

When the door opened, Owen saw the most stunning sight he'd ever laid eyes on. Molly took his breath away every time he saw her, and tonight was no different. She was wearing a dark purple sundress that was fitted at the top and flowy at the bottom. It had tiny little green swirls on it, and it fit her like it was made for her. Her feet were donned with simple strappy sandals, and her toes looked like they were painted a bright purple color that matched her dress quite well.

In her eyes, Owen swore he could sense need and sexuality. He guessed they matched his own. He felt like someone had just socked him in the gut, but in a good way.

Without another thought, he crossed the threshold and took her into his arms, kissing every possible ounce of fear and doubt away. She was all his, and she was about to find out just how badly he needed her, too.

Twenty

Chapter 19

Owen's hands held tightly to the steering wheel as he drove, stealing glances at Molly beside him. The golden hues of the setting sun danced across her face, casting a warm glow over her delicate features. He couldn't help but feel a surge of gratitude that she was sitting here beside him, safe and sound after the terrifying ordeal of her accident.

His thoughts drifted to Tara. The memory of her battle with the cancer still weighed heavily on his heart, and the mere thought of losing Molly, too, was a thought he couldn't bear. He had watched his precious wife wither away to nothing before his eyes and seeing Molly in that hospital bed had brought back too many memories that he'd tried to bury for years. Still, despite the risks, he knew that loving her was worth every moment of fear and uncertainty that he might feel.

As they drove, conversation flowed effortlessly between them, the tension of the day melting away with each passing mile. Molly told Owen about the cake she had made for the Andersons' anniversary party, reminiscing about the years of friendship her parents shared with the couple. Owen listened intently, captivated by the warmth in her voice as she spoke of old memories and cherished friendships.

He felt a tinge of jealousy as she talked about their son, Josh, who had been her first kiss and her date to the prom her junior year of high school. Things hadn't worked out between them, but he couldn't help wishing that her first kiss had been with him. He'd have enjoyed that *very* much. Josh was apparently a doctor now, and according to Molly he was married with three kids already.

Owen, on the other hand, regaled Molly with tales of the last baseball game of the season, his passion for coaching shining through with every word. Molly giggled at his enthusiasm, finding his dedication to the sport endearing.

"They played their hearts out, and I can't ask for more than that as their coach," he said, frustration clearly still present in his tone. "I just wish they'd have gone all the way this year. I have a great group of seniors that were very disappointed."

"I'd imagine so," she replied, finding his frustration adorable.

The pizza parlor came into view, its inviting facade illuminated by the soft glow of twinkling lights. Owen parked the truck and walked around to Molly's door, opening it with a gentlemanly flourish. He scooped her up in his arms, planting a tender kiss on her lips before setting her gently on the pavement. Molly leaned into him, reveling in the warmth of his embrace and the scent of his cologne. Together, hand in hand, they walked to the entrance of the adorable little restaurant.

As Owen held the door of Salicia's Pizzeria open for her, the savory aroma of freshly baked pizza floated through the air towards her, filling her senses with anticipation. The tantalizing scent of melting cheese, tangy tomato sauce, and aromatic herbs beckoned her hungry stomach further inside. Taking her hand, Owen guided her towards the heart of the restaurant and to a cute little table that was empty.

The interior of Salicia's was cozy and inviting, with warm, earthy tones and rustic wooden accents lending a homey atmosphere to the space. The walls were adorned with framed photographs of Italian landscapes and bustling piazzas, transporting guests to the charming streets of Italy.

Red checkered tablecloths adorn the tables, adding a touch of traditional

Italian flair to the quaint family setting. The tables were each set with simple white plates and silverware, inviting patrons to sit down and savor a delicious meal in good company.

Above, soft lighting casted a warm glow over the room, creating an intimate ambiance that was perfect for a romantic date night or a casual gathering with friends and family. The gentle hum of conversation filled the air, mingling with the soft strains of Italian music playing softly in the background.

Behind the counter, the bustling kitchen was a hive of activity, with chefs tossing dough and topping pizzas with a flurry of motion. The sound of sizzling cheese and bubbling sauce drifted through the air, heightening Molly's anticipation for the culinary delights that awaited.

Owen pulled out a chair for Molly to sit in, then followed suit in the chair across from hers. Molly looked around, mesmerized by the atmosphere in the cute little restaurant. From the bustling kitchen to the cozy dining area, every corner of Salicia's exuded warmth and hospitality, making it the perfect destination for a memorable meal shared with loved ones.

After ordering their drinks and their pizza, Owen and Molly continued their conversation with ease, discussing their favorite foods, movies, and books. They shared stories and anecdotes, their connection deepening with each passing moment.

Before they knew it, their pizza arrived, a steaming masterpiece of ham, onion, and tomato that had Molly's mouth watering in anticipation. They dug in eagerly, savoring each delicious bite as they basked in the joy of each other's company.

"I would have never thought of that combination on a pizza," Owen said, putting one last piece into his mouth to enjoy.

"Yeah, it was is mom's favorite pizza, so I learned to love it too," she replied, enjoying her last few bites.

"Huh… well, I look forward to eating it many more times in the future then!" he said, giving her a mischievous grin.

The owner of the restaurant stopped by their table, chatting amiably with Owen as if they were old friends. Owen introduced Molly with a proud smile, the warmth in his eyes unmistakable as he spoke of her.

After they finished their meal and paid the bill, they headed back outside to get into Owen's truck again.

"Hey Molly, would you mind if we went back to my place for a while? I have something I'd like to show you, and I'd really like to spend some more time exploring that kiss we shared earlier. What do you think?"

Molly looked at him, cocking one eyebrow up in suspicion. "Oh really?" she asked.

"Yes, really," he replied, smirking at her.

"I would imagine that would be fine… my curfew isn't for a few hours anyway," she said, poking fun of the way he'd asked her.

"Very funny. Feeling like a comedian tonight, huh?" he said, nudging her arm as they walked together.

"I'm just teasing. Anyway, I have some things to talk to you about too, so that sounds good to me," she said, smiling back at him.

Owen could get used to seeing that smile, that was for sure. She was so beautiful when she smiled, and it felt like his guts were in knots when she looked at him with that naughty grin.

Molly's heart leapt with anticipation at the thought of sharing more time with Owen. She was pretty sure she'd have found any possible excuse to use to extend their evening together even longer.

As they drove back to Owen's house, the air between them crackled with unspoken desire, the sexual tension palpable in the confined space of the truck. But more than that, there was a sense of connection and intimacy that left Molly feeling breathless with anticipation for what the night might hold.

When they got to the house, Owen unlocked the door and stepped aside, allowing Molly to enter first. Molly couldn't help but feel a flutter of excitement in her chest. She walked inside, taking in the familiar surroundings with a sense of warmth and comfort. The soft glow of lamplight filled the cozy living room, casting a gentle illumination over the space.

The room was tastefully decorated with comfortable furniture and warm, earthy tones that exuded a sense of hominess. The air was filled with the faint scent of vanilla candles and the subtle aroma of Owen's cologne, sending a shiver of anticipation down Molly's spine.

As they stepped further into the room, Owen turned to face her, his eyes sparkling with affection. Without a word, he leaned in and pressed his lips to hers in a tender kiss. This time, though, something was different. This time, it was filled with a fierce need and longing that ignited a fire within Molly's chest.

She melted into his embrace, returning the kiss with equal fervor, her heart racing with desire. They sank down onto the plush couch together, their bodies pressed close as they lost themselves in each other's arms.

Breaking the kiss, Owen looked into Molly's eyes with a soft smile, his hand reaching out to caress her cheek. "I love you, Molly," he whispered, his voice filled with sincerity and adoration.

Molly's heart swelled with emotion at his words, her own feelings pouring forth in a rush of warmth and affection. "I love you too, Owen," she replied, her voice trembling with emotion.

Taking a deep breath, Molly gathered her courage and spoke again. "I've been thinking a lot about it, and I've decided that I'd really love to move in with you and Oliver, if you'd still like to have me."

Owen's eyes widened with joy and elation, his heart soaring at the realization that his deepest wish was finally coming true. "Molly, I can't tell you how happy that makes me," he said, his voice filled with gratitude and excitement. He quickly let Buck out the door to do his business, thankful he was quick.

When Buck was back in the house and fed, he returned to Molly's side, leaning in once more to capture Molly's lips in a passionate kiss, his need for her burning with a feverish intensity. In that moment, they surrendered to the raw, unbridled passion between them.

Suddenly, Owen pulled away, looking into Molly's lust-filled eyes. "I don't want to hurt you, Molly. Are you sure it's okay to be doing this?" he asked, obviously worried about her injuries from the crash.

"You are the sweetest and kindest man I've ever known, Owen West. Yes, it's okay. I had my checkup yesterday and everything is healed up and as good as new. I got the go-ahead to partake in any adult activities that I feel up to partaking in…"

"Oh really?" he asked, his grin becoming very naughty as the all the possibilities crossed his mind at once.

"Yes, really," she replied, reaching up to caress his face in her hands.

"And, what, in particular, are those adult activities you'd like to partake in?" he asked, grinning at her as he gently kissed her neck.

Molly nibbled at his earlobe as she whispered, "I want to make love to you, Owen."

That was all the invitation he needed. He scooped her up in his arms and took her to the bedroom, laying her on his bed so he could undress.

Molly lay back, watching Owen strip naked. Her stomach was doing flips, and her heart was beating loudly in her ears. He was so handsome, and he was hers. She could hardly believe it. She watched as he pulled his shirt over his head, exposing his hairy chest beneath. She thought about what it would feel like to run her hands through that hair, scratching at the chest beneath it.

Next, he unbuttoned his jeans, pulling them over his lean hips and allowing them to fall to the ground. As he stepped out of them, Molly could see his throbbing erection now pressing out of his underwear. Her body reacted, and she felt a pleasant pain between her legs.

Owen moved to the bed, sitting next to Molly. He kissed her gently, and then carefully lifted her dress up over her head, exposing her bra and panties beneath. He reached around her body, unclasping her bra, slowly pulling the straps down over her arms. Molly felt exposed, and her nipples were hard in reaction to his glaring eyes.

He slowly slid her panties off next, leaving her completely exposed on the bed. Before she could say anything, he lifted her onto his lap, allowing her to straddle him. Then, he went to work kissing her, first on the lips, then down her chin and neck, nibbling and kissing his way down her body. He stopped at her collar bone, licking the outline of it. Then, he moved downward, capturing her nipple in his mouth, teasing it with his teeth before suckling on it.

Molly thought she was going to explode. She'd waited so long for this, and now the time was finally here. She was going to make love to Owen. She could feel his manhood through his boxers, slowly moving her hand down his body until she reached it. He was large and erect, and she wanted him in her hand.

"I think you forgot something," she said in a breathy tone she barely recognized.

"Oh yeah?" he asked, a bit breathless himself. "Maybe you should fix that problem."

Looking into his eyes, she replied, "happily."

She stood, gently pushing his body down onto the bed. When he was lying flat, she pulled his boxers off, exposing his pulsing erection beneath. Dropping his boxers to the floor, she moved her hands up his thigh, causing him to gasp lightly. Then, she gripped his shaft in her right hand and rubbed him. He gasped even harder. Moving towards him, she replaced her hand with her mouth, putting him all the way in. He tasted so good. She slowly moved with him inside her mouth, tantalizing and teasing him.

"Molly, you need to stop. I can't hold off much longer," he said, trying to sit up.

Molly climbed up onto Owen, kissing her way up his torso until she got to his mouth. Her breasts hung onto his chest and his hairs teased at them, sending wonderful sensations through her body. Slowly, she lowered her body onto his, taking him into her fully. She moaned with pleasure, feeling him so deep within her.

She started to move slowly, and then with more need and urgency. Owen knew he wasn't going to last very long. He pulled her gently towards his face and looked into her eyes.

"I love you, Molly," he said as he came, bucking hard against her body. He kissed her and she accepted the love he poured into her.

"I love you too, Owen," she said as he reached down to flick her center, sending her over the edge with him.

After their bodies finished convulsing with pleasure, they lay together on the bed, snuggled in each other's arms. Neither knew just how miraculous this night truly was, but they both knew that they had found someone worth fighting for, somehow whose love was worth the fear of losing them one day. There, with the moonlight flowing in the window, they both slept in the loving embrace of one another's arms.

** * **

As the soft morning light filtered through the curtains, Owen stirred awake, feeling the weight of Molly nestled in the crook of his arm. She looked peaceful and serene, her chest rising and falling rhythmically with each breath. He couldn't help but feel a surge of affection as he watched her sleep, her features bathed in the gentle glow of dawn.

Careful not to disturb her, Owen gently extricated himself from the bed and made his way to the kitchen. He filled the coffee pot with water and scooped out a generous portion of ground coffee, relishing in the comforting routine of his morning ritual.

As the coffee brewed, Owen's thoughts drifted back to Molly, still nestled in his bed. She looked like an angel when she slept, her delicate features softened by the faint light of dawn. He couldn't help but feel a swell of love for her, his heart overflowing with affection for the woman who had captured it so completely.

When Molly finally stirred awake and joined him in the kitchen, Owen couldn't help but notice the way her eyes lingered on his shirtless torso, the admiration evident in her gaze. He wasn't built like a bodybuilder, but years of coaching baseball and exercising whenever he could had left him with a lean, muscular physique that Molly seemed to appreciate. Her look made him feel powerful as a man, and he had never realized that it would feel so good to be looked at like that.

Handing her a steaming cup of coffee, Owen smiled warmly, his heart swelling with affection. "Good morning, beautiful," he said, his voice soft with tenderness. "I hope you slept well."

Molly smiled back at him, her eyes sparkling with affection. "I did, thank you," she replied, taking a sip of her coffee. "And thank you for making me coffee. You really are too good to me, Owen."

Owen chuckled, shaking his head. "Nonsense," he said, reaching out to gently brush a stray strand of hair from her face. "You deserve all the happiness in the world, Molly. And if I can help make your mornings a little brighter, then I'm more than happy to do so."

Molly's smile widened at his words, her heart swelling with gratitude and love for the man standing before her. She reached out to take his hand, intertwining their fingers together as they stood together in the warm embrace of the morning light.

"I don't know about you, but I think I need a shower," she said, kissing his cheek as she sat her coffee back on the counter. "Care to join me?"

Owen grinned. "You are a little vixen, aren't you?" he asked, laughing as he sat his coffee next to hers.

"Well, is that a yes or a no?" she asked, smirking at him.

"It's one hundred percent a yes," he said, adding, "First one there gets to stand in the water first!"

Just like that, the race was on. Molly won, of course, and they both stripped down and hopped into the shower together. They took turns soaping each other up and wiping each other off, with kisses placed carefully in between each crevice.

They made love in the shower, their passion evident in every kiss and every caress. When they were finished, they toweled off and got dressed for the day. Molly was pleasantly sore and was thankful she'd thrown some extra clothes in her bag just in case.

After showering and getting dressed, Owen and Molly returned to the kitchen to finish their coffee. The warm midmorning sun filtered through the windows, casting a gentle glow over the room. Molly sat at the small kitchen table, her fingers wrapped around her steaming cup of coffee, her eyes bright with anticipation. The air was filled with the rich aroma of the fresh brew, mingling with the scent of soap from their shower.

As Owen took a seat opposite her, he couldn't help but feel a sense of closeness between them, a feeling that had only grown stronger after the intimacy they had shared the night before… and again that morning. He reached across the table to take Molly's hand in his, his heart swelling with love for her.

"I'm so happy you've decided to move in with us, Molly," he said, his voice filled with sincerity. "I can't wait to have you, Oliver, and myself all under the same roof."

Molly smiled warmly at him, her eyes shining with happiness. "I'm excited too, Owen," she replied, her voice soft with emotion. "I feel like this is the right next step for us. I seriously felt a weight lifted off when I made the final decision, and that's how I know it was the right one."

They sipped their coffee in comfortable silence for a moment, the warmth of the room enveloping them like a cocoon. Then, Molly broached the topic that was lingering in the air between them.

"I was thinking maybe we could start moving my stuff this weekend," she suggested, her eyes meeting Owen's. "That way, we'll have plenty of time to get everything settled before Oliver comes back from his grandmother's place on Sunday afternoon. Do you think that would work okay?"

Owen nodded in agreement, a smile playing at the corners of his lips. "That sounds perfect, beautiful," he said, his heart skipping a beat at the thought of having her with him full-time. "I'll make sure everything's ready to go before then."

"I do have a few things to pack back up after being at my parents' place for the last month or so. For the most part, though, it's all ready to go!"

"It shouldn't take us too long. I'll bring the truck by, and we'll load it up. We can take as many trips as we need, especially since it's only a few blocks away!" he said, laughing.

Molly laughed too. "I completely forgot it was that close! Wowsas."

"Of course… if you plan to make any 'unexpected' visits between now and then to get a little more acquainted in the bedroom, you can bring a suitcase or box with too. Then it will go even faster…" he said, his tone implying he already knew she'd be stopping by for some 'unexpected' visits.

Molly looked at him incredulously. "Who, me?"

"Uh… yes, you. And I *definitely* don't mind one bit myself if you stop by. Heck, if it was up to me, you'd get back in my bed now and not leave it until it was time to move!"

Molly laughed, falling even deeper for the goofy and adorable man in front of her.

"I can't say as though I'd object very loudly to that," she added.

As they continued to talk, Molly couldn't help but feel a twinge of nervousness about how Oliver would react to her moving in. Her brow furrowing with worry.

"Owen, I'm a little nervous about how Oliver will take the news. Do you think he'll be happy that I'm going to be living here? I don't want him to think I'm trying to take his mother's place or anything. I'd never do that," she said, her smile changing to sadness.

"Don't worry, Molly," Owen reassured her, squeezing her hand gently. "Oliver adores you. He asks about you every day when you're not here. He's going to be over the moon when he finds out you're going to be living with us."

Molly smiled at Owen's words, feeling a wave of relief wash over her. She knew she had nothing to fear with Owen by her side.

"And about his mother…" he added seriously, "Oliver doesn't remember her very well. He was only two when she passed away. I keep photos of her for him to look at in case he ever would like to, and I tell him about her often, but he really doesn't remember her very well. I think it's important that she remain in his life through my memories, but I also know that he will be okay with you stepping into that role for him when you are ready."

"Thank you, Owen. I just worry about him. I don't want to mess this up, and I'm nervous that I will. I don't know anything about being a mother."

"First of all, you *are* a mother. Your little girl is an angel, but you are still her mother. Second, you are going to learn as you go, just like every mother and every father do. I promise we will do this together."

Molly smiled, feeling a little better. Maybe he was right… maybe she *would* be okay.

As they finished their coffee, Owen remembered something he had been meaning to show Molly.

"I almost forgot… I have a gift for you!" he said, putting his coffee cup down and reaching for hers. As he walked to the kitchen to place them in the sink, he added, "I made it for you while you were in the hospital."

"You made me something?" she asked with surprise.

"Yes, it's something I'm hoping you'll find useful and special. If you sit in the living room for a minute, I'll go grab it quick for you."

Molly smiled skeptically. She wasn't sure what he was up to, but she couldn't wait to find out either. She walked to the living room and sat on the sofa, hugging a pillow in her arms. She watched as he walked into the back laundry room area.

Owen reached into the closet in the back of the laundry room, grabbing a large box that was on the bottom shelf. He had placed it there for safe keeping while she was in the hospital. He felt his heart pounding with nervous anticipation.

As he turned around to head back to the living room, Owen paused for a moment, his hands trembling with nerves. He hoped with all his heart that Molly would love his gift as much as he had hoped she would when he built it.

"What was I thinking? What if she hates it? Even worse, what if she gets really sad because of it? She just got happy again!" he thought as he tried to steady his hands.

Taking a deep breath, Owen shook his head as if to shake the thoughts back away. Then, he willed his feet to move, slowly making his way back to the living room, his stomach churning with anxiety.

Setting the box down in front of Molly, Owen felt a lump form in his throat as he told her how much he hoped she would like it.

"Like I said before, I made this for you while you were in the hospital," he said, clearly nervous. "It's nothing fancy, but I hoped it would be special. Go ahead and open it and then I'll explain," he said, worried for her reaction.

As she lifted the lid, her eyes widened in disbelief at the sight before her. Nestled inside the box was a beautiful wooden chest, crafted from ash wood with delicate carvings adorning its surface. And there, etched into the wood in elegant script, was Hannah's name.

A gasp escaped Molly's lips as tears welled up in her eyes, cascading down her cheeks in a torrent of emotion. She couldn't believe it – Owen had made this for her with his own two hands, a tangible reminder of her precious little girl.

Owen watched her reaction with bated breath, his heart pounding in his chest as he waited for her response. When Molly fell into his arms, tears streaming down her face, he held her close, his own eyes misting over with emotion.

"I love you, Molly," he whispered, his voice filled with tenderness and love. "I wanted to give you something special, something to hold all of Hannah's precious items in. I know you didn't like putting them into any old box, so I made you one that you feel good about. I wanted to help you to hold those special memories close to your heart."

Molly looked up at him, her eyes shining with gratitude and love. "Owen, I... I don't know what to say," she choked out, her voice trembling with emotion. "This is the most beautiful thing anyone has ever done for me."

Owen brushed a tear from her cheek, his heart swelling with love for the woman in his arms. "You don't have to say anything, Molly," he murmured, his voice soft with emotion. "Just know that I'll always be here for you, no matter what."

Molly looked into his eyes, her heart overflowing with love for this kind and thoughtful man who had captured her heart so completely. He hadn't been there when she'd lost her precious baby girl, but he seemed to feel the love she had and the loss she felt just the same. How could that even be possible?

Cupping his face in her hands, she pressed her lips to his in a tender kiss, pouring all her love and gratitude into the gesture.

"I love you, Owen," she whispered against his lips, her voice filled with sincerity and affection. "I can't wait to spend the rest of my life showing you just how much you mean to me."

"I love you too, Molly," he replied through tears. "Always and forever."

Twenty-One

Chapter 20

"Hey Molly, what kind of cake did you say Oliver decided on for his birthday party tomorrow?" Mia asked as she gathered the ingredients for a large cupcake order that had come in the day before.

"He said he wants chocolate cake with chocolate frosting and blue sprinkles," she said, laughing.

"Oh yeah, how could I forget that one? Chocolate on top of chocolate. That boy's going to turn into chocolate!" Mia joked.

The two women worked side by side as usual, talking about Mia's pregnancy and Oliver's birthday party. Molly had missed this a few months ago when she'd been off work. It had been so nice to get back into the swing of things and have time here with her friends again. She loved her customers, and she loved baking for them.

"Is there anything in particular he wants for his birthday?" Mia asked. "I told Jeff I'd let him know so he can stop at the store quick on his way home today. I was going to get it last weekend and totally spaced it. I swear this baby brain I have is going to drive me insane!"

Molly laughed at her friend. She was right, she'd been forgetting things like crazy lately, but Molly remembered when that had happened to her too. It was just part of the process.

"Uh, well… let's see. He loves trucks and diggers and anything that involves dirt. He also loves dinosaurs, playing board games, and coloring. Does that help?" she asked. "He's pretty easy to please at his age."

"What did you and Owen get him?" Mia asked.

"We got him one of those cars that you ride on… you know, those bigger ones with the good wheels and the battery in them?"

"I've seen those… my nephew has one. They are pretty cool! I bet the little dude will love it!"

"I hope so. It wasn't the cheapest thing in the world, but we both saw it in the store the other day and grabbed the tag at the same time, knowing he'd love it. I guess great minds think alike," Molly said laughing.

"Maybe we should get him a slingshot… that could be fun!" Mia said, testing the waters and looking for a reaction from Molly.

"Absolutely not!" Molly said, rewarding her friend's teasing with a nudge in the shoulder. "Lord only knows what that kid would be 'slinging' around!"

They both laughed, the sound echoing through the kitchen. When they finished the projects they were working on, they cleaned up and then made Oliver's cake. It was very 'chocolatey' but looked and smelled amazing. On top, Molly piped: *Happy 6th Birthday, Oliver!*

When they were finished up for the day, they hung their aprons and headed out the front door, locking up behind them.

"I'll see you tomorrow morning at the party!" she called out to Mia as she got into her car. It was windy today, and she didn't want to drop the cake on its way to the seat. Molly had a million things to do before the party tomorrow, and she still had to stop by the grocery store to grab some balloons and a few other things.

Molly loved Oliver very much, and she wanted to make sure her debut party as a mother figure for him was perfect. Now, if she could just find the right color of balloons! Of course, she'd waited until the last minute to do so, so there was a good chance it wasn't going to happen.

"Oh well, I guess I'll have to settle for whatever I can find!" she said to herself, sighing. She backed out of her spot, on a mission to find the perfect blue balloon with a construction vehicle on it. Easy peasy, right?

***

The morning of Oliver's sixth birthday dawned bright and sunny, filling the air with anticipation and excitement. Molly had spent the past week meticulously planning every detail of the party, from the decorations to the menu, wanting everything to be perfect for Oliver's special day.

As the guests began to arrive, Molly felt a flutter of nerves in her stomach. This was her first time hosting a birthday party for a child, and she wanted to make sure it was a memorable one for Oliver. Plus, she had a secret mission to show everyone that she could do this… or maybe she was trying to prove something to herself more than everyone else. Either way, it was game on.

Joe and Cheryl arrived first, their arms holding gifts for their grandson. Molly greeted them warmly, feeling a sense of gratitude for their support and acceptance of her into their family.

Buck was next to greet the newcomers, wagging his tail furiously as they gave him a pet on his way in. Snowflake, on the other hand, didn't give a hoot about anybody who was walking in the door. She sauntered off to the bedroom, obviously not feeling very social today.

"Good morning, Molly. Everything looks amazing!" Cheryl said, looking around the room at the adorable decorations Molly and Owen had strung up all over the place. "How in the world did you get my son to help you with all this decorating? I couldn't even get him to help me put up the Christmas tree when he was at home!"

"Well, truth be told, it was mostly me, but he did help some," Molly replied, laughing.

Next came Molly's parents, Lily, Mia, and Jeff, all eager to celebrate Oliver's birthday. Molly's heart swelled with happiness as she hugged each of them, feeling grateful for their presence at the little boy's party.

"Did you guys *plan* your grand entrance or something?" she asked them, laughing.

"Yep, Mia here said she was too scared to go in alone, so we waited for the calvary!" Jeff said, earning himself a whack on the shoulder from his loving wife.

"Ouch!" he said, rubbing the injured appendage.

"Well, either way, come on in and make yourselves at home. Oliver just ran in the other room to show his grandma his new Legos he got from the lady next door," Molly said, moving out of the way so the crowd could enter.

Not long after that group came, the doorbell rang again, and this time it was Owen's dad. He was finally back home after his heart surgery and doing quite well. He was a little slow-going, but definitely better than he had been the day she saw him at the hospital. Molly gave him a hug, earning herself a kiss on the cheek.

"Hello, sweetheart. I can't believe you're still dealing with that son of mine. Are you a glutton for punishment or something?" he asked, laughing.

"Yep, I sure am! It's nice to see you, Chuck."

"It's good to see you too, Molly. Now… where's that grandson of mine?"

"He's in the other room with Cheryl. Go on in and find them!" Molly said, gesturing towards the kitchen.

As the party got underway, Molly watched with a mixture of excitement and trepidation as Oliver began to open his presents. She held her breath as he unwrapped each gift, relieved when his face lit up with delight at the sight of his new toys. She'd given most of the guests advice on what to get for him, and she'd hoped she hadn't messed it up.

"Here you go, buddy," Joe said, handing Oliver two wrapped packages. One was big and one was smaller. "These are from your grandma and me."

Oliver ripped into the biggest one first, excited when he uncovered a new comforter. It was blue with bright yellow and orange construction vehicles all over it.

"Grandma, can I open it? Please?" he begged.

"Why don't you open all your gifts first, pal? Then we can go put it on your bed together, okay?" she asked, attempting to keep the little boy on task.

"Ah… okay," he whined, grabbing the second gift. In it was a pillow that matched the comforter. It was shaped like a dump truck. He loved it, running to them and hugging them close. "Ahh…" and "Oh, how sweet," were heard throughout the room.

Molly's parents had chosen a set of monster trucks, knowing how much Oliver loved playing with toy cars and trucks. He quickly handed the box off to Owen.

"Please daddy? Please can you open it?" he begged.

"I will work on that while you open the next one, okay sport?" Owen said, again trying to re-focus the boy on the task at hand. Molly was starting to understand the saying *"It takes a village!"*

Lily was next to hand Oliver his gift. It was a big box wrapped in bright blue wrapping paper that had dinosaurs all over it. Oliver excitedly opened the box, tearing paper this way and that. Inside, he found an art easel, paper, and markers. Oliver hugged her tightly, obviously in love with the gift. The art set was a thoughtful gift that would allow Oliver to unleash his creativity… something Lily was passionate about.

"Okay, kiddo, you better keep going or you're going to be here all night with all those gifts!" she said, smiling at the boy.

Lily walked over to Molly, standing next to her. Leaning over, she whispered quietly enough that only Molly could hear her. "That kid seriously makes my ovaries throb!"

Molly tried to hold it in, but she couldn't help it. She laughed so hard she thought her belly might explode. Everyone in the room was looking at them, and she couldn't control herself. Soon, everyone was joining in with no idea of what they were even laughing at. Eventually they all calmed down, wiping the tears from their eyes. It felt good to laugh that hard, and Molly hugged her friend for helping to break the awkwardness in the air.

Mia and Jeff were next in line, and they gave Oliver a gift bag with a big blue ribbon on the handles. Owen cut the ribbon and handed the bag back to Oliver. He pulled the tissue paper out, revealing the gift beneath. His eyes grew wide as he pulled out a remote-control tractor, a gift that had him squealing with delight as he imagined all the adventures he would have with it in the backyard.

Even with all the wonderful gifts he had gotten from everyone at the party, the highlight of the day came when Molly and Owen unveiled their gift—a big ride-on truck they had wrapped with a bow in the back yard. Everyone followed the excited little boy out into the yard, amazed that they had actually found one that was an almost exact match to Owen's. Oliver's eyes widened with wonder as he climbed onto the truck, immediately taking it for a spin through the grass.

For over an hour, the guests all stayed outside, visiting with one another and watching Oliver ride his new truck. Eventually, they went inside to have some finger foods and visit some more. Oliver looked happy, and that made Molly's heart swell with pride and love. As she leaned against the wall and watched him draw a picture with Lily on his new easel, Molly felt familiar hands wrap around her.

"Hey, beautiful," Owen said, nuzzling her neck with his face. "You did an amazing job with his party. You are definitely hired!"

Molly nudged him in the side with her elbow playfully. "Ha, ha."

Owen laughed, kissing her on the cheek. "Seriously, though. Everything is perfect and Oliver is having the time of his life. I'm really proud of you."

Molly looked into his eyes, thankful that he hadn't given up on her when she'd been at her worst just months before.

"Honestly, all I am feeling at the moment is exhausted. I think I could sleep for two days if I had the chance!"

"I bet. Maybe we can all lay around tomorrow and have a movie day or something before starting back to the grind on Monday," he said, cupping her cheek in his hand.

Molly leaned in, kissing him quickly and softly. "Sounds perfect to me."

"Seriously, you two! Get a room or something!" Mia said, laughing as she came over to hug Molly. "We need to get going now," she said. "I am tired and need a nap and Jeff has some paperwork to run over to a house over on the west side of the city this afternoon."

"Okay, well thank you both very much for coming," Molly answered, giving her friend one last hug. "Oliver and Owen and I really appreciate it."

"Of course! We wouldn't miss it for the world," Mia replied, motioning to her husband that she was ready to go.

As the afternoon wore on, Molly found herself swept up in the joy and laughter of the party. She watched with pride as Oliver played with his new toys, his laughter echoing through the house.

When it was time for cake, Molly brought out the homemade chocolate cake she had spent hours baking the day before. The guests said *"ooh,"* and *"ahh"* at the sight of the cake, and Molly felt a swell of pride at their reactions.

As they dug in, Owen's family raved about how delicious it was, insisting that they would be ordering from Molly's shoppe for all their future celebrations. Molly beamed with pride, feeling a sense of validation for her baking skills.

As the party drew to a close, Molly felt a sense of contentment wash over her. The day had been a resounding success, and she couldn't help but feel grateful for the love and support of her friends and newly acquired family.

As the guests began to leave, Molly and Owen found themselves alone with Oliver once again. They began cleaning up the mess together, laughing and joking as they tidied up the house.

As Oliver played with his toys in his bedroom, Molly and Owen shared a quiet moment together in the kitchen, remembering the memories of the day. The birthday party had been a whirlwind of excitement and joy. Oliver had laughed and played with his new toys, and Molly had felt a sense of pride as she watched him enjoying himself. Now, though, she felt tired.

"Hey, Owen, I'm going to go sit down for a bit if that's okay… I've got a bit of a headache," Molly said, rubbing her temples with her fingers.

"Sure, go ahead. I'll be in there in a minute too," Owen said. "Do you want some Tylenol or something?"

"Owen…I" Molly said, fading off.

Before he could react, Owen saw her stumble slightly, reaching for the counter to try to steady herself. She gripped the corner of the island, trying to will the dizziness away.

Owen rushed to her side, concern etched on his face. " Molly, are you okay?" he asked, his voice laced with worry as he looked into her pale face.

Molly forced a weak smile, trying to brush off her symptoms. "I'm fine, just a little lightheaded," she reassured him, though she couldn't shake the feeling of unease gnawing at her insides.

But before either of them could say another word, Molly's vision began to swim, and she felt the world tilt dangerously to one side. With a gasp, she pitched forward, darkness swallowing her whole.

Owen's heart leapt into his throat as he watched Molly crumple into his arms, slowly being led to the ground. He knelt beside her, panic rising in his chest as he tried to rouse her. "Molly, wake up!" he urged, his voice trembling with fear.

But Molly remained unconscious, her breathing shallow and uneven. Owen's mind raced as he frantically dialed for an ambulance, his hands shaking with adrenaline.

Within minutes, the sound of sirens filled the air as the ambulance arrived, and Owen watched helplessly as the paramedics loaded Molly onto a stretcher and rushed her away. She was finally starting to come to as they loaded her into the ambulance.

As the ambulance disappeared into the distance, Owen's mind was a whirlwind of worry and fear. He couldn't bear the thought of losing Molly, not after everything they had been through together.

With a heavy heart, Owen made his way to Molly's parent's house to drop Oliver off. He tried to put on a brave face for his son, but inside, his heart was breaking.

"Please call us as soon as you know anything, okay?" Laura asked Owen as she gave him a hug on his way back out the door.

"I definitely will. I am so worried. She's been having some headaches lately, and I am scared that maybe they have something to do with her accident and the concussion she had," he admitted, feeling his own world spinning on its axis.

"I'm sure they'll get to the bottom of it, Owen. You just have to trust them and be there for her."

"I hope you're right," he replied, turning to run to his truck.

The ride to the hospital felt like a blur. His mind was racing a hundred miles an hour, and he felt like someone had punched him in the stomach. He couldn't lose Molly. First, he lost Tara. Then, he almost lost Molly in that car accident. Now this… how much more could his heart handle?

At the hospital, Owen parked his truck in the lot and walked as quickly as he could into the building. He found the reception desk and asked for Molly. They led him to a waiting room just outside the emergency room and said someone would be out to talk to him soon. For what felt like hours, Owen paced the waiting room, his mind consumed with thoughts of Molly. Every passing minute felt like an eternity, and Owen prayed silently, over and over, for good news.

Finally, a doctor emerged from the emergency room, and Owen's heart leapt into his throat. "How is she?" he asked, his voice barely above a whisper.

The doctor offered Owen a reassuring smile. "She's stable," he said, his voice calm and steady, "and she's asking for you. Why don't we head on into her room and we can talk about everything there, okay?"

"Okay," Owen said, willing his feet to move from their spot. He needed to see her, to hold her and see for his own eyes that she was okay.

When he got to the room, he had a moment of déjà vu, only this time Molly was smiling at him and awake, not like the last time when she'd been in a medically-induced coma and covered with tubes and wires.

Tears filled Owen's eyes as he sat on the bed next to the woman he was so madly in love with. He kissed her gently, and she assured him she was okay.

"Molly, your vitals are looking great, and we seem to have ruled out any major issues that may have caused your collapse," the doctor shared.

"If everything is fine, what made her pass out?" Owen asked, worry filling his voice.

"Well, we think we may have an idea of why Molly got dizzy. When she got here, we ran a whole slew of tests, and we found something unexpected we think could have caused this."

Owen's stomach clenched with apprehension as he listened to the doctor's words. "What is it?" he asked, his voice barely audible over the pounding of his heart. He squeezed Molly's hand, willing his strength into her for whatever news they were about to hear.

The doctor hesitated for a moment before speaking. "Molly," he said, addressing her directly. "It appears that you are pregnant," he said, his tone gentle but firm.

For a moment, Owen felt as though the ground had been pulled out from beneath him. Pregnant? It was the last thing he had expected to hear, especially after everything that had happened. He looked at Molly, trying to figure out what was going on in her mind. She looked just as shell-shocked as he did.

Molly's heart raced as she sat in the sterile hospital room, the doctor's words echoing in her mind. Pregnant. The word hung in the air, heavy and laden with emotions she wasn't sure how to process.

She had known that something wasn't quite right when she had passed out at Oliver's birthday party, but she never could have imagined that she was pregnant. Not after everything she had been through after losing Hannah, not after finally finding happiness with Oliver and Owen. She still hadn't quite figured out how she felt about having another baby one day, and now, to find out she *already was*?

Tears pricked at Molly's eyes as she struggled to comprehend the news. She felt a mixture of joy and fear swirling within her, a tumultuous storm of emotions threatening to overwhelm her fragile heart.

"How…how can this be?" Molly whispered, her voice barely audible above the sound of her own racing heartbeat.

The doctor, a kind-faced woman with gentle eyes, reached out and placed a comforting hand on Molly's shoulder. "Sometimes, life has a way of surprising us," she said softly. "And sometimes, those surprises come when we least expect them."

Molly nodded, her mind spinning with thoughts of what this unexpected pregnancy meant for her and Owen. Would she be able to handle another loss if something were to go wrong? Could she bear to go through the pain and heartache all over again?

But amidst the fear and uncertainty, there was also a glimmer of hope—a tiny spark of light in the darkness that had enveloped her since losing Hannah. She couldn't deny the warmth that spread through her at the thought of bringing new life into the world, of holding a precious little baby in her arms once again.

"I… I don't know what to say," Molly murmured, her voice thick with emotion as she looked at Owen's teary eyes.

"Are you okay, sweetheart?" Owen asked, sitting on the chair by her bed so he could be at her level. "I know this must be a lot for you to comprehend."

Molly thought for a second. *Was* she okay? Owen reached up and took her face in his hand, a concerned smile on his face.

Leaning into Owen's hand for comfort, she admitted, "I'm scared, but I'm also…happy."

The doctor nodded understandingly, his eyes filled with compassion. "It's okay to feel scared," he said gently. "But try to hold onto that happiness, too. This is a new beginning, a chance for joy and love to fill your life once again."

"Thank you, doc," Owen said, standing to shake his hand as he turned to leave. Owen felt like his entire world had just been turned upside down… but in a good way for once. A new baby… imagine that! Looking at Molly, he couldn't imagine anyone on this Earth he'd rather be on this pathway with than her.

For the next few hours, the nurses came in and checked Molly's vitals and gave her something to eat and drink. They wanted to be sure she was okay before releasing her to go home. At one point, they wheeled her up to radiology to do an ultrasound where they were able to determine she was about eight weeks pregnant. She felt like everything was a big blur around her, and she was watching from another corner in the room.

When the doctor came back in to release her, Molly thanked him for his kindness and compassion. He told her to take it easy for a while and to be sure to eat something small every few hours to try to avoid passing out again. Molly assured him she'd do her best, and he gave the nurse the go-ahead to release Molly.

When the doctor and nurse left the room, Molly got dressed again. Owen helped her and then sat with her on the edge of the bed as they waited for the nurse to return.

"Owen, I'm scared," Molly admitted, looking up at him with her big eyes.

"I know you are, sweetheart. I am too, but I promise we are going to take this one day at a time… together," he assured her, hugging her close to his chest.

Molly felt safe and secure in Owen's arms. She knew that they could tackle any obstacle as long as they did it together.

"What if I do something wrong and this baby dies like Hannah did?" Molly asked, tears pouring down her cheeks.

"Oh, Molly. You didn't do anything to cause Hannah to be stillborn. Surely the doctors told you that…" Owen said, trying to reassure her.

"Yeah, they said that, but they also didn't know what went wrong, so nobody can tell me that it *wasn't* my fault for sure!" Molly was crying now, and it broke Owen's heart to see her like that.

"Molly, you need to try to calm down, and trust that everything will be okay. Either way, I'm right here by your side and not going anywhere, okay?"

Molly sobbed in Owen's arms. She needed to cry it out, and he knew that he needed to let her, even though it was so hard to watch. He wanted to fix it but knew he couldn't with this. He just needed to give her time to process the news and to figure out her own feelings about it.

A few minutes later, the nurse came in to wheel Molly out. Owen went to grab the truck and meet them at the door. When they got to the curb, the nurse turned towards Molly, looking into her tear-stained eyes.

"Molly, I know you're scared, and I can't say that I wouldn't be either. All I can tell you from my thirty years of experience here is that I've seen many more rainbows than I've seen storms," she said, her smile a comforting balm to Molly's injured heart.

"Thank you," Molly replied, tears gently flowing down her cheek.

"You're welcome, darling. I just don't want to see you so sad at a time when you deserve to be the happiest," she said, reaching out to squeeze Molly's hand gently.

Molly thought about the kind woman's words all the way home as she looked out the window at the sidewalks filled with families enjoying their fall evening together. She could do this… she knew she could. She just had to take a breath and leap.

"I love you, Owen," she said, holding his hand.

"I love you too, Molly," he replied, smiling that intoxicating smile back at her.

She was going to be okay… it was time to stop being scared. She was done fearing the storms that 'could' come in her life. Instead, she was going to embark on a new journey, leaving the storms behind and *following her rainbow.*

Twenty-Two

Epilogue

February in Wisconsin meant crisp, clear air and a chill that went all the way to the bone. Molly and Owen packed Oliver into his seat and covered him with his fuzzy blue blanket, headed for Owen's father's farm. Today was the day of her baby shower, and she couldn't wait to see everyone. Chuck had agreed to allow her to have her shower at his large farmhouse, and Cheryl had spent the last few days cleaning and decorating the home. Molly couldn't wait to see it.

Looking out the window as Owen drove, she saw the hilly landscape blanketed in a pristine layer of snow that shimmered in the early morning light. The temperature hovered just below freezing, the air tinged with a chill that hinted at the depths of winter.

As the sun rose higher in the sky, casting long shadows across the snow-covered fields, the world seemed to come alive with activity. Wisps of smoke rose lazily from the chimneys of cozy homes, blending with the frosty air in delicate tendrils that danced in the breeze.

Outside, the trees stood tall and bare, their branches etched against the pale blue sky like intricate lacework. The ground was carpeted in a soft layer of snow, pristine and untouched except for the occasional footprint left by a passing animal. Molly absolutely loved this part of the country. It was picturesque in the summer, but in the winter, it absolutely came alive with beauty.

Despite the cold, at the farmhouse there was a palpable sense of warmth and excitement in the air as preparations for the baby shower were underway, and Molly couldn't wait to get there and see all they had done to transform the old home.

When they finally arrived, Owen carried Oliver into the house and then came back to help Molly. He was always doting over her… making sure she was okay. Molly settled herself in a comfortable chair that had been set in front of the room, and prepared herself for the chaos that was about to ensue.

Molly's parents were next to arrive, and she spent the next twenty minutes telling her mom about her swollen ankles and growing midsection. Before long, the air was buzzing with excitement as friends and family gathered to celebrate the impending arrival of Molly's baby. The sun shone radiantly overhead, casting a bright reflection off the freshly fallen snow. The light brightened the room with sunshine.

Molly looked luminous, her face glowing with the joy of motherhood that awaited her. She was excited to see Mia and Jeff drive in. She assumed they weren't coming, especially since Mia had just gotten out of the hospital a week before after having Sarah. She couldn't wait to hold Sarah again! She was so tiny and precious.

As the guests mingled and chatted, laughter filled the air. They played games together. There was a diaper-changing race, where the men had to race against the clock to see who could change a diaper the fastest, much to the amusement of the women watching. There was also a baby food game, where blindfolded participants had to guess the flavor of different pureed baby foods—a game that elicited both laughter and grimaces as some of the flavors proved to be less than appetizing.

But the highlight of the afternoon came when it was time for Molly to open her gifts. She unwrapped adorable onesies, soft blankets, and tiny booties, all lovingly chosen for Owen and Molly's precious baby-to-be. Everyone was captivated by the beautiful colors and amazing new items that were available for new moms nowadays.

Mia's eyes sparkled with delight as she unwrapped a tiny baseball jersey and miniature cowboy boots for her little boy.

As the pile of gifts dwindled, Owen stood up, a mischievous glint in his eye. "I almost forgot," he said, his voice filled with excitement. "I have a gift for you too, sweetheart."

Molly's brow furrowed in confusion as Owen disappeared out the door, leaving her wondering what he could possibly have gotten her. When he returned moments later, he was carrying a large box, which he set down carefully in front of Molly. She could see that it was very heavy, which made her even more curious about its contents.

Curiosity piqued, Molly eagerly tore into the wrapping paper, her heart racing with anticipation. When she finally opened the box, her breath caught in her throat as she saw the most beautiful handmade wooden horse she had ever laid her eyes on.

"It's stunning," she exclaimed, her eyes shining with delight as she reached out to run her fingers over the smooth wood. "Oh… Thank you, Owen."

But the surprises weren't over yet. As Molly admired her gift, Mia called Oliver over to her side, a small box clutched in her hand. "It's your turn to give *your* gift to Molly," she said, her voice filled with warmth.

Oliver bounded over to Molly, his face lit up with excitement as he handed her the small box. "I love you, Momma," he said, his eyes shining with love.

Tears sprang to Molly's eyes as she pulled the sweet little boy into a tight hug, overwhelmed by the love she felt for him in that moment.

"I love you too, Oliver," she said, snuggling the little boy close. She'd waited a long time to be called momma, and it meant more to her that Oliver trusted her with that title than anyone could ever know.

With trembling hands, she opened the box, her heart pounding with anticipation.

Inside, nestled among tissue paper, was a ring—a simple yet elegant band with a beautiful diamond that glinted in the sunlight. Molly looked up at Oliver, her eyes wide with surprise, before turning to Owen, who was watching her with a mixture of nervousness and hope.

And then, in a moment that took her breath away, Oliver asked her the question she hadn't even known she had been longing to hear.

"Molly… will you marry me and Daddy?" he asked, his voice filled with innocence and love.

Molly's heart swelled with emotion as she looked around at her friends and family, who were all watching her with eager anticipation. Tears streamed down her cheeks as she nodded, her voice choked with emotion. "Yes," she whispered. "Yes, of course I will."

A chorus of cheers erupted from the crowd as Molly looked at the beautiful ring, her heart overflowing with happiness and love.

"I think I'd better wait to put this on until I'm not swollen like a balloon!" she said, laughing as she helped Oliver down from her lap, using the arms of the chair to stand up, She suddenly wanted very badly to hug and kiss her husband-to-be.

As she stood, she suddenly felt a gush, followed by wetness down her legs.

"Um… Owen… I think I just peed!" she said quietly as he leaned in for a kiss.

"What?" he asked, looking at her with a confused expression on his face.

Before she could answer, a pain in her stomach had her reaching to sit back in the chair. "Owww…" she cried. Suddenly, the excitement in the room heightened as everyone got out of the way so Owen could help Molly into her jacket and out to the truck. Molly couldn't believe this was happening!

"Owen, it's too early!" she said, suddenly scared. "He's not due for another four weeks yet! What if something's wrong?"

Molly had tried to trust that everything would be okay, but this wasn't part of that plan. Now, she was terrified that she was going to lose her little boy before she even got a chance to name him.

"It's okay, sweetheart. Oliver was born three weeks early, and he did perfectly fine! Let's just breathe, okay?"

Molly tried to calm down. She remembered her class on breathing and did her best to follow the pattern they'd taught her. They got to the hospital in record time, and Owen helped her out of the car and into a wheelchair at the entrance, covering her with Oliver's blanket so she wouldn't freeze since she was still wet from her water breaking. When he got her settled, he ran to park the truck quickly, before meeting her back inside the doorway. The warmth of the hospital was a comforting contrast to the bitter cold outside.

Nurses greeted them with warm smiles as they were led to the labor and delivery ward, where Molly was quickly settled into a room and hooked up to monitors to check the baby's heartrate and monitor Molly's contractions.

The baby's heartbeat echoed through the room, a steady rhythm that served as a comforting reminder of the life growing inside Molly's womb. With each contraction, she felt a surge of energy coursing through her body, bringing her one step closer to meeting her little one.

Hours passed in a blur as Molly's labor progressed, the pain intensifying with each passing moment. She had always been determined to experience childbirth without intervention, and it had gone well with Hannah, but as the contractions grew more intense, she knew she needed relief this time.

"I think I want an epidural," she whispered to Owen, her voice trembling with exhaustion.

He nodded, his hand squeezing hers in silent reassurance. "Whatever you need, Molly. I'm right here with you."

The anesthesiologist arrived soon after, his calm demeanor a welcome sight as he administered the epidural with gentle precision. As the medication took effect, Molly felt a wave of relief wash over her, the pain fading into a dull ache as her legs warmed and she drifted into a peaceful sleep.

When she awoke, the room had transformed, the nurses bustling about as they prepared for the final stage of labor. The doctor smiled warmly as he approached Molly's bedside, his hands gentle as he checked her progress.

"Well, Molly, it's time to push!" he announced, his voice filled with quiet excitement. "How about we go ahead and meet this little guy?"

Molly took a deep breath, her heart pounding in her chest as she prepared to meet her baby. With Owen by her side, she pushed with all her strength, each contraction bringing her closer to the moment she had been dreaming of for nine long months.

Molly found herself in tears as the end neared. She had done this before, and it hadn't ended well. She had waited to hear her little girl's cries, only they had never come. She wasn't sure she could go through that again.

Seeing that she was struggling with her emotions and correctly guessing what was going through her head, Owen leaned down, gently caressing her cheek. "It's okay, sweetheart. You're doing an amazing job. I love you so much… we're about to meet our son…"

And then, finally, after what felt like an eternity, he made his grand entrance into the world. For a moment, there was no sound. Molly closed her eyes, praying as hard as she could, not even aware that she was holding her breath.

Suddenly, as if her prayers were being answered, she heard it. The sweet sound of her baby's first cry filled the room, bringing tears of joy to Molly's eyes as she collapsed back against the pillows, exhaustion and relief washing over her in equal measure. She sobbed, only this time the tears were those of joy instead of sorrow.

Owen leaned in close, his own eyes glistening with tears as he kissed Molly's forehead. "You did it, Molly," he whispered, his voice filled with awe and wonder.

The doctor placed their baby boy on Molly's chest, his tiny body warm and fragile against her skin. She looked down at him, her heart overflowing with love as she whispered a silent thank you to the precious angel watching over them.

In that moment, as she held her son in her arms for the first time, Molly knew she had weathered the storm and found her rainbow.

About the Author

Lyla Davis is a contemporary romance author from a small town in Wisconsin where she lives with her husband and children. She enjoys spending time with her family outdoors camping and fishing, and also loves to sing and play piano. She loves writing stories that captivate her audiences and steal their hearts. She writes characters that her readers can not only connect with but also love and feel close to. She uses her own life experiences to shape and guide the stories she writes. Lyla also enjoys speaking in public and sharing her books with audiences both large and small at public events and venues.

The **Strong** Women Series tells the stories of six women from different backgrounds and different states in the upper Midwest who survive a major trauma. The stories follow their healing journey as they find their way from heartbreak to love.

Trusting Her Heart (Book 1 in Series)

Sadie Benson knows the saying 'love hurts' more than anyone should. After 5 years of verbal and emotional abuse that turns physical, she takes her little girl on a journey across the country to find hope, healing, and love. When she meets a local firefighter, her world will be forever changed. Still, can he save her when her past comes threatening to undo all the progress he's worked so hard to help Sadie find? Will they get a chance to find the love she has always dreamed of finding? Will she ever be able to trust another man when she doesn't even know if she can trust her own heart?